ISBN 978-1-907571-23-7

A CIP catalogue record for this book is available from the British Library.

Cover design and Book layout by Agent Design Ltd.
117, High Street, Hastings, E. Sussex, TH34 3ET

Printed and bound by CPI Group (UK) Ltd, Croydon, CR0 4YY

The Last Grand Adventure in British Aviation?

D. R. Kay

Antony Rowe
Publishing

Contents

Acknowledgements   i

About the author   ii

Introduction   iv

Chapters   Page No.

1	Start Up	1
2	Agrarian Foundations	11
3	Marine Interlude	19
4	The Dream Recurrs	26
5	Full Throttle	35
6	Re-organization	56
7	Pressing On	69
8	Turbulence	91
9	Amalgamation and Separation	110
10	More Turbulence	129
11	Reprieve	144
12	Running Down	160
13	Endgame	170
14	Retrospective	177

Illustrations - abbreviated captions

Between Pages 10 and 11

1.1   Peter Gatrell and Jimmie Jamieson
1.2   Front of original Bembridge Airport Hangar
1.3   Peter Gatrell displays BN-1 Wing
1.4   John Britten and Peter Gatrell installing original BN-1 Engine
1.5   Fuelling-up part-finished BN-1
1.6   John Britten taxying part-finished BN-1
1.7   The BN-1 nearly ready for First Flight
1.8   The BN-1 in Bembridge Hangar following modifications
1.9   The BN-1F taxying to Bembridge Hangar
1.10 John Britten and Companion standing under BN-1 Wingtip
1.11 The Prototype A-100 Atomiser
1.12 A Production A-100 Atomiser mounted on DH Tiger Moth
1.13 A Damaged DH Tiger Moth awaits conversion at Bembridge
1.14 A Completed Micronair A-100 Atomiser packed in its Transit Case
1.15 The Yacht 'Encore'
1.16 'Encore' at Bembridge Harbour
1.17 Mrs. Britten Prepares to Launch 'Encore'

Between Pages 18 and 19

2.1   Jim McMahon Spraying Potatoes
2.2   J. M. McMahon as a Young Pilot
2.3   Part of The Original Team for the first Sudanese Expedition in 1955
2.4   Another picture of Team Members, in front of the Avro Anson
2.5   The First Sudanese Crop Spraying Expedition 'Awaits the Off'
2.6   Jim McMahon gets into G-ANRL
2.7   Sudanese Field Workers

Between Pages 25 and 26

3.1   First 'Flight' of The CC-1: 1960
3.2   Personnel beside The CC-1
3.3   First Extension to Original Hangar
3.4   'Encore' sailing at Spithead
3.5   The CC-2 with Builders and Designers
3.6   The CC-2 in Etch Primer
3.7   The CC-2 at Rest
3.8   John Britten at the Controls of The CC-2
3.9   The CC-2 at Earl's Court Boat Show
3.10 Sea Trials of The CC-2 in Bembridge Harbour

3.11   The Second Production Model, CC-2-002
3.12   The CC-4 on Trials at Bembridge
3.13   Work in Progress on The CC-5 at The Duver
3.14   The CC-5 on the Beach at St Helen's
3.15   Artistic Impression of The CC-6
3.16   The CC-7 on Sea Trials at Bembridge

Between Pages 34 and 35
4.1   Bembridge Airport Original Hangar
4.2   John Britten and The BN-2 Prototype
4.3   The BN-2 Islander Prototype in 1965
4.4   The Duke of Edinburgh visiting Bembridge Airport in 1965

Between Pages 55 and 56
5.1   The Prototype Islander on a Test Flight
5.2   Rigging some of the Improved Micronair AU-5000 Atomisers on a Crop Sprayer
5.3   A Wing Set of AU-5000 Atomisers and their Mounting Booms
5.4   Production Islander, Const. No. 21
5.5   Desmond Norman viewing The New Assembly Hangar Construction: 1966

Between Pages 68 and 69
6.1   Islander Wing Construction at BHC's Falcon Works in East Cowes
6.2   Islander Fuselage Construction at the Falcon Works
6.3   The Combined Wing and Fuselage Assembly Lines at East Cowes
6.4   Semi-completed Fuselages and Wings Awaiting Transport to Bembridge
6.5   Final Assembly of Islanders in the New Assembly Hangar, Bembridge
6.6   N.D. Norman and F.R.J. Britten, in front of a Typical Production Islander

Between Pages 90 and 91
7.1   The BN-3 Nymph in Flight
7.2   Specimen Component Build Instructions for the BN-3 Nymph
7.3   The BN-3 Nymph Taxying at Bembridge
7.4   The Scale Model Trimotor
7.5   Constr. No. 2 Islander (G-ATWU) as The Trimotor Prototype
7.6   'Whisky Uniform' flying after initial extension to its Tail Fin

Between Pages 109 and 110
8.1   An Islander Equipped with Warloads
8.2   The Pre-Production Trislander (Constr. No. 245)

Between Pages 128 and 129
9.1   Islanders and Trislanders under construction at FSA Gosselies
9.2   Islanders in Final Assembly at Bembridge
9.3   Artistic Impression of Projected Mainlander in comparison with Trislander
9.4   Early Production BN-2AIII-2 Trislander in service in The Pacific Islands
9.5   Constr. No. 1012 Trislander in Flight

Between Pages 143 and 144
10.1   One of the Belgian Army Islanders
10.2   An Indian Navy Islander at Bembridge
10.3   The First Turbine Islander Project
10.4   The Upgraded BN-2B Series Cockpit

Between Pages 159 and 160
11.1   Second Hangar and Terminal Building
11.2   BN-2T Turbine Islander Demonstrator
11.3   Two Military Turbine Islanders

Between Pages 169 and 170
12.1   The Final Production BN-2T Version

Between Pages 176 and 177
13.1   A Pilatus PC-7 at Bembridge 1995
13.2   A Pilatus PC-12 at Bembridge 1995
13.3   A Birthday Flypast in 1995.

Acknowledgements

DRK March 2008

For their unstinted co-operation and material help during the preparation of this work, I take pleasure in thanking friends, colleagues and acquaintances of those contemporary times:

Peter Gatrell for his generous supply of photographs, including permission to reproduce them, and his incomparable reminiscences; David Williams for his inexhaustible anecdotes and for just being himself; Penny and Garry Turnbull for their recollections during odd out-of-the-blue telephone conversations; James P. Birnie (Jim's son) for providing me with detailed information on his father's career; Graham Goold for his background information on BN Hovercraft Division activities; Peter Graham, former Commercial Manager of Britten-Norman Ltd. and Allan J. Wright, of BN Historians, for the supply of and general permission to reproduce some specific aircraft and production-related photographs from the latter's archives.

Thanks are also due to Pilatus Aircraft, of Stans, Switzerland, for permission to reproduce certain photographs from the post-1980 era.

Special thanks go to Peter Gatrell for reading and commenting upon the early chapters of this work. Similarly, I have to thank Ron Dack for his valuable guidance and discerning comments, following his appraisal of the chapters dealing with the post-1964 period.

For her work in transcribing my sometimes scruffy manuscript into Word files, I am indebted to my daughter Diane Livesley. Nor must I forget the patience and tolerance of my wife Alice.

Finally, my thanks must go out to all those other associates, once within the British aircraft industry or its essential supporting services, whose tireless efforts in the aviation cause have conspired to give me the inspiration to complete this book. Most of them, alas, now deceased or long-removed from a fading scene.

About the Author

Descended from Yorkshire farming families, Derek began his industrial career at the age of 15, in 1943, as an apprentice with Blackburn Aircraft Ltd. Working at the Olympia factory on Roundhay Road, Leeds and studying at evening classes, until that factory closed in April 1946, shortly before his 18th birthday. With only about 3 months to go before his call-up for military service, arrangements were made for his transfer to the Yeadon factory of A.V. Roe & Co. Ltd, along with several other young men similarly affected. Being, also, a keen ATC cadet at this time, he was accepted for service in the RAFVR and trained as a Flight Mechanic (Engines) at No.11 S of TT (School of Technical Training) then based near Hereford. After training he was posted to No. 10 ANS (Air Navigation School) where he worked on the Bristol Hercules engine power plants, installed in their Vickers Wellington Mk X aircraft. Further service followed on the Rolls-Royce Merlin power plants of de Havilland Mosquito T3 aircraft, on the establishment of No. 204 AFS (Advanced Flying School) until his demobilization in August 1948.

Returning to A.V. Roe & Co. Ltd, but this time to Woodford in Cheshire, Derek worked on the 'cabin pressurization squad' of the ill-fated Avro Tudor airliner until the cessation of that project, following a succession of disastrous accidents. Thereafter employed on a variety of work, on many of the Company's continuing products – including, lastly, the Vulcan – he finished his time at Woodford in 1956 as an AID (Aeronautical Inspection Directorate) Approved Inspector. Taking an opportunity to train as a Technical Author, he joined Blackburn & General Aircraft Ltd at Brough, East Yorkshire, in the autumn of that year. The intention was to employ him in the preparation of engineering manuals for the Buccaneer aircraft, then in prototype form and known as the NA39. Instead, however, Derek was put to work on the origination of modification leaflets for the Beverley transport aeroplane (née General Aircraft Universal Freighter). Production of the Beverley was in full swing and he worked on most of its technical manuals until the design authority was transferred to the Armstrong Whitworth Aircraft Co. at

Coventry about 1962.

Then began his association with the Buccaneer and its Repair and Overhaul Manual in particular. That aeroplane has proved to be the last 'All-British' designed and constructed military type to enter service with the Royal Navy and, later, the Royal Air Force. An inevitably declining industrial base, offering fewer opportunities for the future, led Derek to seek employment in the field of civil aviation, once more, by joining the embryo company of Britten-Norman Ltd on the Isle of Wight at the beginning of 1966. The culmination of his experiences, across his working lifetime in the British aircraft industry, has prompted him to produce this book.

Introduction

Most readers attracted to this book will have some knowledge of, and interest in, the development of aviation during the twentieth century. Many will have thoroughly good knowledge of the subject, others seeking to gain further insight, perhaps, and some, caught by the title, just looking for an interesting read. I hope their verdicts will be favourable. My story concerns the Britten-Norman enterprise, from its inception in 1950 and its place in the Great British Aviation Industry, until the decline of both into virtual obscurity forty years or so later. Facts and figures concerning production, variation of aircraft models, fields of operation and the like, have been published elsewhere over the years but this narrative account seeks to shed light on behind-the-scenes efforts. It does not purport to be a Company's Corporate history, but aims to convey to the reader some sense of the vision, the dynamism and the goal of the founding members of the enterprise. Not only at the topmost level of the organisation but throughout its makeup and its buildup. In this context the activities of the various disciplines and the interplay of the personalities involved, provide a vivid insight into the final stages of the 'Grand Adventure in British Aviation' as woven into the larger canvas.

Some people may take issue with the title, thinking it to be contentious, pretentious even. But I will defend it on the following grounds. Remember that the British aircraft industry, raised by its pioneers into powerful and capable units, was past its zenith by the mid-nineteen fifties and facing an inevitable rundown of factories and personnel. The driving forces of the 'hands-on' pioneers such as Alliot Verdon Roe, Richard Fairey, Frederick Handley Page, Alan Cobham, Robert Blackburn, Freddie Miles, Geoffrey de Havilland, Edgar Percival and T. O. M. Sopwith had all but disappeared. Only Sir George Edwards, at the Bristol Aeroplane Co. was still fighting a corner towards the eventual launch of Concorde. How remarkable then, given the circumstances, that two young men were able to envisage a future and make an autonomous start in such a complex and waning business arena. In so doing they raised themselves and their enterprise into an internationally respected place in the annals of British aviation.

It was towards the end of 1965 that I first became aware of the Company's existence when I noticed an advertisement in 'Flight' magazine under the heading of Situations Vacant. At the time I was, myself, seeking a change of direction and a fresh challenge. Remembering, now, the first impressions of the advertisement and the potential that seemed to be on offer, I discussed the import of the situation with a colleague. He had no knowledge of the Company either. Being a matter-of-fact sort of chap himself, he opined that the undertaking was probably '… a couple of blokes in a barn somewhere, experimenting all over again.' He little knew how near to the truth he was with that observation. My application was duly posted and not long afterwards I was invited to Bembridge for an interview – it was on 12th December 1965 to be precise. Disembarked from the Portsmouth/Ryde steamer and chuffing down Ryde pier, behind one of the small British Rail tank engines of the time, on that very rainy morning, I had time to wonder if my journey was really necessary. Waiting for me at Brading railway station was the Company's little Ford Anglia estate car and its driver, so well known to so many other people as I was to discover. So far as could be seen, not another person or animal abounded in that wind- and rain-swept landscape.

First introductions over and motoring across the downs, I was momentarily surprised when the car turned into a petrol station forecourt. What? out of petrol already, was the first thought that occurred but, no, we're there – 'this is it' declared the driver. A keener look then took in a flat-roofed pub frontage, behind which rose the pitched roof of a small hangar on the west side of the petrol pumps and the attendant's wooden shed. The rain-swept field, across, evidently served as an aerodrome, denoted by a tired-looking windsock. Through the outer doors, into the hangar and threading a way through the busy workbenches, stepping over work in progress – not at all tired-looking in here – on the way upstairs, guided by the driver, to my interview with the Chief Technical Executive. Out of the corner of my eye, to the right, I had seen an aeroplane across the threshold of the closed hangar doors. To be truthful I had already been able to do a bit of initial research and, therefore, knew what kind of aeroplane to expect. Nevertheless I could not suppress a buzz of excitement upon seeing this still crysallis-bound butterfly for the first time.

Well, the remainder of that day passed very quickly indeed; friendly discussion, negotiation and, yes, an offer, subject to confirmation, before being collected once again by the little Ford Anglia for my return journey back up north. The brief was to set up and run an Air Technical Publications support function for this new aeroplane, the Islander, with utmost urgency. Timetables had already been planned and the crucial first date, that of certification for service, was slated for the following June – 1966. It was evident that everyone concerned was working flat-out towards that end. The prospect was intriguing. A completely new start from a clean sheet of paper, as it were, a free hand (within the bounds of common-sense) but a late entrant, and so little time. I had glimpsed the drawing office in action and the translation of its designs into finished parts, large and small, on the workbenches below, for assembly into the chrysallis. All of this was not new to me of course but the scale was tiny, compared with the large plants in which I had worked and had my being up to that point. Perhaps that was a bonus. The challenge was there. Even as I sailed away from the Isle of Wight that day, I had a strong feeling that I should soon return.

Decision time; arrangements; starting date (the beginning of January 1966) – a change of direction indeed. A challenge accepted and, for me also, that other, insistent clock began to tick.

Chapter 1

Start-up

Forrester Robin John Britten was born in 1928. He was the second of three children born into a prominent Isle of Wight family, his father Colonel Britten being an influential man in island business circles. The Britten family had strong naval connections, but Colonel Britten owned and operated a chain of cinemas, both on the Isle of Wight and on the mainland. One such cinema was the Commodore in Star Street, Ryde, and his young son spent a good deal of time in the film projection room whenever he had the chance.

After completing his formal education John, as he preferred to be known, enrolled in the Royal Navy as a cadet at the Dartmouth Naval College. He was, however, gripped by the fever of aviation and soon decided against a career in the Navy. This was the Navy's loss because the young cadet had proved himself to be a consummate mathematician as well as a skilful navigator. Although strongly lured by aviation, never losing his affinity for the sea as a true Islander, he continued to be interested in boats and sailing throughout his life. A lively and charismatic young man, he had a great gift for infusing others with his own enthusiasm and carrying them forward in the pursuit of progress. John was more interested, perhaps, by the engineering aspects of aviation rather than the practical flying activities. He was more taken by the design challenges and nurtured ambitions to build his own aeroplanes. To those ends, after a short time at Dartmouth, he went on to study at the then prestigious de Havilland Aeronautical Training School. This school was set up by the de Havilland aircraft company to train its own apprentices, initially, and John spent three years there between 1946 and 1949. Whilst at that establishment he met a kindred spirit in the form of one Nigel Desmond Norman, universally known as Desmond. Desmond, about a year younger, was a gregarious and dynamic personality, an 'Old Etonian' with a tremendous zest for life and flying in particular. His grandfather had been a baronet and a pioneer airman who distinguished himself in the First World War. During the inter-war years his son Nigel (Desmond's father) became one of the founding directors of the internationally active aviation contracting company Airwork Ltd. before going on to serve in World War II. Tragically, he was killed in a flying accident when Desmond was only fourteen. Following his death the title passed to Desmond's older brother, a tall dignified 'Wykehamite'. Desmond, himself, stood 6ft 3in (1.9m) tall while a younger brother was even taller, approaching 6ft 7in (2.0m) in height. All three men possessed great charm and a high degree of personal magnetism.

John and Desmond became firm friends during their time at the de Havilland Aeronautical Training School and realized that their shared ambitions could be effectively combined. On completion of their training the two friends had decided to work together on the design and manufacture of a new small aeroplane. This was something of a momentous decision given the austerity of the times applying in 1949. Petrol was still rationed and materials of all kinds were in short supply after the wartime demands. A thriving government surplus market in ex-service machinery and equipment could be tapped, however, for those people who knew what they wanted and how to adapt it. Where to start was the question and when. With John's studies completed Desmond was about to embark on his period of National Service as a Royal Air Force pilot, leaving the pair only able to work together as opportunity permitted. As a first resort it was agreed that they should start their work at the Britten family home in Bembridge – no doubt with one eye on the potential of the nearby Bembridge Airport. Accordingly it fell to John to begin the design work on their first project, designated the BN-1. It was to be a small parasol winged sporting aeroplane of wooden construction, initially powered by a 36hp twin cylinder Aeronca JAP engine, and later by a 55hp horizontally opposed Lycoming engine.

To find space for a design/drawing office, the former nursery room of the Britten household was cleared out and re-furnished with the necessary impedimenta for creating working drawings. By the end of 1949 things were far enough advanced to contemplate a start on construction. Materials had to be specified, ordered and brought together for this event. A young man by the name of Peter Gatrell was given the job of translating the design into a finished article and it was then that an arrangement was made to effect the work at the aerodrome. Bembridge Airport consisted of a small airfield, offering about 900 metres grass runway length at maximum, with a single hangar of typical 1920s flying club style approx. 60ft x 60ft (18m x 18m) square and adjoining brick built offices, housing a bar and club lounge. Alongside the hangar was a lean-to construction which had housed earlier reception facilities. There was a gravelled forecourt with several petrol pumps and an aircraft refuelling point, having two aviation fuel pumps with adjacent wooden hut for an attendant. The wooden hut was divided into two and the second part served as an ice-cream kiosk during the summer season. Indeed, it was the home of the Sandown and Bembridge Flying Club but was only rented to the club by a local farming family who were the sole owners. At that time the club's fortunes were in decline and the principals may have been pleased to accept the partners' approach for space to rent in their hangar. Thus it was that in January 1950 the first fruits of BN's design work began to take shape in a corner of the original flying club hangar.

Working on his own, Peter Gatrell, a skilled woodworker, began to make headway on the construction, using the first of John Britten's design drawings, supplemented by verbal information as necessary. At weekends he would get further, sometimes amended instructions from one or both friends and, perhaps, some physical assistance too. As to be expected both partners held strong opinions of their own and did not always agree on matters of detail. John Britten was a prodigious thinker, worker (and smoker) having an uncanny knack of getting his own way by 'worrying on' about things. Desmond would be often, grudgingly, mollified for the sake of progress. He was, of course, mad keen to get the project flying and onward towards the next milestone. As the work progressed, regular stage inspections were necessary, by the Air Registration Board's representative, in the cause of airworthiness certification requirements. This work and the overall supervision of the project was handled directly by M. J. D. Inskip, the very able surveyor of the ARB's Southern Region Office in Southampton. In that situation, Mike Inskip served the Authority and kept his association with the eventual BN Company for many years. It took about a year to build the BN-1 and Peter Gatrell remembers the exciting time of the first engine installation and the 'roll-out', for ground running tests, when he had the full, unbridled effort of the two progenitors to spur things on. At first, these initial engine runs - and taxiing runs - were done even before the wing was attached, such was the enthusiasm of all concerned. *Fig 1.5 and 1.6 refer*. An experienced test pilot, named Geoffrey Allington, first flew the BN-1 on 26th May 1951. (Allington was Chief Test Pilot for the Airspeed Company, at Bournemouth, during the Ambassador airliner project). He was airborne in the BN-1 for 20 minutes and then again, in a second flight, for 30 minutes. After some alterations and adjustments, Allington flew the machine for a further 2 hours during May and June. Following upon that, a number of minor modifications were made, taking the model no. designation to BN-1F and Desmond himself flew the aeroplane on numerous occasions, before it was dismantled and stored, due to lack of space, in 1953. It appeared that too much time and effort was necessary to progress matters further, which would have interrupted other ideas then flowing between the partners. Reluctantly their first project was shelved in the interests of other, more promising, business.

Although they were not without financial means, it was obviously necessary that work and effort should produce a regular and increasing cashflow if their ambitions were to succeed. The prospects had presented themselves in the form of aerial crop spraying activities in which the partners had begun to take a keen interest. During 1951 a business partnership between John Britten and Desmond Norman was formalized and, a little later on, an offshoot company was formed under the name of 'Crop Culture (Aerial) Ltd.' This latter Company was, in fact, the main operating arm of Britten-Norman Ltd. which, itself, became something of a holding company. The following year saw the demise of the Sandown and Bembridge Flying Club which left the way open for the Britten-Norman enterprise to negotiate a takeover of the facilities. In between whiles the partners, with Peter Gatrell's help, had embarked upon the design and build of an advanced yacht with a high tech aerodyamically inspired hollow keel. This work was done in one of Colonel Britten's cart sheds at the family home, before being transported to Bembridge harbour. It was named 'Encore' and was 21ft (6.5m) long at the waterline. Some time was taken in establishing their headquarters, however, because it was not until 1957 that the Company could claim that it had a suitable permanent home. Things had begun to move more quickly for the partners in 1953. They had become acquainted with a like-minded expatriate Australian pilot who had experienced crop spraying back home, and who had brought his ideas with him to the UK.

James Matthew McMahon, about three years older than John Britten, had designed a special hopper and distributor device suitable for installation in de Havilland Tiger Moth aeroplanes. He was then involved in designing a container tank to feed the hopper and an association began between the men which resulted in J. M. McMahon being invited to join the two existing directors. Prior to that particular event, however, John and Desmond were already sourcing ex-service de Havilland Tiger Moth aeroplanes of their own, from a Ministry depot in Wiltshire. Peter Gatrell recalls that the three of them would borrow Mrs Britten's car, loading his tool kit, two rigging boards and a clinometer, before driving off to Wiltshire early in the morning. Once there, they would fit the wings to the Tiger Moths, rig them correctly, pump up the tyres, make necessary checks of engine oil and fuel states and so on, patching any tears in the fabric covering and around the inspection holes with '100 mph' Lassovic tape, to make the journey home to Bembridge. These aeroplanes were bought for between £50 and £60 each – John and Desmond would fly them back, later the same day while Peter was left to drive the car back to the Island, with one eye always on the ferry timetable. The pattern of hectic days of long hours of work was established in this way and was always a feature of life with Britten-Norman. Next day the trio would dismantle the aeroplanes and take them, to the old Unity Hall in Star Street, Ryde, to be refurbished. This building was adjacent to the Commodore cinema and was also owned by Colonel Britten. It was pressed into service to accept work that could not be accommodated at the Airport. Transport of the fuselages was effected by towing them tail-first, with Peter Gatrell sitting in the boot of Mrs. Britten's car – legs over the rear bumper – holding onto the tail skids. The wings would follow, in due course, in Lacey's local furniture van. Wings and fuselage coverings

5

were completely stripped, structure inspected, repaired and converted, as necessary, before being re-covered with new linen fabric, doped and re-sprayed with new paint schemes and civilian registration marks. ARB licensed ground engineers had to be contracted in, either privately or from Airworthiness Approved firms, to assist with and oversee, this work as it progressed.

The first two Tiger Moths re-juvenated by Crop Culture (Aerial) Ltd., were adapted for 'top dressing' agricultural crops with granular fertilizer and were supplied, under contract, to a buyer in New Zealand. They were dismantled, crated and shipped to that location later in 1953, or early in 1954. It seems likely that these were the first two aeroplanes to be equipped with the McMahon Hopper distribution system; by this time completed with the front cockpit-mounted container tank. Again Peter Gatrell remembers driving up to Broxbourne, in Hertfordshire, where J. M. McMahon was then based, to collect the wooden mock-up of the tank shape. It would have been in 1953, before the arrival of J. M. McMahon as a director of Crop Culture (Aerial) Ltd., maybe later that year, but certainly before the middle of 1954 when he was an active participant in the partnership. The container tank was fabricated from aluminium sheet, patterned from the plywood mock-up shape, and lined with glass-reinforced polyester (GRP) for installation in the front cockpit of a Tiger Moth.

***

Moving in parallel with all this activity were considerations of crop protection and pest control, by the use of insecticide liquid spraying from the air. An economical and effective method of laying down the treatment was paramount if the new chemicals then coming into use, were to be exploited to the full. DDT was one such agent which had high potential for the elimination of mosquito populations. Ground-borne equipment such as fitted to tractors, using nozzle booms, showed severe limitations in the anticipated applications, as studied by a Swedish entrepreneur named Edward Bals. Bals had designed a small – approx. 1.5in (38mm) dia. x 1.5in (38mm) long – wire-gauze-covered cylinder device, to mount onto the spray booms, instead of the conventional nozzles. These cylinders were rotated at high speed, by compressed air, and fed by liquid pumped up the booms, to produce a fine 'fog-like' distribution of minute droplets, 50 – 100 microns in size, over a wider swathe than could be achieved with ordinary nozzles. Edward Bals was approached to act as consultant to the Britten-Norman partnership for the proposed installations in their Tiger Moths. Early in the association, John Britten was taken by the potential of the rotary atomiser system but was already thinking out their own solutions for the necessary airborne installations. They would use free-running windmill-driven cylinders, much larger than Bals' devices, and capable of being braked against the slipstream when required. They would mount these cylinders on the lower wing of a Tiger Moth and feed them, by pumps and pipework, from the cockpit container tank. While further Tiger Moths arrived at Bembridge for re-furbishment, work on an aerial rotary atomiser went forward as a matter of urgency. To test the device it was necessary to build a wind tunnel of sorts, so that the distribution 'plume' could be studied and quantified. By now, a small workforce was employed and Desmond's business acumen was fully engaged in drumming up constant financial support. In this role he was superb and revelled in any PR aspects that could be exploited in the quest for cash.

While John Britten was fully immersed in the technical side of things, Jim McMahon took on the responsibility for running the works affairs with Peter Gatrell acting as Works Manager. Using the engine from the BN-1F as a power plant, a wind tunnel was built and erected in the Star St. premises to prove the installation. The intention was to set it up in open ground for operational testing but Peter Gatrell remembers that Desmond insisted on it being run, before being dismantled for re-location. A noisy interlude in Star St. followed when the Company's newly appointed driver/mechanic David Williams, was called upon to assist them in this task. Liberally speckled with oil, and partially deafened by the row, the 'testers' declared the event a success and the wind tunnel was duly taken to pieces for transfer to another site. It was moved to the bottom of Col. Britten's garden at Bembridge, where it was set up again for use in testing the first aerial rotary atomiser. About this time, one of John

Britten's ex-Naval friends paid a visit to the family home in Bembridge. He remembered asking for John and receiving the reply 'Oh he's down in the garden working on an engine.' Upon making his way down to that location he found a cheery figure in oil-stained overalls almost ready to start up the rig. For these tests the rotary atomiser was fed with water and run in the slipstream of the wind tunnel to produce its 'plume' of fine spray. Edward Bals' objective was to achieve an economical and uniform distribution of droplets, each not exceeding 100 microns in size, and his equipment met that objective when running at around 40,000 rpm. The rotary atomiser designed by Crop Culture (Aerial) partners was about 4in. (102mm) in diameter and maybe 18in. (474mm) long – much larger than Bals' units – belt driven from a windmill and with a friction brake attached to the front face. John Britten had calculated that the design would meet the same criteria as those advocated by Edward Bals and, additionally, would produce a wider 'plume' when running at only 10,000 rpm. In the aerial spraying role the wider 'plume' contributed to a wider swathe which aimed, at least, to better the wing span of the distributing aeroplane. (Later models had adjustable windmill vanes directly attached to the cylinder). Results from the ground testing were promising and it was soon time to get a pair of rotary atomisers onto a Tiger Moth for air testing. At first this was done using water as a medium, to evaluate the set-up and with Edward Bals acting as adviser.

Later tests were made using DDT solutions, to treat a known colony of mosquitoes on the Bembridge side of Brading Marshes, adjacent to the aerodrome. Edward Bals did a percent count, after only one spray run there by Desmond Norman, and found that a 'kill rate' of 90 percent had been achieved. Crop Culture (Aerial) Ltd. partners decided that they had a marketable system and went ahead with production on what was designated the 'Micronair A-100 Rotary Atomiser'. The great benefit of the Micronair system of aerial spraying was, of course, in the economy of liquid application. Previous airborne spraying systems, utilizing nozzles and booms, would consume as much as ten gallons (38l) per acre, with very little finite control. Using Rotary Atomisers, a more controlled application could be achieved, over the same area, with only about two pints (0.95l) of liquid. Patents were applied for and were duly granted about 1955. Meanwhile the Tiger Moth conversion work could now be confidently adapted, from the start, to accept the Micronair installation and a significant milestone was approaching.

Desmond's always-active business antennae were now on the trail of lucrative overseas aerial spraying contracts. One such opportunity arose for the treatment of Sudanese cotton crops in the 1955 season. This would be a wonderful way to put their combined talents and equipment to the test, in field service conditions, thought the partners. Accordingly, some careful planning and preparation was necessary to catch the right time for treating the crops – departure from Bembridge would be in August 1955. Two Tiger Moths were earmarked for the duties, their front cockpit-mounted spray tanks were adapted to serve as extra fuel tankage for the long flight out to the Sudan. These two little biplanes carried the registration marks G-ANRH and G-ANRL. A good deal of equipment, baggage and spares would be needed for the expedition and so an Avro Anson was purchased to act as a 'mother ship' in support of the party. On this first practical field expedition the Anson was flown by Desmond and John, Jim McMahon flew G-ANRL and G-ANRH was flown by another pilot, a friend of Jim's, named Brunicardy, engaged for the task. Travelling in the Anson were ground engineer F. Lindsey and David Williams, the Company's driver/mechanic acting as ground crew. A fifth person was also present in the form of F. H. Mann who was a fruit importer from Devon. Frank Mann was a long standing friend of John and Desmond who had helped to finance them along the way, ever since the BN-1, in fact. He was at the time, or about to become, the fourth and final director of Crop Culture (Aerial) Ltd. Frank Mann was always a remote and non-executive director of the Company.

From Bembridge the party flew down through France to Corsica and on to Palermo, crossing the Mediterranean to Tunis, then Benghasi, to Cairo. Finally the flight out took them to Luxor, Khartoum and the worksite, near Kost in the Sudan. They had endured a long outward flight and now faced five months of hard work on the business they went to do. From all accounts the season went well, important experience being gained as well as the completion of a profitable contract which would lead to further business in future years.

9

There was no let-up at Bembridge, however, whilst the expedition was abroad. Work continued apace in the manufacture of Micronair Rotary Atomisers, pumps, tanks and associated equipment, to satisfy orders then beginning to arrive. Work was still in hand on Tiger Moth re-furbishment simultaneously, so that Peter Gatrell and his small workforce had their hands full at all times. Over three or four years, seventeen Tiger Moths were handled in this way and found places in Crop Culture (Aerial) Ltd operations, or were sold on, to other operators in similar lines of business. As well as the Tiger Moth, it was found that the Auster J1N was a useful aeroplane for crop spraying purposes. There was, also, the purpose-built Auster Agricola which was becoming available at that time. A number of Austers were acquired, during this period and underwent similar conversions to fit them for a new use, alongside the Tiger Moths. Most of the Austers, like the Tiger Moths, were fitted with windmill-driven pumps to feed the pesticide fluid up to the rotary atomisers. In those aeroplanes the Micronair units were installed on the wing bracing struts. It is interesting to note, however, that some of the Austers were equipped with more sophisticated systems using electric pumps and control mechanisms. These systems were developed and improved and would, later, be used in the newer and more specialized aircraft coming under consideration. The Company had a young electrician named Jim Roberts who was cutting his aviation teeth, so to speak, on this early array of equipment.

Although still precariously situated, the fledgling company had found a niche which promised well for its hard-working founders and their loyal staff.

1.1 Peter Gatrell - alongside Tiger Moth cockpit, with 'Jimmy' Jamieson (Chief Engineer of Sandown and Bembridge Flying Club) in cockpit – 1949

1.2 Front of original Bembridge Airport hangar, with adjacent flying club bar – c. 1951

1.3 Peter Gatrell displaying the partially finished BN-1 wing

1.4 John Britten (on the right of the picture) and Peter Gatrell (centre) offer up the original engine to the BN-1 mounting frame, with an unidentified helper

1.5 Fuelling up the part-finished BN-1 for a trial engine run

1.6 John Britten taxying the wingless BN-1 across the airfield from the hangar

1.7 The BN-1 nearly ready for its first flight – with original engine, fin and undercarriage configuration ; at this stage the wingtips had a 'squared-off' shape – in 1951

1.8 The BN-1 within the Bembridge hangar, following alterations to engine installation, undercarriage and fin profile. Wingtips, too, were tapered and 'rounded off' at this time

1.9 The BN-1F (by now) taxying back to the Bembridge hangar in 1951

1.10 John Britten, and companion (possibly his sister) standing under BN-1 wing tip

1.11 The first prototype A-100 atomiser. It was turned from alloy and was belt-driven from a fan to produce droplets of 100microns, it rotated at 12,000rpm

1.12 A production Micronair Rotary Atomiser mounted on the lower wing of a DH Tiger Moth. Fluid feed piping can be seen behind the support structure

1.13 A damaged DH Tiger Moth awaits its turn for repair and conversion, outside the Bembridge hangar

1.14 A completed Micronair A-100 Rotary Atomiser, packed in its transit case ready for delivery to a customer. The attachment brackets, other fixings, and accessories went in another similar case

1.15 The yacht 'Encore' receives her final coat of paint to the topsides, from Peter Gatrell, while Col. Britten addresses an 'on-board meeting' from a ladder

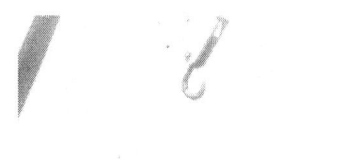

1.16 'Encore' on the Redwing quay at Bembridge harbour before her launch

1.17 Mrs Britten prepares to launch 'Encore', with John closely watching his special keel

Chapter 2

Agrarian Foundations

Back at Bembridge, in the Spring of 1956, the three active partners of CropCulture (Aerial) Ltd. were able to review and absorb the experiences of the first Sudanese expedition. The pilots, and therefore the Company, had been well rewarded for their efforts over nearly five months of intense flying and groundwork, such that a repeat operation was planned for the following season.

Cotton plantations in the Southern Sudan were laid out in huge blocks, each approximating to 90 acres (36 hectares) across flat and featureless landscapes. Flying conditions were excellent for the work concerned apart from the pitiless heat of the sun. There were no recognised landing strips, however, and it was necessary for the personnel involved to clear their own convenient strips as the work progressed and they moved on. Likewise with amenities – there were none. Fluids, oil, petrol, pesticides, water, arrived in 40 gallon drums together with the barest rations to support life. Any shelters had to be made by the personnel, themselves, from empty drums and left-over packaging. The crews began work early, while conditions were still cool, and continued for as long as possible until forced by heat and/or sheer exhaustion to take a rest. Mostly they slept in the shade, under the wings of the Tiger Moths, before readying things for the next cycle of operations. Whilst conditions in Britain at that time were moving, so most people thought, towards a more balanced and equitable society, renouncing the trappings of empire or suggestions of colonial exploitation, here was a little bubble of activity in the true tradition of the empire builders. Of course it was almost an inverse situation in reality, with the *conquistadores* having to do all the hard labour themselves. Perhaps the 'Winds of Change blowing through Africa,' had something to do with affairs! Nevertheless, it was all done in that great spirit of risk and daring which had motivated so many earlier generations of British adventurers. The aeroplanes may have been small, the machinery simple, but this was aviation, and an application of it, with capital 'A's in the hands of determined men. Desmond Norman and Jim McMahon had pioneered the business plans and the flying routes, as well as the crop spraying operations themselves, whilst John Britten had overseen all of the engineering challenges and had seen his rotary atomisers and associated equipment perform well under the most rigorous conditions.

Despite the demanding schedules, not all of the time consisted of bone-crunching work and opportunities did exist for local exploration at certain stages en-route. In particular, John had been profoundly impressed by a visit to the Valley of The Kings. Such an experience was still a matter of privilege at the time, since the package tourist industry had yet to be developed. The scale and splendour of the ancients' original architecture left an indelible impression in the mind of this modern-day thinker. In the forthcoming seasons it would be unlikely that all three active partners would, together, share the experiences again. It was neither practicable, nor politic, for three of the Crop Culture (Aerial) Ltd. directors to be absent, together and at the same time, from the hub of the enterprise at Bembridge. With the increasing business commitments and the requirement to keep decision-making times to a minimum, at least one director needed to be on hand all the while. One has to remember that the communications of the period were mainly conducted by telex or cablegram over long distances, telephonic and even radio links being either unavailable or unreliable in many instances. In the Company's general office, tucked away on the first floor of the hangar, above the workshops, the company secretary, Roy Newnham, and his chain-smoking clerk, battled a constant tide of paperwork. 'First floor' was something of a misnomer, since it was not much more than a mezzanine gantry, along three sides of the hangar, with partitioned-off wooden rooms as became necessary. Order forms, permits, pro-formas, licences, endless workshops process sheets, stock cards, insurance, import/export certificates – or correspondence concerning their absence – and a myriad other missives, ensured that people went home tired.

Desmond Norman and Jim McMahon occupied offices to one side of the general office, while John Britten had his office on the other side.

His drawing board had pride of place in this room and he would, more often than not, be employed thereon, rather than behind his desk. Indeed, he was accustomed to working very late, sometimes until the early hours of a new day. Because of his bachelor status he was able to devote all of his time to his work and his business interests. Unsurprisingly, therefore, it was usually John Britten who was most often the resident director. At extra busy times when the shop floor members may have had to work extended overtime to fulfil a valuable order, or to complete some experimental project, relative to the main work in hand, Mrs Britten (John's mother) would drive her pony and trap up to the airport, loaded with picnic suppers. Mrs Britten's visits – generally at 9:00pm – were much appreciated by those upon whose efforts the final outcome depended.

From this base, against this background, the 1956 crop spraying season's expedition was launched in the month of August. Again the small party of entrepreneurs set off for their distant goal, like migrating birds, while work progressed at home. So it was that the pattern of the Company's growth took shape and substance over the next eight or nine years. A few more hands would be taken on and the internal facilities extended and improved; a small machine shop, an electricians bay, stores department, heat treatment baths, and so on. The beginnings of a dedicated drawing office with a small plan printer, and a buying office, perched on the mezzanine gantry, followed in due course. A positive result from one of Desmond's flirtations with the media happened in late 1956 when a contract to build a small two-seat monoplane of French design was awarded. This was the Druine Turbi, with which the Popular Flying Association of Great Britain sought to publicise its cause, in co-operation with Associated Rediffusion Television, by filming the complete construction for the then current television programme "This Week".The 1957 season was a repeat success during which a contemporary writer and aviator, John Freeman, was persuaded by Jim McMahon to join the party in the pursuit of material and money. Many years later he wrote a fascinating account of the season's activities for an Australian publication, in which he described the return flight – on that occasion across central Africa, to the West African base of Crop Culture

(Aerial) Ltd. at Tiko in the Cameroons. John Freeman's recollections of his first association with Crop Culture (Aerial) Ltd., when he flew one of the modified Austers on the outbound trip, appeared on the internet in 2005/6 under Ag/Air Update, entitled: "Tiger Moth to Sudan".

Co-inciding, almost, with the return of that season's effort, a veteran RAF pilot was leaving the service after 16 years of flying many and varied aeroplanes. This was one James (Jim) Birnie who had begun his career in 1942 after ab-initio training on Miles Magisters. Though not made on a big frame, Jim was a great, larger-than-life, personality and a fund of good humour who could always appear busy, even if (and when) still. Looking for a civilian job, after flying Hawker Hunters in his final service assignment, he had almost decided to take up farming for his future life. Jim had become increasingly impatient of beaurocracy and stifling officialdom in all its forms and sensed that a return to natural rhythms would be good for his soul. Very soon he was pointed in the direction of crop spraying. Well, it was close to farming wasn't it? He could keep his hand in with the flying too! Thus, in May of 1958 he was invited to have a dual control check-out, with Jim McMahon, in a Tiger Moth preparatory to joining Crop Culture (Aerial) Ltd. All cleared, and mutual agreement reached, meant that Jim's immediate quest for employment was satisfied and, in due course, he arrived at Bembridge. During an early conversation with Peter Gatrell he announced that he had '… laid aside his Hunter hard hat for a Tiger titfer.' He described the latter as '… a nondescript leather affair' but, no doubt, he was glad of it when he joined in that 1958 season's August migration to the cotton fields of the Southern Sudan. A vivid account of his experiences on this trip, typical for all of them, was written by Jim some years later. The article: "By Tiger to the Sudan", appeared in the 1986 Spring issue of "The Moth" Magazine.

Three or four avenues of business expansion were unfolding in the Company about this time and their individual developments were to have a substantial effect on its future course. A co-operation of interests in crop spraying activities had existed, for some time, between Desmond and John and an American entrepreneur named Leland Snow in Florida. It happened that Snow was in business making purpose-built crop spraying aeroplanes which were more rugged and better equipped to carry heavier loads than the Tiger Moths. The aeroplanes were fabricated, using the large supplies of US Government war-surplus material, from basic training aircraft originally manufactured by companies such as Stearman, Curtiss and Ryan. While Desmond and John were interested in the Snow aeroplane as a potential replacement for their ageing Tiger Moths, Leland Snow was alive to the better distribution systems offered by the Micronair rotary atomisers. It would not be for another two years or so that Crop Culture (Aerial) Ltd. could put the first Snow, with Micronair rotary atomisers, to work but, by 1960, the faithful old Tiger Moths were phased out in favour of the Snows. Over the following four years Crop Culture (Aerial) Ltd. had contracts in place which progressively expanded its fleet of Snow aeroplanes to 80 or so, in order to cope with the work.

Extensions of crop spraying work were blossoming in West Africa too, where bananas as well as cotton were grown. To deal with this business a subsidiary had been set up at Tiko in the Cameroons where the principal activities were situated. Across in Central America, in Panama, the United Fruit Company (also in the business of banana cultivation) was to become a customer of Crop Culture (Aerial) Ltd. It was to that area of operations that Jim Birnie soon gravitated. Spraying banana plantations is dangerous work for pilots and there were some very serious accidents. Unlike the flat conditions of the cottonfields, bananas were usually planted across valleys, the rows going downhill to the bottom and then uphill on the other side. Since the treatment had to follow the rows, the spraying aircraft had to descend from one high point of the plantation, to the valley floor, and climb up the other side. Expert flying skills were called for in maintaining correct heights and treatment distribution; hour after hour and day after day. Pilots employed on those duties earned every penny of their pay.

***

As if the mounting pressures of work, concerned with the above developments, were not enough, John Britten had become fascinated by the potential of hovercraft. He was determined to have a foothold in that field and spent any time he could afford in scheming possible designs. Space was at a premium, however, and it became necessary to extend the original hangar to almost double its length in order to handle the hovercraft project. This was accomplished in 1958/9, followed a year or two later by the addition of extensions to the old club room/bar, to form the Propellor (sic) Inn, along the forecourt side of the hangar. Under the management of the Company's nominated licensee, the Propellor did a useful trade, particularly during the holiday seasons. The person charged with this all-important function was a member of the accounts department named Tony Edmunds. Tony was a suave pipe-smoking ex-Kenya police official who took these additional duties in his stride. His great challenge, apart from being the costs accountant, was to keep the elixir of life flowing from all the fountains of choice. The bar of the Propellor Inn (over which hung a large wooden prop from a World War I fighter) served as a meeting-point-cum-clubroom for all the company personnel and was regarded as the beating heart of the enterprise. A big brick-built open fireplace emitted volumes of log-fired heat during the winter months to keep the patrons cheerful. Some time during early 1959 John's deliberations gradually crystallized into working drawings for this new venture. By the autumn of the year the thrust of progress was being felt in the workshops below and Peter Gatrell had yet another project on his hands.

Simultaneously, business activities in the Cameroons had gathered pace and generated further local needs. It was necessary to provide transport links between the townships of Douala, on the sea coast, and Tiko, lying further inland and at the opposite side of the wide estuary formed by the the rivers Mungo, Abo, Jebak Wouri and Dibamba. To accomplish this, the partners of Crop Culture (Aerial) Ltd. decided to set up their own airline. Beginning in 1960, Cameroon Air Transport operated a scheduled service, carrying mixed passengers and freight cargo in a Piper Apache. Soon the Apache was replaced by the slightly more competent Piper Aztec. Neither aircraft completely suited the purpose, however, and there did not seem to be a likely contender for the job. Probably late in 1961, or early 1962, a review was put in hand to study

16

the capabilities of all existing light aeroplanes in the desired category, as well as any forthcoming projects that might fit the bill. Capacity was the main problem. The aeroplane needed to be able to carry at least 50 per cent more passengers, or cargo; to be more easily loaded/unloaded, but not to be significantly larger or heavier than the ones already in use. Principal duties of the operations involved transporting surveyors and prospectors, together with their equipment, and other personnel, into the hinterlands. Return journeys would bring back native people, women and children in particular, for medical attention or other humanitarian purposes. Some of the equipment airlifted consisted of long and/or bulky items, not always very heavy, along with the ubiquitous 40 gallon drums. In consequence, therefore, the defining requirements for a suitable replacement aeroplane emerged as: a minimum cabin length of 12 feet (3.66 metres) – capable of carrying 10 people (including pilot) with passenger seats removable for carriage of freight but the ability to carry those in stowage, for use after freight removal – and a cabin width, over that full length, sufficient to accommodate those 40 gallon drums, when loaded athwartships. To achieve the ideal solution, of course, a low loading sill height and wide enough doors, commensurate with passenger/cargo bulk, without the need for access steps or hoists, was predicated. Overriding all the foregoing were the necessities for getting into (and out of) short rough landing strips in difficult weather and terrain, with maximum economy and minimal servicing attention.

Disappointed by the negative results of their review, the partners considered their next move. It was resolved by John Britten; they would design and build their own small airliner for the job in hand and aim to sell the product to other similar operators to help finance the project. This approach was enthusiastically endorsed by Desmond Norman, perhaps less so by Jim McMahon. Over the years to 1961 Crop Culture (Aerial) Ltd. had done well and had built up good reserves. Jim was a canny businessman himself, as well as an experienced flyer, who emanated from farming roots in Australia. He would rather have built on those reserves a little longer. There was also the unfolding vision of an increasingly labour-intensive undertaking with all its attendant cost and complexities. Jim preferred the itinerate, short-term contract way of working with

17

proven costings, known end-dates and the ability to hire and fire people according to the dictates of a situation. It was thought that about £160,000 could be made available from the Company's resources to finance the initial design and prototype building programme, with further funding being provided by grants and loans. In the 'Export or Die' climate of the times, there were all sorts of opportunities to raise finance on what were judged as good prospects. Desmond's powers of persuasion would soon be put to the test. The initial business plan for this new aeroplane, known colloquially by the partners as the 'Mammy Waggon', was very ambitious from the start. If John Britten were to shelve his activity in the hovercraft work, to lead the new design effort it might (just) be possible to unveil the prototype at the Paris International Air Salon of 1965. This event alternated with the British Farnborough Air Show of the period, biennially, but attracted a more truly international clientéle. Success there would ensure that the little Company's endeavours gained a world-wide recognition.

Once the decision to commit was made there was no turning back. John's hovercraft work (and Desmond's, because he was equally involved) had moved on from the experimental first craft – as will be seen later. Crop spraying activities, along with Micronair and ancillary production, were largely handled by Jim McMahon. The new and urgent shift of emphasis occurred in January 1963, when design work began in earnest on the new aeroplane. Up until this point in the Company's existence, a generally predictable course of action leading to subsequent consolidation had been the order of the day. The foundations had been diligently laid but now, suddenly, there were a lot of balls in the air and a set of imponderables began to emerge.

2.1 Jim McMahon spraying a potato crop at Godshill on the Isle of Wight – c1957/8. Modified Micronair installation typical for that time

2.2 J. M. McMahon, as a young pilot in Australia

2.3 Part of the original team for the first Sudanese expedition in 1955. In front of one of the Tiger Moths, from the right, are : J. M. McMahon, pilot ; F. Lindsey, engineer ; D. Williams, groundcrew ; F. R. J. Britten ; Brunicardy, Pilot and F. H. Mann. (only N. D. Norman is missing)

2.4 Another picture of team members, this time in front of the Avro Anson. From the left are : D. Williams, F. H. Mann, Brunicardy and F. Lindsey. This photograph and the one above were taken the day before departure

2.5 The first crop spraying expedition to the Sudan, in 1955, 'awaits the off'

2.6 Jim McMahon getting into the cockpit of G-ANRL in the Sudan ; the Anson in the background

2.7 Sudanese field workers and a 40-gallon drum!

Chapter 3

Marine Interlude

Following upon the successful early seasons of crop treatment which had expanded into other parts of Africa and, thence, to the West Indies, John Britten's mind had time to cultivate another area of interest. Christopher Cockerill's invention of the hovercraft had been taken up by the Saunders-Roe flying boat constructors at Cowes and they were beginning to build experimental passenger carrying craft. These were heady days, towards the end of the 1950s, when it looked as though a completely new kind of vehicle would become increasingly active and in widespread use. The potential of such vehicles was enthusiastically debated and a great deal of national interest generated. As John saw it, however, the vehicles being developed were likely to be disadvantaged because of using aircraft techniques in their build rather than less expensive and more durable nautical methods. The efforts at Saunders Roe Ltd. held a deep significance for that company, in the vacuum created by the failure of its majestic flying boat, the 'Princess', to win commercial airline acceptance. Another project, for which that company held high hopes, was a flying boat fighter concept but the military requirement for that was cancelled, soon after a prototype had been flown and evaluated. Together, these two aircraft programmes would have ensured a continuing position at the forefront of British aviation for the long-established company of Saunders Roe Ltd. As it was, however, and in the spirit of the times, that company was soon to re-invent itself as 'The British Hovercraft Corporation' (BHC) and to devote its further immediate efforts to the design and manufacture of air-cushion-vehicles, or ACVs as they were known.

John Britten's inventive genius, spurred on by Desmond Norman's unbounded optimism and insatiable commercial aspirations, found effect some time in 1958/9 when their own ACV was first designed. This vehicle bore the designation CC-1 and, once again, Peter Gatrell was heavily involved in its construction. At first the early Britten-Norman ACVs were built in the airport hangar at Bembridge. 'CC' was derived from the company's term 'Cushion Craft' for these activities which were additional to, but separate from, the existing business. For the next few years work went on under the umbrella title of 'Britten-Norman Hovercraft Division'. It was not until 1967 that a new company 'Cushioncraft Ltd.' was formed to carry forward the business. Construction of the CC-1 began during 1959, going through into 1960 when it was readied for its first 'flight'. This took place on 21st June 1960 on the Bembridge airfield, outside the hangar there, to the delight of all concerned. Desmond was at the controls, while John Britten and Peter Gatrell stood to left and right sides respectively, holding on to the main platform and steadying the machine against a sudden unexpected tilt and possible resultant damage. In the event the CC-1 rose about 15in. (0.38m) above the grass and was supported by its own cushion of air during limited manoeuvring trials, thus vindicating the objective of the designers.

It was powered by a marine-type Coventry Climax engine driving a large peripheral lift fan, of approximately 18 feet (5.49m) diameter built into a circular platform hull, which carried a control cabin between two propulsion propellers. This vehicle had the distinction of being the second full-scale hovercraft in the world to 'fly'. It is more than likely that John's ideas owed something to his experience with the earlier wind tunnel construction and associated Micronair unit testing. At any rate, however, work went on with the ACV's which gradually required more space and effort over the next few years. Once again long hours of work and development, at this out-of-the-way place, kept people at it with regular overtime and Mrs. Britten's attendant nightly visits with tea and refreshments were much appreciated. The Propellor Inn, when first commissioned, did not supply any food but a goodly consumption of liquor continued between whiles. The late Arthur Rayner, who was a foreman at the time, remembered those visits very well; the little pony drawing Mrs Britten's yellow and brown trap clip-clopping into the forecourt with the eagerly awaited sustenance. More of a test vehicle than a practical craft, the CC-1 was not developed further but the lessons learned were put to good effect in the next ACV design – the CC-2.

Also feverishly working in the ACV arena was a young director of the Red Funnel Shipping Co. which, years before, had pioneered the first regular ferry services and mail packets to the Isle of Wight from Southampton. Moving in the same social and business circles as John and Desmond, his activities were devoted towards the initiation of a high-speed crossing link between Ryde and Southsea, using the Saunders Roe Ltd. ACVs. The company set up to begin those operations was Hovertravel Ltd. and the man in the lead was Christopher Bland. A cultured and gracious man, Chris Bland was paving the way for that most important intermediate stage between the manufacturer's creation and the public's expectations, and acceptance, of ACV usage. Although committed to the Saunders Roe series of craft for the work envisaged Chris Bland, nevertheless, was drawn into association with John's and Desmond's efforts. He became increasingly involved in the design and development of their CC series, eventually becoming a co-partner in the emergent Cushioncraft company. His influence may have been responsible for the fact that BHC (née Saunders Roe Ltd.) ultimately took a 20 percent shareholding in Cushioncraft Ltd, no doubt helping the always cash-strapped partners over some immediate hurdles. The first CC-2 was completed about one year after the CC-1 and first 'flew' in September 1961. This craft was still largely experimental at first and its configuration was progressively changed from a vehicle without external flexible skirts, or external propulsive power units, to one which incorporated both these features. The hull was also significantly modified during which the beam width was increased by 12in. (0.3m), although the length remained unaltered at 30ft. (9.1m).

Increasingly frequent absences, on overseas work and business commitments, by John Britten and Desmond Norman either singly or together, detracted from their 'hands-on' ability to move the projects forward as quickly as was desirable. The services of a chief design engineer were predicated and, in due course, a man named Peter Winter was appointed as the first Chief Designer of the Hovercraft Division. His were to be the responsibilities of seeing through the development of the CC-2 and further projects then mooted. For some unknown reason a CC-3 design never existed and no such machine was ever built. About the time such a project might have been expected, the whole works programme was affected by a massive upheaval to make way for the Islander work then about to start.

Late in 1963 John Britten's second aircraft design, the BN-2, was far enough advanced to consider 'cutting metal'. His and Desmond's original dream was about to be realized – again. Towards the end of the year arrangements to move the Hovercraft Division to a new home at the Duver, St Helens, were finalized. This was an area of low lying marshy ground, round the corner to the north of Bembridge harbour giving direct access to tidal inlets. Stretches of sheltered water there, were ideal for the purposes of testing ACVs. The buildings were less suitable, perhaps, for construction purposes, being a collection of disused boat-building sheds, known locally as Woodnutts Boatyard. It was to these premises (which were rented from a gentleman living in St Helens) that the Cushioncraft operations were progressively transferred so that by 1964 they were completely installed, leaving the Bembridge facilities to accommodate the burgeoning Islander work. For this purpose the hangar was extended for the second time. In the new location at the Duver Works, as it became known, work resumed on the CC-2 development and three craft were eventually completed. Two of these were sold to the then Ministry of Technology for experimental and trials work; one went to the Royal Aircraft Establishment (RAE) at Farnborough and the other to the Royal Aircraft Establishment (RAE) base at Bedford. The third CC-2 went to an operator in Libya for extended dust filter trials. Although the sales prospects had been disappointing, design work continued, along with construction, and the next craft – the CC-4 – emerged in 1964.

All the while Peter Gatrell had been overseeing works progress, first at the Airport location, then throughout the move, and now at the Duver. Still having responsibilities for the Micronair production work, his time was divided between the two facilities for a while to come. Meanwhile, though, Peter would have one last connection with the Airport business before the Islander programme, under a new administration, took hold. It was already foreseen, when the prototype Islander work began, that additional production space would be needed. An area of scrub land, just outside the north-east boundary of the airfield, was under the partners' review for the purpose of erecting a large assembly hangar. Acquisition and approval processes, through the local Council and Planning authorities, had to be put in motion in readiness for an expansion if and when it came. These duties were discharged by Peter Gatrell, before being handed over to a successor to put into effect. His time was then fully concerned with the Micronair and Cushioncraft activities until a re- organization in 1967, when the Britten-Norman Hovercraft Division formally became Cushioncraft Ltd. Before that stage was reached, another ACV made its appearance in the form of CC-5, built during 1965/6. This machine was damaged during trials in 1966 when it capsized. Although recovered, it was written off in October of that year. All the ACV designs up to that point were of a similar size, powered by piston engines driving quiet-running shrouded fans and intended to carry between 6 and 11 passengers, or equivalent freight loads. The next design, the penultimate Cushioncraft vehicle, CC-6, was a much more ambitious project. It was to have used the same quiet shrouded fan methods of lift and propulsion as those which had been worked out and tested, in the preceding ACVs, but was approximately twice the size. This time, though, instead of using piston engines, two gas turbine engines, each developing 1850 shaft horsepower were specified and their jet effluxes would contribute to propulsive forces. This craft was now approaching what John Britten and Desmond Norman had in mind as their optimum product. It was designed to carry 4 to 6 cars and 30 to 40 passengers, or equivalent freight, at a cruising speed of 40 knots.

In the absence of positive financial backing for what would have been a very expensive programme, however, it was not possible to progress matters beyond the design stage. The following year saw the debut of the final Cushioncraft product, the CC-7. This craft was developed from the CC-5, being of a similar size, but different in that it was the first one to be powered by a gas turbine engine. It 'flew' for the first time in March 1968. In this craft experience was to be gained by the company, in the employment of gas turbine engines in ACVs. By that time, senior personnel in the Britten-Norman companies knew that plans were made to separate them and sell them off. Peter Winter, who had a great interest in the design and use of sand-yachts for racing purposes, left Cushioncraft Ltd. to start out in a business of his own. About the same time Peter Gatrell (who had finally moved the Micronair work out of Bembridge to make further space available for the Islander in 1967) joined the newly formed autonomous company of 'Micronair Ltd.' and, himself, left the Duver Works.

For the next three and a half years or so, work at the Duver was concerned with the progression of the CC-7 and three craft were laid down. The prototype was purchased by the Ministry of Technology and used in trials at their Hythe establishment. Selling price for this craft had been established at around £30,000. Among the small group of design engineers remaining with the company was John Ackroyd, later a designer of Thrust 1 and 2 World Landspeed Record breaking cars and the high altitude balloon of Richard Branson. Graham Goold was another of the design team at the Duver works, for a short time, and he remembers the Nymph wing undergoing its 'Static Testing' sequence there. He recalled that it passed with 'flying colours'. Tony Edmunds was running the Finance and Accounts function and there was a 'test pilot/driver' by the name of Tommy Tomlinson. Before him, one of Chris Bland's founding member colleagues from Hovertravel Ltd, had been on intermittent loan to the Duver Works to carry out the necessary service trials. He was Capt. Peter Phillips, a powerfully built, heavily featured man who was a reassuring figure at the controls of Hovertravel's ACVs on the Ryde - Southsea regular service.

All this time the Britten-Norman Hovercraft interests had been strongly financed by money earned from the overseas operating companies, under the aegis of Crop Culture (Aerial) Ltd. Indeed the original idea had been borne as much out of a commercial need, as out of a pure desire to further the cause of ACV design. Desmond Norman had witnessed the difficulties in transporting banana crops from the Cameroon hinterlands to the seaboard for export, and had visualized how much everything could be improved upon by the use of suitable hovercraft. That insight and the determined design and development work, coupled with the dedicated construction programme, over a period of ten years or so, deserved a better outcome than it all received. Under-capitalized from the start, lacking firmly confident orders and approaching a time of national as well as local crises, the writing was on the wall for Cushioncraft Ltd. In 1972 the company was bought by the British Hovercraft Corporation who also took over the loyal workforce of about 35 people who had transformed the ideas into reality. Work did continue at the Duver for a while and BHC did make proposals for a stretched version of the CC-7 which would have carried up to 17 passengers, or equivalent freight. It was not to be however. The ACV market, once full of promise, never really developed into the vigorous industry that had been expected. BHC withdrew from the Duver Works and they were later used by a hovercraft contracting and maintenance company by the name of Hoverwork Ltd, an offshoot of Hovertravel. Unfortunately the uniquely motivated inventiveness and latent productiveness of the Britten-Norman enterprise had departed, for ever, from the Duver

3.1 First 'flight' of the CC-1 : 1960 – Desmond Norman at the controls, with Peter Gattrell on the left of the picture and John Britten on the right, steadying the craft

3.2 Pete Southcott (Fitter), David Williams and Jim Roberts (Electrician) beside the CC-1

3.3 Light coloured surface areas show first extension to original hangar, effected during 1958/9 in preparation for construction of the CC-1

3.4 'Encore' sailing out toward the review of the fleet at Spithead in 1953

3.5 The CC-2 with builders and designers. Desmond Norman on back row, extreme right, with John Britten on his right, pictured in 1963

3.6 The CC-2, in etch primer, pictured in 1961 on early trials at Bembridge Airport

3.7 The CC-2 at rest showing lift fan apertures and entry steps

3.8 John Britten at the controls of the CC-2 at Bembridge Airport in 1961

3.9 The CC-2 at Earl's Court Boat Show in the early 1960s

3.10 Sea trials of the CC-2 in Bembridge Harbour – before being modified with different arrangements of flexible skirts, inflated fenders and external propulsion engines

3.11 The second production model (CC-2-002) runs past the Bembridge Sailing Club, with propulsion engines stopped to reduce noise for the members including Col. Britten. Two Lycoming Aero Engines and an all-round inflatable fender were fitted

3.12 The CC-4 on trials along Bembridge beach – outside the harbour. Chris Bland is at the controls on this occasion

3.13 Work in progress on the CC-5 at the Duver works in 1965

3.14 The CC-5 on the beach at St Helen's with forward deck combing removed. Chief Designer Peter Winter is on deck and Col. Britten is in the background (in duffel coat and trilby hat) to the right of Chris Bland, in blue, centre

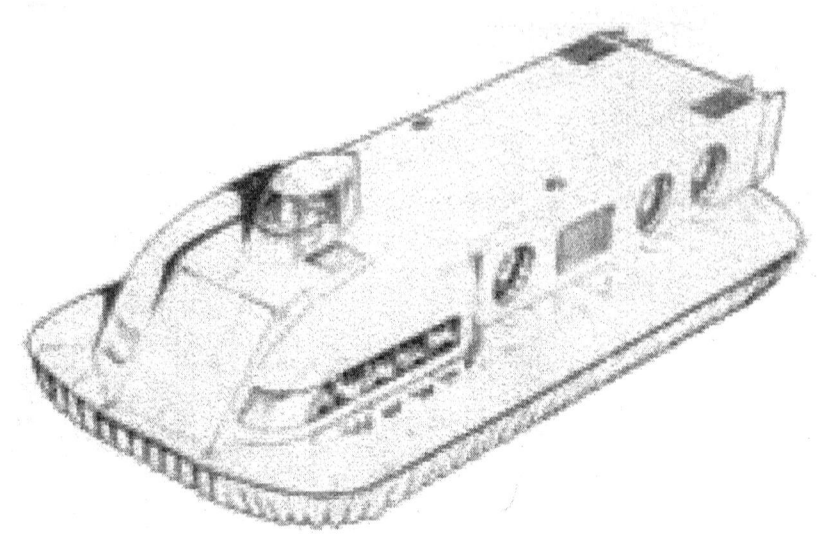

3.15 Artistic impression of the CC-6 as projected

3.16 The CC-7 on sea trials off Bembridge Harbour

Chapter 4

The Dream Recurrs

Although the full implications of creating an aircraft production facility were recognised at the outset, they were consciously relegated to the background in the white heat of enthusiasm at the end of 1962. For John and Desmond, their dream of building and flying their own aeroplanes was once more revealed. Another step in the Grand Adventure of which Desmond, in particular, saw as the Company's destiny. A great deal of attention was paid to this facet in the choice and design of 'in-house' stationery and the adoption of the B-N logo for example. This latter item was greatly prized by the partners, being a registered trade mark to which no alteration, or variation in style, was permissible. A good working relationship existed, by now, with the Air Registration Board, through its Southern Region representative, Mike Inskip, at Southampton and the first thing to do was to study the relevant airworthiness requirements. These were set out in a series of official publications known as BCAR's (British Civil Airworthiness Requirements) which constituted the 'working bible' for the civilian industry. There were, also, similar American requirements, published by the Federal Aviation Agency, as FAR's (Federal Aviation Requirements) applying to the American Industry. In connection with the review which the partners had conducted, and using the airworthiness requirements to illuminate the way ahead, John Britten began work on their second aircraft design in January of 1963 – the BN-2 – which would be a 10-seater, including the pilot. As the work proceeded it was soon realized that the colloquial name 'Mammy Waggon' was unsuitable for official use and the name 'Islander' was chosen.

Throughout 1963 John and Desmond, together, formulated the parameters and the provisional specifications of the aircraft, committing the results to working drawings as they went along. There is little doubt that John Britten had already visualized the outline shapes and sizes, along with much of the specification, before the main work began, but a great deal of effort was required to translate ideas to hard and fast manufacturing instructions. Desmond's forte was the cockpit accommodation and ergonomics; much attention being devoted to the windshield, control column, engine and other control levers and media. Assistance in preparing these design drawings was necessary if the timescales in mind were to be achieved. Gradually a small nucleus of design personnel was formed by employing some key staff and making use of sub-contract draughtsmen to support the overall work. Among those people taken on was an ex-Handley Page designer, A. D. O'Connell, and a draughtsman named Phil Swindells. To help with the wing design Peter Winter was temporarily co-opted from his hovercraft duties. The Company already had a young electrician, Jim Roberts, in employment who was put to work in the drawing office to handle the aeroplane's electrical and radio design aspects. An instrument and radio test lab facility was run by Bill Boot, a cheerful north-countryman. With design work accelerating and the ever increasing need for working space, both 'upstairs and downstairs,' something had to give; it was the Hovercraft Division that had to move out in 1964 when the first metal was cut for the BN-2 Islander.

Official Design Approval for the project did not exist within the Company at that time. Everything was being handled in a spirit of speculative entrepreneurship which required the oversight of either the ARB, directly, or one of its 'Approved Organizations' by licence. Since the former course of action would have proved exhorbitantly expensive and the ARB had informed Britten-Norman Ltd that it would not handle the work directly, the latter course of action had to be taken. Late in 1963, F.G. Miles Aviation at Shoreham-by-Sea, was suggested by the ARB as a suitably accredited organization. This was an interesting phase of development, bringing into the scene the remaining expertise of the once famous sporting aircraft manufacturers of the 1920's and 1930's. During World War II the Miles brothers, FG and GH, had seen their enterprise grow phenomenally under the national pressures for aircraft of all kinds. Unfortunately, however, they were among the first casualties when the Government's scythe swung in 1947. This action took with it the first British Supersonic Flight Programme, including Prototype 'Work-in-progress', then underway at the Miles Aircraft Company. Judged to be unnecessarily advanced and undesirably risky, it was scrapped by the Socialist government of the time. From a company employing 5000-plus people, they were quickly but surely bankrupted in that form. A background salvage operation had kept the company name and credentials alive for FG, the elder brother but, in the absence of immediate work the younger brother GH (always known as George) took the position of Chief Designer with the Airspeed Company at Bournemouth. There followed some chequered times whilst the Miles brothers were reviving their Company, the latest of which had seen it employed as consultant engineers' to film-makers, as well as other aeronautical enterprises. It was the Miles organization which had engineered and built the replicas used in the films 'Those Magnificent Men in their Flying Machines' and 'The Blue Max', for example. Now those services were needed in another project, for which that Company's experiences were ideally suited.

Still concerned with their own revival and re-structuring, the Miles organization had 'spun-off' two or three new companies to handle sub-contract and consultancy work which they considered to have the right potential for them to handle. Miles Aviation and Transport Ltd was one of these facilities and was then headquartered at nearby Lancing, in Sussex; it was that Company which had been engaged in the film making activities with G. H. Miles as Chief Executive. Thus it was that in January of 1964, George Miles received an information package on the Islander, from John Britten and Desmond Norman, with a most charming invitation for him to meet them for discussion about the project. Being extremely busy just then, with an increasing variety of contract work and not wanting to upset the balance of his slender finances, Miles was reluctant to become involved. Nevertheless he and his right-hand man, Ron Dack (his Chief Stressman/Engineer) went over all of the details together and were convinced that a difficult task lay ahead. In particular, George Miles considered that the Islander's wing structure, as proposed, was unlikely to meet the BCAR criteria and that there were no helpful precedents for UK Transport (Passenger) Category Certification of such a small aeroplane.

His conclusions were to be proved correct later on. Moreover, from his point of view, the aeroplane had none of the traditional 'Miles Style' about its concept. John and Desmond appeared to be paying too much attention to American 'short-life' structural practices and to that country's FAA (Federal Aviation Agency) orientated design procedures. All of these facts were at odds with the Miles' experience and British custom and practice. It must be said, however, that George Miles was a man from a completely different mould to either John Britten or Desmond Norman. He had none of their maverick traits, or tendencies for self delusion in his character. By temperament, he was altogether more professional and humanistic, in contrast to their self-professed amateurism and ambitious ruthlessness. Undeterred, though, John and Desmond succeeded in persuading G.H. Miles to make the trip over to Bembridge to meet them for further discussion. In February of 1964 he and Ron Dack joined the two partners for lunch, prepared by Mrs Britten, at John's family home.

At this epoch-making meeting, Miles was talked into accepting their commission, with himself as nominated Chief Designer and Ron Dack as 'visiting Chief Structural Engineer', on two days per week. That arrangement being necessary in the absence of a recognised Stress Office function at Bembridge and forming a key part in the Design Approval process, pending the Britten-Norman Company's anticipated acceptance, by the ARB, as a Design Approved organization in its own right, at the completion of Miles' brief. The aim was for that stage to be reached at the time when full UK Transport (Passenger) Category Certification was gained for the Islander.

Under the deal set up, Miles Aviation and Transport Ltd would participate in the preparation and checking of design drawings and stressing calculations, for the work then in hand at Bembridge. In addition Miles would also assign two of its own designers, to help out with Islander work, at its own facilities in Lancing. The two men concerned were Dudley Kell and Ernie Perkins, both experienced design draughtsmen. Furthermore Miles would arrange for two more of its design personnel to be seconded to Britten-Norman Ltd to work at Bembridge as soon as possible. Miles also agreed to provide a Chief Technical Executive who would be approved by the ARB, to steer the project through the necessary approval phases on behalf of both Companies. The man to whom these duties fell was R.E. (Dickie) Bird, a former employee of the renowned Edgar Percival whose pre-war sporting aeroplanes were equally famous to those of the Miles organization. Percival's Company had passed through similar post-war convulsions to the ones experienced by Miles, before being enveloped in the Hunting Group of Companies. Dickie Bird, in consequence, had gone to work for the Taylorcraft Auster Company at Rearsby in Leicestershire. That company, too, had been subsumed in an unwieldy merger with one arm of the revived Miles organization, becoming known as Beagle Aircraft Ltd. Business there was not going as well as expected, however, and it was out of those conditions that George Miles was able to recruit the necessary personnel to help in the Islander's programme.

D.A. (Dennis) Berryman and M.J. (Mike) Benjamin were the two design draughtsmen seconded to Bembridge fairly quickly, while Dickie Bird was not able to take up his duties until early in 1965. A short time before Dickie's arrival the Company had recruited a Structural Engineer, named John Brenchley, who had previously worked for the Bristol Aeroplane Co. John was finding his feet at Bembridge, under Ron Dack's guidance, and gradually enabled Ron's withdrawal from regular visitation in order to return to his own full time duties at Lancing, although retaining a discreet overall responsibility until the contract terminated.

Because of the gathering pace of work, in the Bembridge hangar and the need to replace Peter Gatrell, who had gone to the Duver Works with the Hovercraft Division, a new Works Manager was needed to take charge of the Islander construction work. Again George Miles filled the bill with an old hand of his called Jack Sullivan, who was also attracted from Beagle to join the team. Jack was an old-style, no nonsense man who was a real dynamo on the job and pushed the progress mercilessly. Without his concentrated effort it is difficult, in retrospect, to see how the targets could have been met. He had a big sign board erected along one shop floor wall, marked out in 'day spaces' to first flight, with something like: `150 days to go.' These spaces would be crossed through, at each day's end, with pertinent data on delay or shortfall entered in for all to read, digest, and act on.

In this atmosphere of extreme effort and urgency the prototype

Islander took shape. Ernie Perkins, the Miles designer, did the 'mock-up' drawings leading to construction of a full scale wooden replica of the cabin. From this aid it was possible to evaluate and 'fine-tune' the special propensities, for controls, seating and other internal requirements, before the point of 'no-return' was passed in the final design of the fuselage. This would be among the first significant events in Desmond's 'hands-on' appreciation; windshield contours, pilot's viewpoint angles, seat height/elbow room, control placing, and so forth. Certain important instruments such as the main six, concerned with flight attitude, height, speed and direction had to be displayed in standardised positions, but there was much instrumentation and control media that was subject to the dictates of the test pilot: especially when he happened to be the co-owner of the Company. He and John had many, sometimes heated, discussions at this stage in the proceedings. Andrew (Andy) O'Connell was given the responsibility for selecting and specifying equipment and systems, together with their installation aspects, in the Islander. His new colleague, Dennis Berryman had the duties of engine/power plant installation and flight controls design. There were numerous areas of overlap in the work concerned, so it was just as well that the two men got on well together. All of the above activity had to be carried on in close collaboration with the two directors, of course, before finally purchasing 'bought-out equipment items' – large and small – and finalizing the design drawings. It became a usual practice to carry on work, after the nominal finishing time of 5:30pm, until the Propellor Inn opened at 6:00pm, repair to that venue and continue affairs, over drinks, indefinitely! Needless to say, this was not an enthusiasm wholeheartedly shared by the domestic ménages, backing the design and works personnel alike.

For his Islander wing, John Britten had chosen a standard section which had proven low-speed, high-lift, characteristics. In fact it was a very similar wing to the one used on the BN-1 but, this time, all metal. Its performance and controllability at the ultra low speeds envisaged for take-off and landing, was further improved by the use of slotted flaps and slotted ailerons. To progress the wing design work relinquished by Peter Winter after his move to the Duver, a design draughtsman was engaged from Marshall's of Cambridge, who are specialists in sub-contracting services for the industry. The person who took up these duties was a happy-go-lucky Welshman called Elfyn (Taffy) Lloyd. Taffy was a very talented designer, in spite of congenital deformities affecting both hands and feet. He had a wide working knowledge and experience, with a tremendously retentive memory – all of which were invaluable, because these were times before the advent of electronic calculators or personal computers. To see him in action at his drawing board, a pencil behind one ear, a cigarette behind the other (and one in his mouth making his eyes smart) was a revelation.

Fuselage design, being overseen by Ron Dack at Lancing, was handled by Mike Benjamin on site at Bembridge. Both Mike and Taffy were assisted by other personnel, of course, but they (together with others aforementioned) were looked upon as the project leaders and acted accordingly. Evaluation of the 'mock-up' completed, it was soon possible to turn attention to cabin interiors, seating, lining, furnishing, all being quantified and committed to working drawings as 1964 was succeeded by 1965. While the assembly went forward, John Brenchley and his one or two assistants were tracking all of the progress with reams of calculations, determining stresses and strains, gradually taking over from Ron Dack and their counterparts at Miles Aviation and Transport, in the compilation and production of the Aircraft Type Records. Miles actually completed about 50 percent of the Islander design work under the terms of its consultancy. Despite his initial reluctance, George Miles did make a significant input to the Islander design by his choice of control balance ratios that were proved pleasant and positive in use. His long experience left a distinctive imprint (which pleased all of the test pilots) that never changed over succeeding years.

Jigs and tools for many components and assemblies were also being designed and made, some of an interim nature at first, under the guidance of Derek Fitch the Works Engineer. Derek had been recruited from Saunders Roe, up the road at Cowes, and was a constant presence on the hangar floor, if not in his cubby-hole of an office. Fulfilling the role of Chief Inspector was a doughty old expatriate Australian ground engineer, Jim Gobert, who carried ARB licences for both engines and airframes. His duty it was to make sure that the build history of the prototype was properly recorded and chronologically complete alongside the quality control inspection programme, before finally certifying that it was fit to fly.

Preparatory to the flight trials the Company had engaged a young man fresh from college, to estimate performance potential in the way of take-off and landing distances at different loadings and airfield altitudes. Robert Wilson was his name and he was soon joined by a fully-fledged aerodynamicist, recently returned from a spell in New Zealand, named A. J. Coombe who had been working for New Zealand National Airways. Andrew (Andy) Coombe was a colourful and exuberant character who, whilst earlier working for the Gloster Aircraft Co., had survived an emergency ejection from a Javelin, trapped in the then new phenomenon of a 'deep-stall'. These two colleagues were to share the work of practical flight testing and real-time performance measurement, and analysis, when flight trials began with the prototype Islander.

All too soon, and yet not soon enough, the day arrived for roll-out: 10th June 1965 the first Islander (Constructor's No.1) registered G-ATCT, emerged from the Bembridge hangar. Some intensive flying was necessary within the next few days, if the aeroplane was to gain its Special Category Certificate of Airworthiness; the minimum necessary qualification for its appearance at the Paris Salon. Thus it was, after the necessary ground tests, engine runs, and the like, had been satisfactorily accomplished, that Desmond Norman, with John Britten in the co-pilot's seat, took the Islander aloft 3 days later. Desmond expressed his satisfaction after the aeroplane's first flight. His oft-quoted remark, concerning this momentous occasion, was that '...the aeroplane flies like a fully developed airliner.' Both partners realized, however, that there was a need for more power and wing area, to ensure their 'climb-out' criteria were met in full. John Britten was a staunch believer in the rule-of-thumb principle, for light aeroplanes, that 50 hp per passenger was sufficient. Hence he had selected the popular American Continental engines, each developing 210 hp, hoping to make slight gains in economy without sacrificing too much in the way of performance. These initial flight test results showed up the likely deficiencies, at the outset, but did not prevent the Islander from gaining its Special Category Certificate of

Airworthiness and making a successful début in Paris a few days later.

Much interest had been shown in the new aeroplane during the days of the show, with potential customers asking pertinent questions about prices and delivery dates. There was obviously a lot more work still to do but John and Desmond were so encouraged that they immediately set about deciding their programme of changes. Instead of the Continental engines, they would use the more powerful Lycoming engines of 260 hp each and stretch the wing span by 4 feet (1.22m) to 49 feet (14.93m) overall. An increase of 24 per cent in power, with 9 per cent more wing area for a negligible increase in weight or complexity.

Back at Bembridge it was all hands to the pumps to make the changes happen. In the light of these decisions, and the allure of sales prospects, the partners were impelled towards the goal of a fully re-worked prototype, being completely flight tested, and ready for public service transport, with a full-blown Certificate of Airworthiness by the following June – 1966.

It was very obvious to all concerned that another cycle of intense effort was building up. For the two principal directors, however, it was a vindication of their hopes and dreams. A production facility of some capacity would be needed to handle the anticipated orders. Already foreseeing the need for expansion – it had been apparent all along that the existing hangar was too small even with its second extension – feelers were out to acquire some waste ground adjacent to the airfield. On it would be erected a large assembly building suitable for Islander production, provided that the essential certification targets could be met and sufficient customer interest could be held, and built upon, to make the dream a reality. It was a monumental gamble, that would require massive financial assistance, plus the unstinted goodwill of local authorities, business people, and government agencies, to bring the project to fruition. The partners were fortunate to be able to rely on the support of the Isle of Wight Conservative MP of the time, the late Mark Woodnutt, who was able to turn the keys in many official doors, if obstruction or delays were encountered along the way. In the meantime the work and the wages were consistently being financed by Crop Culture (Aerial) Ltd. from the well-established overseas interests on which the Company was founded.

4.1 Bembridge airport original hangar and extensions, photographed circa 2003. The second extension, identifiable by its lower rooflines and the extended club lounge / bar buildings, with the first storey office accommodation over some of them, show how it was in 1965. The only noticeable differences concern addition of a wooden porch structure (at the pub door) and the symbolic propeller – from an Armstrong -Whitworth Argossy – alongside, together with removal of the commercial petrol pumps and attendants' huts which happened 12 or 14 years later

4.2 John Britten pictured during construction of the BN2 prototype in the background. Early 1965

4.3 The BN-2 Islander prototype in original configuration with the Continental engines – summer 1965 – showing the clean rectangular lines of the engine cowlings

4.4 The Duke of Edinburgh visiting Bembridge Airport in 1965. From the left of the picture are: Jim Birnie, Jim McMahon, Desmond Norman, Chris Bland, John Britten and the Duke

Chapter 5

Full Throttle

By the time my own starting date with the Company had arrived – 3rd January 1966 – it was looking almost impossible to meet the full UK certification standard by June. So much work was still necessary in the way of design finalization, before confident orders could be placed for a majority of OEM (Original Equipment Manufacturer's) components and other materials. That would obviously affect manufacturing lead-times and, thus, delivery of the parts concerned, to the ultimate delay of the completed aeroplane. Accordingly, a more realistic (though still unarticulated) date in August 1966 was firmly in the sights. September would bring the SBAC's Farnborough Air Show and the appearance of a 'production aeroplane' at that shop window of British aviation products was crucial. In this particular context, my narrative now changes focus slightly, insofar as progress and events are related from a viewpoint of personal involvement. I had already been advised that I should have the assistance of a young lady by the name of Penelope Mason (Penny) who was a competent typist and a young man called Ted, who '… was doing some illustrations'. Someone had thought to provide, without due cogniscence for the work ahead, a second-hand Gestetner offset duplicating machine. Both Penny and Ted had had the briefest of instructions upon how to use this cantankerous piece of equipment which was only able to accept metal printing plates. Processing these for the printing run was messy and time consuming; if illustrations were to be accommodated they had to be photographically prepared, for transfer to the printing plates, by an outside specialist.

Thus I found my new office on that first morning; another wooden box-like structure, up two flights of wooden steps, on one end of the mezzanine gantry. It was, in fact, a twin box because the first half, at the head of the stairs, was the Works Drawing Stores. A glazed partition and door across the centre gave access to 'our space'. Each of these rooms was approximately ten feet square but 'ours' was compromised by the threatening grey Gestetner, plumb in the middle. With Penny's desk/typewriter at one side and Ted's drawing board at the other, my own working area was across the doorway! It could only be temporary and it was. For a good deal of the time, during the first fortnight, I was absent from the door threshold whilst I made my acquaintance with the 'chrysallis' and the personnel wreaking the changes within her. This was Constructor's No. 2 –Registration G-ATWU, known from its two final letters denoting its radio call-sign as, Whisky Uniform'. The Company's first customer for this aeroplane was Loganair Ltd., based at Abbottsinch near Glasgow. Loganair ran scheduled air services to the Highlands and Islands of Scotland from their Glasgow headquarters. Principal among these services was the connection to the Orkney's. It was a very similar operating profile for which the aeroplane had been conceived, except for climatic conditions, to serve the Cameroon air links. Short hops, between 2 and 80 miles, into rough and ready landing strips – some of them island beaches in Loganair's case and only accessible at low tide. That operator, also, was using Piper Aztecs for the work and was desperately anxious to replace them. The airline was an excellent prospective customer, literally baying at the door for the new aeroplane. Close behind Loganair, in the acquisition stakes, was a company, with associations in the Channel Islands, by the name of Glosair Ltd, based at Staverton Airport near Gloucester. This company was run by Sir Deryck Bailey, another keen post-war pioneer, who was also very impatient to put a new service into place between the constituent islands and Southampton. The ancient Celtic name of 'Aurigny' had been adopted for this new airline.

All of which was a good deal away from my position in the door threshold, of course, but was a pointer to the increasing pressures being felt throughout our small Company. With my first assessments in hand, I was expected to give my new employers an estimate of how much it would cost and how long it would take to provide the essential engineering handbooks for the Islander, as part of its full Certificate of Airworthiness. Strictly speaking there were only three mandatory ones: a Maintenance Manual, a Maintenance Schedule and a Flight Manual. (The latter manual was usually done by the ARB staff at Brabazon House, on behalf of the manufacturer and on commercial terms, of course, but the manufacturers could elect to do it themselves if expedient. Needless to say, John Britten had elected to carry that responsibility 'in-house' at Bembridge). A further three would be necessary to follow on but would not prejudice the UK certification programme: these would be the Illustrated Parts Catalogue, Workshop Manual and Owner's Handbook. As a pattern of what could be acceptable, I had been given a copy of the Beagle 206 Maintenance Manual to serve as a guide. It was a very rough specimen of early draft copy and not really useful, since that particular aeroplane was not proving very successful in service. Furthermore my new boss, with whom I was beginning to forge an empathy, conveyed the message that the Air Registration Board disliked that publication and was insisting on a fuller treatment for the Islander. An early meeting with the ARB representatives was necessary to agree our terms of reference and suggested programme. In his position as Chief Technical Executive, R. E. (Dickie) Bird was responsible for co-ordinating all the design work, along with ground and flight testing data to satisfy the ARB's Certification Requirements.

My diary records that Dickie, Ted and I visited ARB headquarters, at Brabazon House, Redhill, on 25th January 1966 for that initial meeting. We came away having achieved mutual agreement and I was gratified that my credentials, ideas and proposals, were acceptable to the Authority. It meant that I could conclude my estimates of time/costs for the work ahead with a clearer knowledge of the requirements and the milestones along the way. For Dickie Bird, my immediate superior, it meant that he could now remove the question mark against the hitherto blank space concerned with 'Air Publications'. Back home, work continued apace; it was extremely difficult gaining the ear of the relevant design engineers, who were overwhelmed with their own work. A lot of the major design drawings, still fluid in change, did not yield full information, so discussion and observation took on a high level of importance. For a further two weeks or so, armed with a Polaroid instant camera, to record details in certain areas of the aeroplane (likely to be covered up at short notice) along with the work on my estimates and initial writing assignments, I was kept intensely busy. Then, suddenly, we had to move. Somewhat of

37

a relief to me, in that I might have a more amenable work area perhaps.

To accommodate the fuselage design squad, under Mike Benjamin, the Company had leased some rooms in a large house about a quarter of a mile away. Belonging to a single retired man who had fitted the house out in 'holiday-let' flatlets, the arrangements for more permanent guests seemed to suit him fine. Mike and his three or four draughtsmen occupied two of these upstairs kitchen/bed-sitting rooms and we were to join them in occupation of a third one. Not much bigger than the gantry office, the new quarters were (at least) free of the menacing Gestetner machine. Further rooms were taken over as the design workforce expanded and Tom Knight (the owner) eventually relegated his own lifestyle to keeping the central heating system going, from his own smallish kitchen, and moving his bed in there too. Tom had, by this time, promised us the use of his downstairs lounge which was a long narrow panelled room with French doors to the garden at one side. Probably about 24 feet (7.3m) long by maybe 12 feet (3.7m) wide this was an ideal proposition to house additional members of our team. Dickie had mentioned the fact that an 'old Miles hand' was retiring to the island and may be able to help us with illustrating work on a part-time basis. It turned out that Eric Jacobs, as this man was called, came to live at Bembridge having latterly worked for British Railways at Reading. Not only was he keen to take up aircraft illustrating again but was able to work full time, if it could be arranged. Since I was already having to prospect for sub-contract assistance, this appointment was agreed and 'Jake', as he was known, made a start with us in the bedroom. He was a thoroughly knowledgeable, doughty old character who had joined the RAF, as a boy entrant, at Cranwell in the early 1920s. Jake well remembered Bert Hinkler's flight to Australia when the pioneer flyer passed through Mesopotamia where Jake himself was stationed at that time. Jake's abilities, experience and willingness contributed greatly to our performance over the next five years, or so, until his retirement 'proper' occurred.

Back at the hangar, work on the wings, led by Taffy Loyd, was gelling and we could at last plot and number all the access panels with some certainty. John Britten, however, was most upset that the upper surface of his wing had gathered in the region of 40 access holes; all these were necessary to reach controls for adjustments/inspections, electrical equipment and fuel tank compartments. Loganair's Chief Engineer, Walter Ramsey, made a visit and requested that we provide information of that sort for him, on an interim basis, to assist the entry into service of his Islanders. Walter was the archetypal aircraft chief engineer, a Scot of course, clad in a well-worn tweed suit topped by a battered trilby hat, he had a weather-beaten face housing a pair of keen blue eyes that did not miss much in the way of detail, when sizing-up situations or individuals. In return, Walter would give us a copy of his ARB-approved Maintenance Schedule for the Aztecs, to help us in formulating our own. There was a good spirit of mutual co-operation all around, with the object of speeding the new aeroplane's availability to prospective customers. In fairly short order we were also visited by Sir Deryck Bailey and his Chief Engineer, Neville Wright, just as eager as Walter Ramsey to get their hands on as much advance material as we could provide. Glosair's Chief Pilot, Bert Lane, was also an early visitor – wanting the Flight Manual information, in his case, of course.

At about this time Dickie introduced me to an ex-RAF Engineer Officer named Dick Stratton who was doing some local consultancy work. Dick was a very direct and commercially-minded man who enjoyed sparring with the ARB. Bringing with him some specimen work on helicopter inspection schedules, he delighted in showing us how he had been able to convince the Authority that simplification need not compromise safety or accuracy. His advice and incisive thinking helped me a great deal, later on, when we managed to pare down the volume of the Aztec Maintenance Schedule to about half the size; firstly for use as an 'Interim' version and then developed into a 'Final' one for the Islander. All that without losing any vital data, but eliminating a lot of 'officialese' and refusing to bend to previous custom if no good reason could be shown in favour. Dick paid two or three brief visits and, to this day, I do not know whether he was paid for his trouble or if he, like so many others, was caught by the spirit of the overall project.

It is certain that John Britten and Jim McMahon did not welcome the burgeoning expenses. Desmond was not noticeably concerned and, himself, was taking on assistance for potential sales duties. A young pilot enthusiast, who owned a vintage B A Swallow, was taken on in this regard. He was sent off on a Far Eastern tour (though not in the Swallow) to fly the flag for the Company. Meanwhile, a test flying programme was going on with the prototype Islander, Constructor's No. 1 – Registration G-ATCT (Charlie Tango) now with the extended wing and re-engined with the Lycoming 260 hp engines, it was considered more or less representative of a production aeroplane. Returned from the crop spraying arena in Panama, to undertake the Islander's test flying programme was Jim Birnie. Jim's apartment consisted of the wooden shed, formerly used by the forecourt petrol pump attendant, who was now re-located next door in the smaller ice-cream kiosk. Always a dog-lover, Jim was constantly accompanied by his latest canine companion, 'Poochie', an English Bull Terrier bitch with a leary eye and a penchant for seizing and worrying the aircraft wheel chocks by their rope ends. She would lie across Jim's doorway when not engaged otherwise and it was inadvisable to step across her if one wanted to leave with trousers intact, although Jim always maintained '… she was good with children'. Jim's other almost inseparable companion was aerodynamicist/flight test engineer Andy Coombe who shared an office up in the hangar roof, with his performance engineering assistant Bob Wilson. This trio were providers of the data – needed by the operational pilots who would follow – conveyed in the aircraft Flight Manual and Owner's Handbook. Three weeks or so after moving to Tom Knight's bedroom, he notified us that we could move downstairs to his lounge. He'd managed to evacuate what furniture existed there, to places elsewhere, and reckoned that we could have it for as long as we liked. In the event we occupied Tom's lounge for the next eight months and dealt with the main thrust of our preliminary work from there. Several times we were visited by John and Desmond, anxious to ascertain practical progress over that routinely reported.

An early hiccough concerned Ted, who was really more interested by crop spraying activities than illustrating. Sensing that illustrating was going to keep him anchored when more interesting and lucrative work with the overseas spraying tours beckoned, he decided to have a change of employment. He went off to an interview with Pilatus Aircraft, in Switzerland, over the Easter weekend but, unluckily for him, John

Britten found out about the visit. John and Desmond regarded Pilatus as their arch rival, since that company was producing an ultra short-take-off-and-landing workhorse in the form of the Pilatus 'Porter'. Although that aeroplane was completely different from the Islander, the spectre of one of his trusted workers decamping to the opposition was too much for John Britten. Our unfortunate colleague was called into the master's office about a week later, had the equivalent of a Riot Act read out against him, and was summarily dismissed. John and Desmond, in session in the so-called 'Propellor Parliament', liked to think of their organization as a democratic one. In fact, it was more hedonistic, autocratic and paternalistic in its nature, as this particular incident (along with several others) proved. These were times, however, when even the employer was his own master; to a large extent still untrammelled by the effects of socialistic and ideological government legislation.

***

Test flying results were showing up some difficulties that required attention, causing more unanticipated delays. The engine oil radiators had been re-sited towards the rear of the engines for the Lycoming installations, thus being adversely influenced by engine-heated air flowing out of the close fitting cowlings. A remedy for this was eventually devised in the form of baffle plates attached around and above the engine cylinders, with improved air intakes and exits for the oil radiators themselves. Fuel gauging was also problematical, there being an integral compartment at the inner end of each tank which housed the contents float transmitter, along with three or four gallons of fuel and a delivery pump. The idea was to preserve a supply of fuel to the pumps when the aeroplane was in a banked attitude, with lowered fuel states; from this captive amount of fuel the pumps and the contents transmitters were intended to continue steady operation without being unduly affected by sudden level changes due to banking turns. In practice the system worked well but the ARB pointed to possible serious consequences if a blockage of transfer holes between main tank and pump compartment occurred. The Authority did not like the layout and insisted on the Company changing it by a product improvement modification. Changes were made to the wing structure, at the earliest practicable time, to re-site the delivery pumps and fuel contents transmitters to a central position in each tank. The pumps were re-positioned below the undersurfaces of the wing in streamlined sump fairings which also included the fuel sampling cocks.

These latter devices were lethal to Jim Birnie's unprotected bald pate when ducking around the wing doing his pre-flight checks. Oft were the times when Jim incurred another gash before the scabs from a previous injury had healed over. Jim, himself, was also dissatisfied by the rather crude control handwheel and the lack of individual seat adjustment. In the quest for economy John and Desmond had insisted on using five identical passenger seats with folding backs. Each was a twin seat and four of them could be detached and stowed, at the rear of the cabin, if freight was to be carried. These first seats were designed and made by the Company but were, later, improved upon and manufactured by specialist equipment suppliers. For the pilot, however, unless he happened to be in the specific build quartile, it was most unsatisfactory. Jim had to work very hard on the sidelines to get things changed. He had some success, firstly, with the pilot's seat unit. An improved frame carrying two independent sliding seats was later introduced; although much better it still did not include height adjustment. Desmond, no doubt, influenced the situation since he was in the upper realms of build quartile himself. Still later, a new control handwheel was introduced but on an optional basis to begin with; Jim Birnie did not like that one either – but more details about this situation appear later.

As can be seen, the 'Propellor Parliament' had innumerable subjects under discussion, review and change, across the complete aeroplane. Wing structure, engine installation, equipment selection, cabin furnishings and sundry other aspects. In the event, of course, the fever of the work was heightened as the spring of 1966 gave way to the summer and then the autumn. My own work was not made any easier by all these 'ifs and buts' but our particular progress gradually assumed a degree of respectability and I regularly had to provide evidence of this to the ARB at Redhill. It was a bit like being a fictional detective in the novels of yore... 'I have to have the facts, I need the facts, just give me the facts!' How could the designers give me all I needed in good time? Of course they couldn't, until things were decided and tested, step-by-step. Well-knowing their difficulties, I had to cover those parts of the aeroplane that were finalized, in between major enlightenments. A further area of uncertainty concerned the electrical systems. John Britten had decided upon using only one generator as standard equipment – a second generator being specified as an optional extra. To operate in the Public Transport (Passenger) Category of UK Certification, the aeroplane was required to have two generators. This meant that customers would have to pay extra for the necessary second generator and its wiring/control equipment, if they were to carry fare-paying passengers under scheduled airline conditions. While Dennis Berryman and his squad were resolving engine installation affairs and Taffy Lloyd, with his wing structure team, attended to their alterations, Andy O'Connell and Jim Roberts were preoccupied by the fermenting changes to the electrical systems. Not just a matter of bolting on another generator, it was a thoroughgoing exercise in how much wiring and equipment should, or should not, be installed in wing and fuselage – as basic – in order to connect up the second generator when it was fitted.

Needless to say this was a most urgent sector of the design work, since the customers for the first five, at least, aeroplanes required full Transport (Passenger) Category certification and, therefore, dual generator systems. They were not well-pleased, either, when they had to pay for the second system as an optional extra. It took a considerable time to persuade John Britten away from his original decision but he eventually relented and turned the situation around. Dual generators would later be declared standard equipment and the single generator system was the optional one. It was all to do with cost, of course, and John had arrived at a selling price of £17,500 for the production aeroplane, ex-works. Driven as he was, by engineering principles rather than esoteric accountancy rules, John's established price was never a realistic one and could only be held for a limited time before escalation had to occur.

A costing exercise was set up to deal with the manufacturing aspects of the Islander so as to prove and confirm the selling price. In this regard a considerable amount of ground work was done by Tony Edmunds and his assistants, in between more pressing day-to-day responsibilities, but it was dogged by change and delay such that a satisfactory outcome was never achieved. The Chief Accountant, J. P. (Jim) Munn, had so much work on hand at the time, and so few people to deal with it all, that it was amazing how the wages turned up regularly every weekend and the scores of bills, for everything from paper clips to aero-engines, were paid. Some were late – often, but the wages never failed. Tony Edmunds and David Williams, in the little Ford Anglia, collected these from the bank at the appointed time every week. Sometimes the Anglia would be driven by Gwen Burden, a redoubtable island woman driver taken on to assist with the transport duties. Constantly on the road, between the Airport and the several Island ferry terminals, Ryde, Cowes, Wootton Creek, or Yarmouth, the car and its drivers were for ever collecting or delivering people, parcels and paraphernalia. By the autumn of 1966 the workforce at the airport had grown to about 150 people, some of whom were sub-contract workers, in addition to the 30, or so, employed in the Hovercraft Division at the Duver Works. Ironically enough Jim McMahon found himself carrying responsibility for most of this effort, in the absence of a dedicated personnel function. Added to this regular workforce were sub-contract outworkers, such as those employed by Miles, at any one time numbering between 10 and 30 people perhaps.

Among those visitors regularly carried between the ferries and the Airport were the ARB's engineering surveyors tasked with overseeing progress. In addition to Mike Inskip's established liaison with the factory operations, the Company was receiving attention from the relevant design specialists at Brabazon House. At first the Senior Surveyor, working in close conjunction with Dickie Bird, was a man by the name of Harry Ellis. Harry was a seasoned veteran who was nearing retirement and who thoroughly enjoyed his trips to the Isle of Wight. He was supported by the Authority's relevant specialists in electrics, stresses-and-strains, flight performance, and other disciplines as the needs arose. In the flight performance discipline Brian Black was the first man concerned and he was a stickler for perfection. Many were the searching meetings and discussions, concerning flight test data, between he and Andy Coombe before we could confidently commit the results to publication. It was intended that the Company should gain full ARB Design Approval status by the point at which the production aeroplane was awarded its Full Certificate of Airworthiness. Thus, all the related procedures and overall responsibilities would be relinquished by Miles Aviation and Transport Ltd, in favour of Britten-Norman Ltd, at that time. To this end things were moving smoothly and R. E. Bird had been seconded from Miles to act directly for the Company in his confirmed role as Chief Technical Executive.

Activity in the small hangar was intense under Jack Sullivan's 'hands on' leadership, and the fourth wing was now being constructed in the still-not-altogether-complete wing jig which occupied a large amount of much-needed space. A fifty feet (15.25m) long, by eight feet (2.5m) wide steel box member construction for the one-piece wing, dominated the smallish shop floor area. The first two wings, mounted on G-ATCT and G-ATWU, a third one earmarked for a Structural Test Specimen (STS) and now the fourth one, which would be mounted on G-AVCN (Charlie November) Constructor's No. 3, scheduled for delivery to Glosair, closely following the first Loganair delivery. No room in the hangar for the fuselage construction, which had been 'farmed out' to any empty spaces existing at the Duver Works, alongside the hovercraft assembly work. One of Jack Sullivan's foremen was in charge of the construction there with a small party on detachment from the Airport. Harry Hooper was the man responsible, working in conjunction with Mike Benjamin on the design side. Being concerned, as a priority, with the wing attachment brackets but other aspects, such as doors and the floor as well, I paid several visits to this little enclave with my Polaroid camera. Harry was always a willing co-operator and helped me in every way he could to assist general progress.

It was not until the end of August that G-ATWU was rolled out into the light of day. The crysallis stage completed – superseded by the bright new butterfly. Jim Gobert was no longer there as Chief Inspector to sanctify proceedings. For a few months he was replaced by Denzil Humphrey, a mild-mannered rubicund ground engineer with years of experience in Shell Aviation behind him. In turn Denzil was followed by Reg Hobbs, an ex-Handley Page man of South African origin. Reg built up and ran the

Inspection and Quality Control function for many years until his early death. Although 'Whisky Uniform' made its maiden flight just before the end of August, there was no chance of full certification before the Farnborough debut. Another 'Special Category Certificate of Airworthiness' would be necessary to enable its appearance alongside the prototype at the show. For the trade shopwindow, however, the little Britten-Norman company could demonstrate again, a significant degree of progress that ensured further customer interest. John and Desmond were riding high in aviation esteem at this time and the world seemed to be their oyster. In the hangar at Bembridge, Constructor's No 3 – G-AVCN – began to take form, built up from one of Harry Hooper's fuselages and awaiting its wing from the adjacent assembly jig. Meanwhile, Max Wall, one of John Brenchley's structural engineers (who was another ex-Beagle man), was handling the STS wing testing procedure in a polythene tunnel shelter, alongside the western outer wall of the hangar, on the airfield. For a short time the test flying programme was augmented by the availability of two aeroplanes.

Across the corner of the aerodrome, just outside the boundary, steelwork for the new assembly hangar began to make its appearance and at the end of October our time under Tom Knight's roof was over. By now there were seven of us engaged full-time in preparing the necessary engineering and flight manuals for the Islander. Re-furbished office space on the mezzanine gantry was allocated to us and Mike Benjamin's little team was absorbed into other duties within the drawing office nearby. This facility had been expanded by the expedient of joining up two gantry sides with a bridge-like structure, across the centre of the hangar, above the shop floor work area. Somehow or other extra space had been found to accommodate our estranged Gestetner machine (for which we now had an operator) and a small photographic darkroom, to house platemaking equipment and a likely new process camera. Things were looking up. In the drawing office a much improved new plan printer was installed to replace the earlier small one.

**

Notwithstanding all of the efforts and improvements, however, it was now evident that the chances of attaining full UK certification for the Islander by the end of 1966 were remote indeed. On the 9th of November we were all struck by a hammerblow. The prototype Islander, Constructor's No. 1 (G-ATCT – Charlie Tango), returning from an assignment on the continent, had crashed in Holland. Bad weather, icing conditions in particular, had contributed to the disaster in which the freelance pilot lost his life. Someone in authority, from the Company, had to go there at once to make an assessment of the wreckage. In the event it was Desmond Norman himself who went, accompanied by Ron Dack. Desmond would not allow anyone else from Britten-Norman Ltd to attend the crash scene and it proved to set the pattern for future accidents, when they occurred. Being a Chartered Engineer, whose findings were acceptable to the insurance companies, Ron would be called upon a number of times in the future to make similar assessments. A detailed and time-consuming official inquiry was necessary to establish all the facts, in case of other possible defects. In the light of the inquiry findings, some modifications were introduced to stiffen the wing spars and undersurface skinning, together with improvements to the elevator attachments, rendering them less likely to be affected by ice accretion. No major problems existed, however, except that the delays and the necessity for the Company to retain one aeroplane for continued flight testing, set the programme back by a further three or four months. An arrangement was made with Loganair to retain Constructor's No. 2 (G-ATWU), for the remaining development test flying, provided the airline could have it on lease to do its route proving trials, at least a month in advance of the arrival of their first production aeroplane. This was now re-scheduled as Constructor's No. 4 (G-AVKC), there being no change to the Glosair allocation of Constructor's No. 3 (G-AVCN). By the turn of the year everyone in the Company was working just that little bit harder and longer to try to make up lost ground.

In our particular case we had been providing small batch samples of our publications (ten or a dozen copies, perhaps) for comment and to follow the position as it developed. Concerning the electrical supply diagrams, which were extensive enough to need two or three 'fold out' pages, I had to get these processed and printed by an outside agency because our own equipment could not handle them. This action was necessary to save paper and effort, of course, but as the situation became clearer and more stabilized we were able to increase some quantities to fifty off and set them aside for incorporation into the finalized manuals later on. I had an agreement, with John and Desmond, upon the stylized loose leaf binders to accommodate our manuals and these were on order from a specialist manufacturer in Gloucester. John Britten had also wanted to price the emerging manuals, for sale to Operators. He and I had several sessions upon the subject, before establishing a pricing formula which, initially, set the price of the Islander Maintenance Manual at the truly English value of 12 guineas! John was understandably irritated by the length of time it was taking, on all fronts, to achieve the full certification requirements; cold weather flight trials in Iceland or Finland, followed by trials in 'hot and high' flight conditions, in East Africa, had to be arranged and pursued, to complete the performance scheduling data. All these things in mind, John paid me a searching visit early in February of 1967 to ascertain the exact situation as it affected the preparation of the relevant manuals. I was able to show him my 'suspended' drawer which contained a lot of half-finished illustrations and draft copy material, awaiting design decisions and 'go-aheads'. The pilot's seat unit was one such; no fewer than three possibles were still being evaluated. Looking back, now, at my diary for 1967 it seems probable that the ARB was making waves in the background, because their representative Theodore (Ted) Tonkin (my mentor on the engineering manuals) telephoned me a few days later, asking what progress we had made since November, when he was last up-dated.

On the broader front the new assembly hangar was taking shape and would have space for about 16 Islanders, in two lines abreast. In the event, however, the right-hand line would not be viable because it was decided to set up the wing, fuselage and tail unit assembly jigs on that side. Building delays, in one form or another, affected the completion of the hangar. These sprang from numerous hastily-arranged and ill-thought-out sub-contract jobs, interfering one-with-another, together with a considerable amount of on-site pilfering. Following a Sunday morning visit, by John Britten himself, and several instant dismissals, the latter situation improved somewhat. Early in 1968, as soon as it was practicable, the main jigs were brought together for the first time and installed as planned. In the summer of 1967, however, this was still some distance away and the immediate target, apart from those of the ever-present certification programme, was once again the Paris Air Salon in June. This date came and went in the usual welter of haste and special arrangements but light was appearing at the end of the tunnel and August was set to be the time of UK Transport (Passenger) Category certification. R. E. Bird had been working flat out to prove completion of all design and test requirements, against a master check list, in conjunction with the ARB departments concerned. My area of responsibility was just one of the many which had involved him in an exhausting routine of meetings and exchanges over many months. Dickie was always urbane and courteous throughout, he had a precise and totally unflappable manner which engendered confidence in those who worked with him, although I became aware that he was not a universally popular man within the Company.

Accordingly, I note from my diary (and remember vividly) that three or four of us, Penny included, worked until approximately 2:30am on the night of Wednesday 21st June 1967 to get advance copies of several publications corrected and made up for transit, by hand with Dickie Bird, to ARB on Thursday 22nd June. This was to be his penultimate meeting with the Authority before, hopefully, gaining the final seal of approval for the Islander in August. When complete, the two or three fairly heavy packages were labelled, as requested, and placed on and around his chair ready for him to convey that morning, while we went home to bed. Several days earlier I had had meetings with Vic Stevens of the ARB (an associate of Ted Tonkin), concerning the Maintenance Schedule for the aeroplane, and with Brian Black, in connection with the Flight Manual. This latter manual was the most complete one, the Maintenance Schedule being classed as an 'interim' version, whilst the Maintenance Manual itself was about 65 per cent complete but would reach its full standard of completion by the turn of the year, through amendment action as mutually agreed. A few last minute changes were required when these publications were assessed and, about one week later, I had a telephone call from Ted Tonkin to say he would be arriving at Bembridge on 14th July for the Official Acceptance Meeting of the Islander Engineering Publications.

A final effort to clear up outstanding issues over the next few days, led on to an all-out printing effort, beginning on Friday 7th July until Wednesday 12th July, to complete the first production batch of publications for the final Assessment Meeting on Friday 14th July. It had been done. We had satisfied, if not completed, our brief and the UK Type Certification process had not been compromised through a lack of acceptable technical publications for the Islander. On 18th August 1967 the Islander was awarded its full Certificate of Airworthiness, in the UK Transport (Passenger) Category, allowing deliveries to begin. The first two aeroplanes away had already beaten the official gun, in fact, Constructor's No. 3 (G-AVCN) and No. 4 (G-AVKC) having been delivered to Glosair and Loganair on 13th August and 15th August respectively. Desmond's sales initiatives were never held up for long by official procedures. Constructor's No. 5 (G-AVOS), built in the same rudimentary conditions, first flew three weeks after the official certification date and was delivered 19 days later – on 28th September 1967 – to Britten-Norman's USA agent in New York.

Thus another new pressure point was created, because the aeroplane had yet to receive American Federal Aviation Agency (FAA) Type Certification. Although a reciprocal agreement for such matters was in existence, there were some significant differences in the US requirements. Some of these caused us to have to raise a new and specific Flight Manual for use in the USA and those other countries within its jurisdiction. Other necessary design changes caused similar shifts of emphasis in the Drawing, Weights, Stress and Flight Test offices' work programmes which had to be finalized before Christmas 1967. This was essential because the aeroplane had been delivered to America with a temporary UK C of A for Export and the Agents (Jonas Aircraft and Arms Corporation) in New York, could not achieve American registration until compliance with their regulations was established. Dickie Bird was again fully occupied in drawing everything together for this important milestone in the Islander's development. As well as being a competent engineer,

Dickie was an exceptionally good organizer, a shrewd negotiator and a man with a cosmopolitan background, ready to go anywhere in the world at short notice. These were valuable attributes, seldom found together in one individual's package. In many respects he was more akin to Desmond Norman than John Britten, who had been prevailed upon to appoint a new Chief Designer earlier in 1967, with a somewhat vague brief since, he, John Britten, still insisted on leading the design initiative. It turned out that the ARB had insisted upon the Company taking on an experienced engineer to control things, in the always likely situation that R.E. Bird should decide that he had had enough and wanted to move on. The man appointed was John Allan, a Diploma Engineer, who had worked for Handley Page Ltd on their 'Herald' airliners. Before that, John had been employed by the Blackburn Aircraft Co. Ltd where I had, myself, started out as an apprentice in 1943.

***

Arising now, almost in parallel with the American certification work, were preparations for Constructor's No. 15 – not yet ready but destined for delivery to the Australian Department of Civil Aviation in mid-February of 1968. Again specific requirements pointed up urgent actions necessary to comply with the Australian airworthiness regulations. This time, besides being required to produce another specific new Flight Manual, there was a definite requirement for an Illustrated Parts Catalogue (IPC) as part of the Type Certification documentation, leading to the ultimate award of an Australian Certificate of Airworthiness. Although work on the IPC had been mooted, it had not been possible to start anything because of other pressures and the fact that the publication had been seen, hitherto, as a commercial proposition only. Convinced, in the event, that the work was essential, John and Desmond sanctioned a limited sum, one-off, sub-contract job late in 1967 which was left to me to expedite. The only person I knew of, likely to be reliable in this commission, was P. S. Braisby who ran a company by the name of Gloster (sic) Designs Ltd, based in the old Gloster Aircraft factory, at Hucclecote, near Gloucester. It was all that remained of that once famous organization. The sum in question amounted to £5000 and represented about four thousand man-hours of work to get the catalogue readied for typesetting and printing. Additional expenses would be involved in that final process. This position, as established from my own estimates, was accepted in good faith by Percy Braisby who paid a quick visit, was introduced to John and Desmond, and assured us of his fullest co-operation. Two or three days later Percy's office manager, Tom Durrant, arrived at Bembridge and made himself aware of the prevailing situation over the next two days. During that time we got together five packages of prints from design drawings and as many of our Maintenance Manual illustrations as we could spare, for him to take 'photographic pulls' from, in order to save duplication of illustrating work. Gloster Designs put every available person onto the job and made it their top priority, so long as we could keep them fed with the necessary emerging information.

On Friday 16th February 1968 we air-freighted a bundle of Islander Air Publications, 2 each of 8 titles, amongst which were two advance copies of the Illustrated Parts Catalogue (not yet complete but a portent of good faith) to the Australian Department of Civil Aviation in Melbourne. Dickie Bird was to leave for that destination on Sunday 18th February to meet with the Authority in preparing the scene for the arrival of Constructor's No. 15 some days later. Stopping off briefly in Singapore, Dickie was carrying with him a smaller package of Islander publications for the ARB's Far-Eastern Surveyor, who would soon be concerned with local operators and transit flights in that region. On the same day, Friday 16th February, I note that we also air-freighted a similar package of Islander publications to the Canadian Department of Transport in Ottawa. This action was to assist that Authority with its own forthcoming acceptance of the aeroplane for Canadian certification and operation. Constructor's No. 23 was the Islander concerned and it was earmarked for delivery, through Jonas Aircraft and Arms Corporation, to Jim Wright in Edmonton sometime in May 1968. Jim ran a company called 'Big Wiel', having as his logo a prairie wagon wheel with that lettering running through it. WIEL stood for 'Wright Industrial Enterprises Limited' and Jim would have liked to have had a full Canadian agency for Britten-Norman Ltd. Background circumstances prevented that development, however, and the particular aeroplane soon went to another owner.

These were fruitful and formative times for Britten-Norman Ltd. Design documentation, static testing, flight testing – and even technical publications – now hardening into a decisive definition for the small airliner so fervently desired by its founding partners. Several ARB test pilots had flown the Islander, of course, but the man who was doing regular flight test checks, on behalf of the Authority, was a Canadian ex-patriate pilot named Hugh Kendall, who lived on the Isle of Wight as it happened. Hugh lived across to the western end of the Island and had enough land for his own airstrip, thus allowing him to commute to Redhill in his Jodel monoplane. When working at Bembridge his little white and blue Jodel was a familiar sight at the Airport. Later on, after retiring from the Authority, he would be taken on as an additional test pilot for the Company. More people than ever were employed when the new hangar gained enough shelter to house the production jigs, down the right hand side, as initially planned. Over 200 people were now employed directly by the Company. Mrs Britten still drove her pony and trap up from Bembridge now and then, but the workforce had outgrown her capacity to provide them with picnic teas or suppers. Another local character who visited at certain times, was 'Cocoa' Fry. His nickname derived from his surname and the fact that his weatherbeaten, wizened appearance resembled the eponymous bean. 'Cocoa' was an old Bembridge boatbuilder, employed by John and Desmond to look after their yacht, moored in Bembridge harbour. He would come up to the Airport to receive his instructions, particularly in the time leading up to Cowes Week, exchange banter with anyone he could find willing to listen, before returning to his solitary duties. John Britten was a long-standing member of the Royal Yacht Squadron at Cowes and, together, he and Desmond were regular competitors in the associated racing and social events of that illustrious calendar. On at least two occasions the partners competed in the gruelling Fastnet race.

All the while, wages and expenses were still being carried by Crop Culture (Aerial) Ltd., apart from servicing the heavy loans which now existed to the tune of about £700,000. British Hovercraft Corporation, at Cowes, which had helped in the construction of early jigs and fixtures, had been engaged to augment early production by making a number of Islander components, including complete wings, under sub-contract. Even so, however, the need to expand, further, the existing production potential was having to be accepted. In April 1968 orders for the Islander stood at over 200 aeroplanes and Desmond presided over a Sales Department handling ever more customer interest. Gone was the young enthusiast pilot, John Anning and his B A Swallow; in place as Sales Manager was an ex-RAF pilot by the name of Brian Partridge. Almost as soon as the concrete was set around the jigs down the right-hand side of the new hangar, dialogue between Britten-Norman and British Hovercraft Corporation resulted in that company being contracted to build 240 sets of full Islander components, in the form of kits, for final assembly at Bembridge. Up came all the Bembridge jigs for transport to Cowes, leaving the full floor area free to accept two assembly lines of aeroplanes, instead of one. Needless to say there was a temporary disruption for eight or ten weeks, until the kits began to come through. Entwined with these arrangements was the decision to transfer upwards of 60, or so, production workers from Britten-Norman's payroll to that of BHC, thereby lessening the effects of an emerging cashflow crisis. This was an extremely unpopular decision with most of those people affected, since they had never wanted to work for BHC in the first place.

Jim McMahon's worst fears were being confirmed. Jim would have preferred to have steered the Britten-Norman Company towards public ownership, through a stockmarket flotation but John and Desmond were afraid of losing their influence in, and control of, their Company in such a move. Seeing a more satisfactory alternative, for himself, Jim McMahon negotiated a split from Britten-Norman, under which he would take over the Micronair production and marketing facilities, including the personnel and certain crop spraying interests, as his share of the enterprise in which they had, all three, co-operated up to that time in June 1968. To these ends, Jim had been able to lease the old defence fort on Bembridge Down, built in Napoleonic times. In 1967, Peter Gatrell had carefully moved out all of the Micronair plant and production, from the Airport premises to the Duver Works, to make room for Islander work, as previously mentioned. Now, Peter had accepted Jim's offer to join him at Bembridge Fort and was to move all the Micronair effects once again, separating himself, finally, from the Duver Works and from Britten-Norman Ltd. a couple of months later in August. One could say that these further pruning effects may have been temporarily beneficial to the cashflow situation, but significant difficulties still lay ahead. For the remainder of us, ever grappling with targets and delivery dates, however, there was no time to brood on hypothetical matters because the show had to go on. After all these were the 'Swinging Sixties'.

5.1 Prototype Islander (Constructor's No. 1) on a test flight, off the south-western coast of the Island, near the 'Old Battery'. Photograph clearly shows the different engine cowling shapes, with deep carburettor air intakes, for the Lycoming engines. Late 1965 or early 1966

5.2 Rigging some of the much-improved Micronair rotary atomisers on a dedicated crop-spraying aircraft. This is the model AU-5000, driven by directly-attached windmill blades

5.3 A wing set of model AU-5000 atomisers, mounted on carrier booms, ready for installation. These units are still in limited production at the time of writing

5.4 Production Islander Constructor's No. 21. This aeroplane – and the next off the Bembridge line, Constructor's No. 22 – were delivered to a German operator, Ostfriesische Lufttransport, during April 1968

5.5 Desmond Norman viewing the new assembly hangar construction, at Bembridge Airport, in 1966

Chapter 6

Reorganization

It was about the middle of May 1968 when John Britten and Desmond Norman first informed a small group of us, from the Technical Offices, that major changes were impending. Decisions had already been taken to sell off those overseas companies and associated interests that were of no use to Jim McMahon. We were told of the revised arrangements in hand with BHC for the manufacture of further completed Islander sub-assembled components and the plans to complete the aircraft final assembly at Bembridge. This was to be done using BHC's own workforce initially, some of whom would be ex-Britten-Norman employees, of course, on detachment back to Bembridge. In due course Eric Gilberthorpe, the BHC Works Director, came across to Bembridge to make a formal announcement, along with John and Desmond, to our factory personnel about the co-operation. There was no doubt that an extremely favourable price for the completed aeroplane, in sub-assembled form, had been quoted by BHC. We were told of this figure at the time of our call-together by the two partners and were sworn to such secrecy by Desmond Norman that, even now, forty years later, I would not willingly divulge the cost to anyone. Eric Gilberthorpe's influence and experience, together with BHC's production capacity and expertise played an important part in getting the Islander production work off on the right foot. In its previous incarnation, as Saunders-Roe Ltd., this was the company which had built so many of Short's Sunderland flying boats during World-War II.

To oversee the whole scope of BN's production affairs, a highly-placed Production Engineer, from Vickers at Weybridge, had been recruited. This was Ken Mills, who had recently taken his place at Bembridge. Despite his years in the softer climes of Surrey, Ken was a blunt, hard-drinking Mancunian, who had never quite shaken off his northern accent, or the outlook of his fellow countrymen. Inevitably, in the situation, there were disagreements at top level. During one of these altercations, whilst Jim McMahon was still at the Airport, Jack Sullivan who had done so much to expedite the initial work programme, made a sudden departure from the Company. A man from Fisher-Ludlow, the Birmingham metal pressings firm, took Jack's place for a while, but he didn't stay very long with the Company. Desmond, meanwhile, had hired a high-powered executive from the cosmetics industry to head up his Sales Department. Gerry Maynard, it was, who reckoned that selling aeroplanes was much like selling bars of soap and soon became engaged in overseas tours of business in an attempt to prove it.

Across in the USA Alex Mueller, the president of Jonas Aircraft and Arms Corporation, was so sure of the Islander's potential there, that he was bargaining with the Company to take alternate aeroplanes from the production line, as soon as it was up and running. Alex made several visits to Bembridge early on, sometimes bringing with him his Argentinian lieutenant, Alex Pagliere. This latter gentleman had the distinction of being Jonas' Eastern Representative and he would make many more routine visits as time went on. In that function his area covered everywhere on the globe, eastwards of New York. I suppose there was a Western Representative, who covered the other half of the globe – but who it was and where their demarcation lines met, I was never to find out. Pagliere was a decent sort, however, who was always immaculately turned out and well-informed of customers requirements and whereabouts. Some of them, on Alex's books, changed names and addresses at similar frequencies to their laundry it seemed, so his visits often cleared up anomalies on our mailing lists. John and Desmond, at this time were very captivated by a Portuguese manufacturer and distributor of aircraft accessories, operating out of Lisbon. That company was named Alar and was run by Pedro Reitsch and Jóse Canélas. This was the supplier who had developed a control handwheel, favoured by Desmond, in the form of an inverted 'W – or 'ram's horn' as he liked to call it – similar to the style used in the Concorde. Trials were effected and, despite Jim Birnie showing that interference with the throttle levers could occur in some conditions, a batch of these handwheels was supplied to Britten-Norman and fitted to customer orders.

Jim was not at all satisfied with the situation and determined to design his own control handwheel. With the help of empathetic people in the drawing office and ancillary efforts, both within the factory, and from outside specialists, a very neat ergonomic new control wheel was developed. This was known, internally, as the 'Jim Birnie control wheel', and was trialled to the universal approval of everyone concerned. It became the standard fitment for future production aeroplanes during the up-dating programmes which saw improved cabin trim and seating introduced. Alar, however, continued its association with Britten-Norman for some time, taking over the design of an improved and adjustable pilot's seat, to supersede the use of a fixed passenger seat unit at that position. Only a few initial production Islanders had the fixed seat at the pilot's position. A constantly busy time was experienced by the small buying office at the Airport, led by the Chief Buyer, Vic Lewis, which was tasked to find the most suitable cost-effective supplier for all those other items, not directly held as fashionable or desirable by John and Desmond. There was a strong policy to use American equipment wherever possible, since such materiél was more likely to be acquired by overseas operators than equivalent British stock. Every so often Vic would be quickly dispatched to the USA to sort out alternative suppliers, or mollify the unpaid ones, whilst trying ever harder to improve lead-times and pricing structures. All the while his few colleagues, chief among whom was Pat Pickard, worked with their telephone in one hand and a pen in the other for most of their time. Pat could have done with a third hand since he smoked about 40 cigarettes a day and could never find his ash-tray under the welter of suppliers' catalogues and purchase order forms. In the conditions of the reorganization, as it got underway, it became necessary for the hard-pressed buyers to arrange diversions of deliveries of certain equipment and materials, to BHC at Cowes to avoid double handling wherever possible; another set of complications which they could well have done without.

The temporary stagger in production, caused by the reorganization process, allowed a small window of opportunity to enable the introduction of design changes in the Islander. These were significant major improvements which had been thrashed out by the 'Propellor Parliament' and were vitally necessary in the light of developing experience. Besides the wing and fuel tank improvements, previously mentioned, there were changes to the engine nacelles, undercarriage, undercarriage fairings, wing flaps and wing inboard leading edges, aimed at improving the take-off and climb-out capabilities. If those objectives could be realized it would enable a modest increase in the aeroplane's carrying capacity and, hence, its gross weight. This latter feature had an important effect in the field operations, but could not be achieved effectively without commensurate performance enhancement. The Islander had been designed to comply with that section of British Civil Airworthiness Requirements (BCARs) applicable to small aeroplanes not exceeding 6000lb (2722kg) All-Up-Weight and John Britten had been parsimonious with the weights issue throughout. The Weights Engineer, Peter Ward, had been entrusted with reviews and actions devoted to weight saving all along with the result that the initially certificated Model BN-2 Islander had a stated maximum All-Up-Weight of 5700lb (2585kg). Any excesses over 6000lb (2722kg), in normal operating weight, would have taken the aeroplane into a different class, involving a host of further requirements, outside the scope of the original specification. However, the extra 300lb (136kg) load-carrying potential was worth striving for and the four or five modifications being considered, would enable the ultimate benefits to be achieved, as test flying results had confirmed. This group of interdependent modifications, along with their predicted benefits, was known internally as 'Speedpack" and was submitted to the Air Registration Board for immediate attention. Mutual discussions resulted in a recommendation, from the Authority, that the Company should embody the changes in a package which would have the effect of changing the aeroplane's designated Model No. from BN-2 to BN-2A. Working towards an optimum situation, therefore, it was decided that Constructor's No. 24 should be designated as the first BN-2A and that was done. There were two or three later production aeroplanes, caught up in the changeover period, which remained as BN-2's but their buyers were prepared to accept them, for their own operations, without the upgrades. The scene was now set for an uninterrupted production programme which offered the best possible product within the framework of specifications, price and regulations that could be achieved.

Stepping back a moment, to the first week in March 1968 and to the cabin seat situation, it is interesting to recall that the Company's first experience of in-service failure, concerned the Britten-Norman made seats. Two cases of seat cushion collapse occurred, with two different operators, on those seat units installed at the pilot's stations. The rubberized canvas support straps, under the cushions, were prone to breakage under heavy use it seemed. In my earlier discussions with Ted Tonkin at the ARB, we had agreed that we would cover any field-service defects with three categories of Service Bulletin. These bulletins would be classified as: MANDATORY, RECOMMENDED and OPTIONAL. The two latter classifications would be printed under blue-coloured headings, whilst the former classification would be printed under 'signal red' headings and would, in all cases, impose a time limit by which specified inspections and/or alterations must be completed. Because of the nature of the seat defect, which may have caused a pilot to lose control at a critical moment, this otherwise fairly minor fault gained a 'red-top' status immediately. Our small in-plant printing facility (such a liability in the first year or so, centred as it was around the Gestetner machine) had dramatically improved in recent months since we had taken on Graham Montrose, a tradesman printer, to run the facility for us. Graham had made out a strong case for part-exchanging the Gestetner in favour of a much more capable Multilith 1250 offset-litho machine and we had installed a new little process camera, together with electrostatic plate making equipment. For a modest outlay our capability and flexibility had increased enormously and we were now well-prepared to respond quickly to any extra technical field service output that may be required.

As soon as the terms of rectification for the seat failure had been decided and agreed with the ARB, formally printed 'red-top' copies of the resultant Service Bulletin were mailed to all known Operator's and Airworthiness Authorities' addresses, in 'Priority Flight Safety Information' marked envelopes. This occasion was one of a number of recent instances when I had been drawn, more and more, into the orbit of John Allan, the Chief Designer who had been engaged, reluctantly, by John Britten. Due to Dickie Bird's increasingly frequent absences, on initial Customer liaison and Airworthiness Approval duties, John

Allan was my obvious 'next-of-kin' when Dickie was away. It was John Allan who would steer the Company policies and technical action, in conjunction with Peter Mallinson who was in charge of the Field Service Department, when defects such as the above mentioned one occurred. All these seemingly digressive facts, in their rather circuitous commentary, are included because the overall picture of the Company's prime activities, capabilities and logistics were under the microscope in the reorganization process, leading up to June 1968. Among the considerations was the question of whether to retain the in-plant printing facility or whether to dispense with it altogether. A review of the situation, firstly by the Chief Accountant, Jim Munn, who had asked me to provide estimated annual costings for the possible use of outside sub-contract printing services and, secondly, by John Allan, on the basis of how much extra space could be released if Graham Montrose could be persuaded to take over the equipment, moving it out and operating it on a freelance basis.

Indeed, Desmond Norman, himself had taken me on one side, some time earlier, about these matters. No doubt Desmond had been apprised of outside printing costs as they had developed, over the first rather chaotic year, contrasting them with increased expenditure on the recent improvements to in-plant equipment and personnel, and coming up with the obvious deduction – why? Desmond approached me with the opening gambit of '... Derek, we are aeroplane designers and manufacturers, not printers. We don't want to set up in opposition to our good friends, the printers...' Just who he was thinking of, when he used the term ' ... our good friends the printers,' was not made clear, but I felt I had to remind him of the alacrity with which the first Service Bulletin issue had been accomplished, compared to negotiating with an outside printer and literally standing in his work queue until the job was done. One could have spent several weeks, at that time in such procedure whilst the embodiment limit for a MANDATORY class bulletin ebbed away on a similar, or maybe shorter, timescale which would also have affected the confidence of the ARB, in an adverse manner.

Nonetheless, however, the proposition of offloading the printing function onto Graham Montrose, had to be considered and couched in terms of the Company's needs taking priority over other potential work which may arise for him. Not just printing alone was involved, because quite a varied stockroom holding of finished and part-finished material for our aircraft technical publications (as well as other company documentation) was, by now, an essential part of the service. Of course, even in the event of Graham being offered all of the equipment as a gift, having to sign an agreement to put Britten-Norman's work always at the head of his priorities, made for a completely unattractive business deal to him. It was not surprising, in the circumstances, that a considerable amount of time and effort was expended to no avail. The in-plant printing function stayed under the Company's direct control after all avenues had been explored.

August 1968 saw the departure of J. M. McMahon from the Company, taking with him the Micronair work and the relevant personnel. Their new premises in the old fort, up on Bembridge Down, were fitted out to cope with the Micronair design and production requirements and a new autonomous Company – Micronair Limited – under the sole ownership of Jim McMahon was formed to carry on the business, formerly based at the Duver Works. Jim McMahon stayed on good terms with John Britten and Desmond Norman, however, and there was a continuing co-operation in crop-spraying activities, when they arose in connection with the use of Islander aeroplanes. The drawing office was further extended, in the Airport hangar, by flooring over the mezzanine open quadrangle above the shop floor space. This was supported by additional steel stanchions and effectively joined up the majority of the mezzanine floor spaces into one large first floor working area to best effect. The whole effort of internal alterations to the factory space, in those times, was a constant testimony to the ingenuity and hard work of the small works maintenance staff under the foremanship of Jan Maley and Works Engineer Derek Fitch, firstly, followed by David Cover. Steel erection, joinery, plasterwork, electrical installation and painting /decorating, all had to be done with least disruption to those other workers so that no delays were experienced. Inevitably there were some areas where self-respecting factory and fire service inspectors were best kept away from, but things usually worked out well in the end.

Andy Coombe moved down into the office vacated by Jim McMahon and Jim Birnie was a constant visitor, naturally enough, in the pursuit of test flying business. Of the few ladies employed at that time, Lyn Maud served as Desmond's secretary, working in the next office. Lyn was a somewhat excitable mature woman who was often left to find her own best way through regular piles of important and mundane matters, whether Desmond was present, or not, as the case may be. Fortunately for her, she was possessed of a tolerant and cheerful disposition most of the time, but there were often amusing exchanges taking place, on the first floor landing adjacent to my own workplace. One occasion I remember when Jim Birnie came up the plain uncovered domestic staircase. from the shop floor, huffing and puffing in mock concern; Lyn, having some particular aviation question to settle and knowing well the manner of the ascender, rushed to the doorway saying '... Jim may I have your advice please?' Quick as a flash Jim replied in his best West Country accent 'Yes m'dear, always keep your knees pressed tightly together'. There was an explosion of mirth all around culminating in Lyn's rejoinder 'Oh, Jim, you are awful!' Installed in a little boxed-in compartment near the staircase was the Company's telephone switchboard, operated by Barbara Ford, another mature lady whose husband Tom was the Chief Storekeeper in the various wired-in compounds along the sides of the hangar. Barbara's distinctive mellow voice always gave the effect of an unflurried BBC announcer. Together, she and Tom had once earned their living in theatrical circles as a duo song-and-dance act. There was an underlying connection with the world of theatre, since John Britten's younger brother was an impressario, or agent, in the London scene and we were visited, on occasions, by celebrities from stage and screen. Roy Orbison, the blind American singer and his entourage were entertained as guests of the Britten family, I remember, during these early formative and enthusiastic times, when the majority of the effort was concentrated in the old hangar.

***

As that important summer of 1968 unfolded, Jim Birnie and Andy Coombe were test flying a programme of largely experimental changes to the Islander, along with routine additional performance measurements and calibrations, often based away for a few days at a time. Still using Constructor's No. 2 (G-ATWU Whisky Uniform) they were evaluating updated undercarriage units and combinations of disc brakes, together with many other aspects as revealed by some of the developing certification requirements. With the American, Canadian, Australian and New Zealand certifications either cleared or within sight of completion, there were French requirements to contend with, for the African and other overseas countries under the French jurisdiction. Gabon was one of the first to materialize, because two operators, under the names of Transgabon and Air Gabon, were in negotiation to purchase several Islanders for use in that country. The pressures and extent of the technical administrative work involved in gaining these certifications, often seemed disproportionate to the initial gains, particularly if only one or two aeroplanes ended up in those regions. Nevertheless, once achieved, they were usually there to stay and we lived in hope that further orders would develop; sometimes they did and sometimes they didn't. By the end of July, partially finished kits of fuselages, wings and empennages were beginning to come on stream to Bembridge, from BHC at Cowes, for final assembly. The part finished sub-assemblies went straight into the new assembly hangar for completion and a quite slick operation soon developed. Because of Jim Birnie's experimental flying commitments, it had been necessary to engage another test pilot, to handle the expected production check test flights of new aeroplanes, as they were completed. In this matter the Company had been very fortunate to acquire the services of John Nielan, who was semi-retired, after a long career of test flying duties behind him. During the late 1930's and early war years John had been employed by Blackburn Aircraft Ltd and had taken part in test flying the Blackburn Botha, a twin-engined light bomber project, similar to the Bristol Blenheim. Thus it was that these newly built Islanders from the co-operative activities, received their acceptance checks at the hands of John Nielan.

With the approach of September and Farnborough's turn for the International Air Show once again, there was an emphasis this time on the Far East. Constructor's No. 28 and 29had been ordered by Aerial

Tours Pty of Port Moresby in New Guinea for their varied operations in that country. These were two of the aeroplanes, not having the upgrades to BN-2A status and would be delivered as BN-2's. As Papua New Guinea was within the Australian jurisdiction of Airworthiness Requirements, this explained our recent intensive efforts to comply with all the necessary regulations. Constructor's No. 28 made its first flight just before the show and No. 29 just after. The significant thing, though, was the fact that our small Company could now, in little over two years, demonstrate a purposeful and increasingly capable presence, with thirty-plus new aeroplanes in service across the world. In England for the 1968 Farnborough event was an Australian millionaire motor dealer and distributor, who had an eye for extending his business into the field of aviation. Harold Hunt was a smallish man in stature but, in his well-cut light grey suit and luxurious hand-made shoes, he shone like some antipodean jewel among our watery Island *nieberlung*. It is quite likely, although not certain, that he had made acquaintance with Dickie Bird during the latter's presence in Australia on certification business, at any rate the two men knew each other quite well. Hunt brought with him two or three of his executives who, between them, took in all of our intentions and potential, during a quick but thorough appraisal.

For many years in Australia, almost since Amy Johnson's time, the deHavilland Aircraft Proprietary had enjoyed pride of place in the service to aircraft owners and operators but Harold Hunt, it seemed, was intent on competition with them. Unknown to myself, at that particular time, but later to transpire, was the broaching of another new project which was probably discussed between John and Desmond and Harold Hunt. Even while the hectic business of initial modifications and shakedown alterations to the Islander, and its certification standards, continued to absorb a great deal of the Technical Offices' time and effort, here was another likely pressure point. More about this will appear later but, at its first mention, the project was simply named 'GDP'. Dennis Berryman and Andy O'Connell, who were by this time functioning as joint Drawing Office managers, first drew my attention to it about a fortnight after Farnborough week. Thinking it somewhat strange that they should approach me, over the heads of John Allan and Dickie Bird as it were, I did not give too much attention or credibility to the subject. It seemed, however, that John Britten's fertile mind (aided again by Desmond's outreach instinct) had conceived an idea for a work-sharing and cost-sharing plan to revolutionize the international private flying scene, In this plan, Australia was to feature strongly as the ideal launching pad for the intentions under consideration.

Getting small aeroplanes to these far-flung places was always an interesting exercise in long-range fuel tankage and human endurance. The Islander had proved itself capable of flying for long periods, without problems, in spite of its originally conceived short range role. Its Lycoming engines were famously reliable power units that would keep on running in all weather conditions, so long as fuel could be fed to them. Those first aeroplanes, delivered to Jonas in New York, had set a pattern of ferry flying which was shortly to be replicated in transit flights going eastwards on a regular basis. Among the test flying jobs done by Jim Birnie and Andy Coombe, was the development of various configurations of overload fuel systems. For the Atlantic crossings, initially, the aeroplanes were flown to Shannon, in western Ireland, where a specialist company was used to install suitable temporary tankage to enable the long hops to Boston (Mass.)USA, via Iceland, Greenland and Newfoundland. Once there, the temporary tankage was removed and carpets, curtains and seats were installed for onward transit to New York – or wherever required. The fuel systems were re-used, wholly or in part, by American aeroplanes on export flights to Europe, using the same route in reverse.

Our Design Department had recently accepted responsibility for long range tankage systems and Dennis Berryman, as the power plant specialist, was busy designing a little family of modifications to cope with the requirements. In horse racing terms, he was only a short head in front of the field because the equipment was coming together almost before a modification number had been released and the ARB was pressing me for formal supplementary flight manual information, even whilst Andy Coombe was quantifying the associated performance degradations and operating routines. Although these were not unusual circumstances, they did make for frayed tempers, up and down the communications chains, sometimes. Jim Birnie was not keen on the fuel gauges, in general, referring to them as '... Mickey Mouse instruments..' and constantly hoped for more 'air man like' dials. The ones fitted in Islanders, together with their contents transmitters, had been originally sourced from commercial truck suppliers, on economy grounds. Electric generators, too, had been chosen in the same way, following American practice it must be said, but a hiccough in the supply of these brought attention to the fact that the particular units were going out of production. Andy O'Connell and Jim Roberts were, at the same time, busily 'designing-in' alternative generators which would have the unwelcome effect, for me, of upsetting our existing wiring diagrams (those large fold-out pages) and maintenance data, along with recently published parts catalogue listings.

Early in October, Dickie Bird confirmed that the Technical Offices would be moved into the new assembly hangar, as we had expected. The factory floor area and the ancillary side service bays were all in commission and the overall impression was that of a wartime production line in full swing. Machine shops and Stores/Equipment bays were sited across the south-eastern end of the ground floor, with a big new rubber-die press in a central compound. Above these facilities were two Bison-floored elevations, the first one already fitted out as office spaces and the second one about to be adapted, in similar ways, as accommodation for our Technical Offices. No side windows up here though – the only light was from large translucent roof panels. There being no false ceilings, we were literally up in the roof vault. Dickie had a difficult job to persuade John Britten that side windows must be installed before we could move in. We did move in, during October's third week, however, and dormer-type side windows eventually caught up with us, to relieve the effect of working in a barn-like loft. Fluorescent lighting was hung from the roof structure, but there was no heating or ventilation system installed initially. In winter the offices were abominably cold and in summer, stupefyingly hot, from the metal and transparent roof panels above. Adding to the generally unsatisfactory conditions, the roof demonstrated troublesome leaks during wet weather which called for an array of buckets, bowls and mops. It took six or seven years to cure the defects, with some re-roofing, suspended ceilings and air-conditioning services.

Meanwhile, though, the co-operative production of Islanders, between Cowes and Bembridge, was working well. By the end of December 1968, Constructor's No. 41 and 42 had been delivered to Singapore, for use by Malaysia-Singapore Airlines in that region. Following upon Cushioncraft's inauguration as a self-standing company, in the previous year, and the recent severance of Micronair – together with crop-spraying and associated overseas businesses – the Britten-Norman core business was once again centred on aircraft design, manufacture and marketing. The seventeen intervening years had been full of dash and vigour, hard work and hard-won experience, but the new foothold was surer and stronger than before. This particular re-organization (there would be others, of course, in the future) had paid off. Now there appeared to be nothing in the way of fulfilling the two partners' goal of 1000 aeroplanes in 10 years. If it could be done, it would put the Company's endeavours at the head of British achievements in post-war aviation successes. If only... there weren't those debentures and those loans, if only... suppliers could wait a little longer for payment, or customers were quicker to settle their accounts.

6.1 Islander wing construction underway at British Hovercraft's Falcon Works, East Cowes. It was a 'wet' wing, with the fuel tank compartments sealed by rubberized compound during skinning

6.2 Islander fuselage construction at the BHC Falcon Works in East Cowes

6.3 Another view of the combined wing and fuselage assembly lines of Islanders at the Falcon Works

6.4 Semi-completed Islander fuselages and wings, at Cowes, being readied for transport to Bembridge for final assembly

6.5 Final assembly of Islanders in the completed new assembly hangar at Bembridge Airport. The technical offices are on the top floor, at the end, with administrative offices on first floor and works facilities on ground floor

6.6 N. D. Norman and F. R. J. Britten photographed in front of a typical, new, production Islander of the time

Chapter 7

Pressing On

It is a truism that most people will do their best work when proceeding along tried and trusted paths, knowing where they have come from, what is familiar around them and that which can be reasonably expected ahead. In such a manner the Islander design programme had been set up and carried along thus far, piloted by the very able Miles organization. Now, however, that influence was on the wane and other somewhat arcane practices began to come into play. John Britten was nothing if not an incorrigible experimentalist who really did not have much time for mundane production matters, their problems, or their solutions. He preferred to leave such relatively 'uninteresting' procedures to other people, whilst keeping himself free to pursue more idyllic fields of thought. In this particular side of his temperament, he was ideally complemented by the similar traits present in Desmond Norman. Desmond was already planning a world-beating jet fighter but both partners had sufficient business acumen to realize that such an undertaking, too early, would be ruinous for them. However, right in the middle of extended workloads, accruing from the latest certification events, relating to New Zealand and France, came the intrusion of 'GDP'. During January of 1969, even while Dickie Bird was 'teeing up' for the likely complexities of French certification standards, I received a call from John Allan – on behalf of John Britten – to attend a meeting on the new project.

In essence this consisted of a single-engined, four-seater, high-wing monoplane intended for the private pilot. Nothing new about that philosophy, one might have said, but this one was a little unusual in having folding wings. Again, that idea was not a new one because similar small aeroplanes with folding wings had been successfully built between the wars. What, then, was 'GDP' all about? The letters stood for 'Grand Design Partnership' and the intention was to specify the initial design of the aeroplane and build it, in kit form, for onward supply to nominated international distributors and thence to individual builders, or small syndicates. Thereafter, it was hoped that, all the tedious and time consuming bureaucracy, associated with national certification matters, could be transferred to the relevant local administrations. For the British version of the aeroplane (which had to come first in the certification stakes) the Type No. BN-3 was allocated and the name 'Nymph' would be assigned later. Wonderful – some good news at least; but could we do it later – perhaps? We were still, metaphorically, picking the technical thorns out of the Islander's hide and everyone concerned was fully occupied with their own best ways through the difficulties that still persisted. But, no, work on the new aeroplane had already started, across in the old hangar, and it was intended that this revolutionary concept should gain its first official announcement at the 1969 Paris Salon, then only a little over sixteen weeks away. The folding wings idea had come about through the shortage of hangarage, or high rentals for storage when hangarage did exist, and easier transportation by surface methods if, and when, necessary.

It was about here that I found out why my own presence at this meeting was required. John Britten had been quietly realizing the benefits of the graphic perspectives in the technical illustrations of our Air Publications and had thoughts to harness them in a different way. He had been triggered, it seemed, by recently having built a scale model racing car, from a specialist kit that included instructional methods published in the same way. Reasoning that one could do without conventional design drawings, for the purpose of assembling kits, so long as one had graphically detailed perspective illustrations to work from, John would apply the technique to full-scale aircraft building. Design drawings were being prepared, of course, but these would exist only within the Master Design Authority of our own company. Another unique feature arose, in this context, affecting the way in which the parts of the new project would be identified. Over the years the SBAC (Society of British Aircraft Constructors, as it used to be known) had evolved specifications for the nomenclature of parts and assemblies, according to their places in the overall build of an aeroplane. Thus, the wing structure had its own identifying part number prefix, as had the fuselage and tail structures, separating them from power-plant, hydraulics, electrics, undercarriage; each with their own identifier, and so on. In this accepted scheme of things, location was the main principle. 'GDP' was to use a different principle, in that every part would bear a number, generated from a 'classification system'. Such a system had been employed by the Hoover domestic appliance manufacturers, it seemed, and had demonstrated the ability to avoid 'design doubles' or 'near doubles', which could occur in organizations without vigilant standards engineers. Someone close to John Britten had got hold of the key to a similar classification system, in which all parts were identified according to criteria set out in circular index diagrams, resembling pie charts.

These diagrams began the procedure of identifying parts according to the materials they were made from: light alloys, ferrous metals, plastics, rubber and so on. Next came size and shape, then the method of manufacture (say, castings, forgings, welded assemblies and so forth). At the end of this 'classification' process the design draughtsmen would come out with an eleven digit number that would be meaningless to anyone, unless the procedure were to be applied in reverse. The end results may have avoided designers inventing similar parts, but did not indicate to maintenance personnel those areas, or systems, on the aeroplane, where they were used. With handy electronic computing devices still some way off, all the 'search and find' processes had to be done manually which was something of a disadvantage to begin with. Minds were made up, however, and that's the way things were ordered. I was given a copy of the infamous racing car assembly instructions, at the end of the meeting and was requested to come up with two initial specimens relating to components being designed by Dennis Berryman and his colleagues. An aileron and the rudder were selected for the trial run. Everything had to be done posthaste, of course, without regard to our existing work priorities, entailed in the pre-existing certification programmes. At that particular time I was deeply involved in negotiating translation of the American FAA (Federal Aviation Authority) Approved Flight Manual for the Islander, into French, in support of Dickie Bird's session of meetings with the Dirécteur Genérale d'Aviation Civile (DGAC) and the Bureau Veritas in Paris. When completed this would be the seventh different flight manual for the aeroplane, all of which had to be maintained in line with current conditions as they developed. Together, we were also trying to avoid a likely possibility of the French Authorities requiring all the Maintenance Manual information translated into their own language. This would have been an enormously expensive exercise, if allowed to develop, and had only been brought about by Desmond's Sales Department's promise to certificate the Islander in the French 'Private Category' of airworthiness, as well as the 'Public Transport Category'. Had the Company stood firm on certificating only in the 'Public transport Category', we could have avoided the complications of having to publish a French language Flight Manual, because arrangements did exist for airlines to accept data in 'American English'. In order to qualify for the French equivalent of a British Air Operator's Certificate, the applicant airline had to declare to the DGAC, that its pilots and personnel were fluent in the use of 'English', as the international language of aviation. However, these were only part of the general scene of activities which began to require additional sub-contract assistance for the Technical Offices, as a whole.

In connection with these latest pressures, Maurice Brennon (then Chief Designer at BHC) was anxious for some of his personnel to help, in a period when they had some slack in their own programmes. Accordingly, George Thompson (BHC's Chief Technical Engineer) and Ken Jackson (my opposite number in BHC) came over to see us with some proposals for the loan of draughtsmen, technical writers and technical illustrators. In my own case the Parts Cataloguing work, with Gloster Design Services, was still far from finished and specialist electrical work was being undertaken by two other sub-contract offices – mainly to do with the alternative and replacement generator systems. Now, of course, there was added pressure on the Drawing and Stress Offices because a number of experimental developments during the autumn of 1968 had taken effort away from more necessary production work. Briefly, these diversions had been caused by John's and Desmond's anxiety to satisfy the always constant approaches from operators, for improvements. A few more seats, a bit more power, additional range, extra baggage capacity and so on. One result concerned the introduction of two extra seats (behind the pilot's station) in a 33 in. (838 mm) stretch to the Islander's fuselage, ahead of the wing. For this purpose the long-suffering G-ATWU (Whisky Uniform) was used to make a 12-seater version that was to have been named the 'Super Two'. Although it flew satisfactorily, certification difficulties prevented further development. Cabin evacuation in the event of a crash, or ditching, was the main stumbling block – literally – because access to a doorway meant the two extra passengers climbing over either the seats in front, or behind, within a specified time limit.

After the abortive 'Super Two' exercise, G-ATWU was not returned to standard but the fuselage was set aside for about a year, to form the basis of the Trislander, which was then gelling in the 'corporate mind', as an economical upgrade to address the many operator desires. The drawing office was working on improved and extended wing tips (which housed integral additional fuel tanks and would give extra climb out ability) as well as other aerodynamic adjustments, mainly prescribed by Andy Coombe. As a result of these changes, when embodied singly or in combination, there came into being a line of discrete Model Numbers which were delineated by 'dash number suffixes' to the root Model No. BN - 2A; e.g. BN - 2A -1. Not to be confused with the above variants, there was an early attempt to improve the Islander's power delivery by using Rolls-Royce Continental engines, each giving out 300 hp. Constructor's No.9 was converted by Miles Aviation and Transport, in conjunction with Rolls-Royce (who had bought out the American Continental Engine Co. and were anxious to extend their influence in light aviation) at the Miles headquarters in Shoreham-by-Sea. This sub-type was designated BN-2S, by virtue of its turbo-supercharged and fuel injected engines, but did not progress beyond the flight testing stage. The aeroplane was bought by Miles Aviation and used as a test bed for further power plant experimentation.

***

Also interfering with the Bembridge production line, to some extent, was the incorporation of special equipment in certain aeroplanes as required by their buyers. Some of these specialist modifications were concerned with the embodiment of aerial survey cameras, air ambulance conversions and Micronair-equipped spraying Islanders. All took their toll of the Technical Offices' attention and got in the way of a smooth running production operation. We did manage to negotiate the loan of technical staff members from BHC and the Company also recruited a number of permanent staff of its own. Early aerial survey camera installations, for example, were compromised by the centrally positioned flight control rods and cables, beneath the cabin floor. To enable fitment and utilization of 'Sterio-Pair' precision cameras, necessary for mapping duties, it was essential to re-design the flight control runs and re-route them along the right-hand side of the fuselage, for the full cabin length. Embodiment of these modifications, in build, resulted in a dedicated cabin floor (fitted to customer's option) with the centre bays of the fuselage free to accept different permutations of aerial camera equipment. Opportunity was taken, at the same time, to re-position other intrusive items while leaving unaltered the normal seating provisions. To handle the design of a standardized camera floor installation the Company took on a veteran draughtsman, who had worked for Supermarine in the Spitfire days under R.J. Mitchell. His name was Jack Phillips and he well remembered some of Mitchell's idiosyncracies when discussing work with his designers. If a certain proposal met with his displeasure, said Jack, Reg would gradually push the drawing up the board until it fell over the back, onto the floor, before walking away, when his man would have to try again!

Production output, however, was still falling behind expectations, such that even further help was needed to keep up the momentum. Britten-Norman could have done with the equivalent of a 'Skunkworks Division' to handle the eclectic spread of work that was always in offing. A solution appeared out of a co-operation that was being arranged, with British Government assistance, between the British Aircraft Corporation and the Romanian state-owned airline Tarom. This took place under very delicate diplomatic circumstances, since Romania was still behind the 'Iron Curtain'. The country required a trade-off, in return for purchasing BAC 1-11 airliners, to enable it to modernize its own under-developed aircraft industry. Shared construction of a relatively simple aeroplane, like the Islander, would be ideal for the Romanians and would give Britten-Norman the advantage of lower-cost eastern European labour rates.

Ken Mills, the ex-Vickers and British Aircraft Corporation production executive, was the ideal man to initiate the contracts and was soon to spend much of his time there. Meanwhile, preparations for the 1969 Paris Salon were hotting up and the BN-3 Nymph was nearing its handbuilt completion. Having its first flight during the middle of May and resplendent in a delicate iridescent lilac colour, chosen by Desmond's wife, we had a brief preview of the finished aeroplane shortly before it departed to Paris. It carried with it a bundle of our example instructional leaflets, devoted to the notional building of ailerons and rudders, which had finally passed John Britten's scrutiny. Desmond had staged a Press photo-call for the occasion and was proudly answering questions from that quarter when one was heard to ask '... what is the colour of it Mr Norman?' Without interrupting his eloquent commentary, and with sufficient gravitas to put down any further reference to that subject, he replied 'The colour is Nymph' and passed on. A week or two after this event the full kit of partially assembled components for Constructor's No. 85 Islander was supplied to the Romanian authorities for their completion and the beginning of their learning curve.

In no time at all Dickie Bird was called upon to go to Bucharest and help the Romanians in the interpretation of design drawings, data sheets, technical record indexes and the like. Dickie had a good working knowledge of French, if not Romanian, but was able to save much time at the beginning of the project by keeping things on the right lines. John Brenchley, the Chief Stressman, had been joined by an assistant, Richard (Dick) Stowe, who had lately come from the Bristol Aeroplane Company where he was previously employed on the Britannia airliner; John was also an ex-Bristol employee. They were soon deeply involved in the co-operation and Dick Stowe became the Company's main design liaison man when John Brenchley left Britten-Norman for the USA some time later. John Oversby, who was assistant to Peter Mallinson in the Service Department, was also a regular visitor to Bucharest, in giving practical help to the shop floor workers. Some hilarious experiences were recalled when the visitors were convinced, on occasions, that their hotel bedrooms had two-way mirrors installed, as well as other subtle devices.

The hotels left much to be desired, by western standards, and Dickie Bird was amused one morning at breakfast, after asking for a boiled egg; in due course the waiter presented him with a plate carrying two eggs but no egg-cup or small spoons. It was soon discovered that beef was the great turnkey which would open almost any door in Romania. Decent meat, of any kind, was expensive and almost unobtainable at that time. It goes without saying that each successive visiting party carried as much of this vital currency as could be practicably handled.

To facilitate all the comings and goings, the Company kept a 'mainland' car in a garage, a little way off the Portsmouth Harbour Hard, where the Isle of Wight passenger ferry docked. This car was for executive use on short-term (day) assignments, if not required by John or Desmond. It was useful for meetings with the ARB at Redhill, where rail connections were difficult, or other similar convocations. When John or Desmond needed the car they would invariably require David Williams to drive for them and often at unsocial hours. Early morning ferries – on a Sunday, perhaps, to catch a USA bound flight – and late homecomings, unless David was returning alone. If they were returning together, David recalls that they would be discussing and arguing, incessantly, in the backseat, whilst one urged him to drive faster, so as 'not to miss the boat,' when, after a while the other would call out '... not so fast David, we mustn't get booked for speeding.' Even then, coming out of London on the Great West Road, could be quite hair-raising. Sometimes they would call a halt at one of their familiar watering holes and disappear inside for a quick snack, leaving David to look after car and belongings. Either John or Desmond would appear a quarter of an hour later, sheepishly bearing a glass of lager for him and saying they wouldn't be long now, or words to that effect. One day, following a run of such like incidents, David lost his temper and told Desmond, very frankly, punctuated by unprintable expletives, exactly what he thought about matters. Fully expecting to receive his dismissal notice the following day, he was gathering together his tools and other effects, in readiness, when Desmond walked into his little workshop with a parcel. Gravely announcing that he thought David was under a lot of pressure, on account of his wife's late stage of pregnancy, Desmond handed over the parcel to him, as 'a present for his wife', and nothing more was said. When David arrived home that evening and his wife and he opened the parcel, they discovered (much to their amusement) that it contained a book entitled: 'Bringing up Baby'.

By the beginning of 1970 more than 140 Islanders had left our Bembridge factory, for all points on the compass. The long-range fuel tank systems, designed by Dennis's little squad and made up by our Bembridge personnel, became a familiar and necessary accompaniment to most deliveries. Consisting of between two and six 40 gallon drums mounted on a wooden cradle, secured by wire ropes, and attached to the cabin seat floor sockets, these installations could prolong the Islander's endurance to more than ten flying hours. Their installation and usage had to be covered by Service Bulletin action and flight Manual Supplement inclusion, respectively. At the front of the wooden cradle was mounted a rudimentary instrument panel, carrying several fuel cocks and electric pumps on a Dexion frame, rising to about level with the pilot's seat back. By half-turning in the seat the pilot was able to reach all the necessary pump switches and fuel cocks to operate the system in flight. Jim Birnie and Andy Coombe had set down the instructions for use on all sorts of bits of paper and passed them to me, at intervals, to edit and formalize. It had been decided that the cabin-mounted fuel must be used first before switching to the aeroplane's main wing tanks for the final stages of the flight. There were other structural considerations to dictate this course of action, too, but Andy was always a little apprehensive about the ferry pilot's condition of alertness, after several hours over the ocean, when the time came to switch over the tanks.

His uneasiness sprang from the fact that the established practice was to run each sequence of tanks until they were dry. Several 40 gallon drums, ganged together, formed 'Tank No. 1' and the others, similarly ganged, as 'Tank No. 2' and so on. When the first 'tank' ran dry it would be announced by an engine coughing and faltering through fuel starvation. Then the pilot, already in expectation of the event, had to smartly switch off that tank cock and pump switches, whilst switching on the next tank cock and electric pumps – fingers crossed – until the engine(s) once more resumed a regular beat. This was all because of the near impossibility of installing reliable fuel gauging devices, not to mention added expenses and complexity. It was difficult for the ARB, in its more regulated atmosphere, to accept the customs and practices of so-styled 'General Aviation' methods, but eventually the Authority grudgingly agreed with the procedure, provided that stipulated 'cautions' and 'warnings' were inserted in the fuel management drills, for the ferry flight fuel systems, published in the Flight Manual Supplements.

When such a delivery took place, it was a real eye-opener to see the little aeroplane fully loaded, seats, carpets, curtains and other 'loose equipment', stowed at the back; its cabin full, to window level, of tankage and pipelines, along with electric cabling festooned around. Our consignment of its relevant Air Publications, contained in a large black carrying case, would be pushed into some crevice, somewhere, somehow, for its journey. The ferry pilots who undertook the often monotonous and dangerous work, in all weather conditions, were usually freelance operators who were well-rewarded for their services. In the case of the men, it was said that they were mostly forced into the job by having to stump up high alimony charges, but there were, also, women pilots involved and I never heard palimony charges mentioned. One slightly-built lady, an ex-wartime ATA (Air Transport Auxiliary) ferry pilot, used to come to the aeroplane, after signing the necessary acceptances in Reg Hobbs' Inspection Department, carrying little more than an overnight bag. In a quietly professional and confident manner she would go through the pre-flight inspections and settle herself in the left-hand seat with her bag on the right-hand one. She carried something like a hammer shaft with which she would, later, wedge the control column against the windscreen side trim when in cruise condition. Not all the aeroplanes boasted an autopilot installation. Once I remember asking her how she passed the time, otherwise, and she pointed to her bag saying it was a good way of doing some serious reading. A week or two later she would be back in England having brought a Piper or a Cessna, in similar ferry condition, eastwards for export from the USA.

Attuned hands, eyes and ears – waiting for an engine to cough and falter, before reacting quickly with the fuel cock selectors and the pump switches; far out over the ocean in the path of the wild goose. Motivation of such people was surely not solely down to money.

Another veteran ferry pilot was Bob Iba, a very large American weighing around 17 stones (108kg). When he took office in the left hand seat, there wasn't much room in the right-hand one for even an overnight bag. One night Jim Birnie invited me to his bungalow, near Bembridge lifeboat station, to meet Bob, who was departing the following day. Jim's wife, Wendy, was an American and so there was some common ground. Sipping our warmish beer (Jim's fridge must have been English) it was interesting to hear their various experiences recounted in the relative safety of the Birnie's lounge, although the ever suspicious 'Poochie' was a constant presence. Bob Iba had been the personal pilot to Admiral Nimitz, in command of the American Pacific Fleet, during the Second World War and had close to 20,000 flying hours in his log book. Shortly afterwards he was to survive an extremely dangerous incident whilst en-route, in an Islander, over Greenland. His report, omitting the official preliminaries concerning identity, addresses and business connections, is set out in the following text, in his own words. It clearly indicates the all-prevailing hazards that were accepted by these intrepid flyers, but which could entrap the most experienced pilots without warning.

***

"I crossed the coast at Nagtoralik at 1505z and at that time could see completely across Greenland, including the several oddly shaped mountains just East of Narssarssuaq (one is 50 miles, and the other about 25 from there). All of this time I was still holding about a +10 degree drift correction angle, and was getting a visual confirmation that it was working out. About half way across Greenland, and in a position about 50 miles west of Kap Cort Adelacz, everything started to become dim. I thought I was running into a haze layer, and dropped down to 9,000. This condition still existed, and I realised a white-out condition, or ice fog condition was setting in. It did so very rapidly, as I was on complete instruments within 5 minutes from the time it started. I climbed back to 12,000 ft. This was at about 1530z. I was not particularly worried, as navigation had been working out, I only had about 30 minutes to go to Narssarssuaq and called the tower on

118.1, and received them loud and clear. They advised me that weather there was 7,000 ft overcast, visibility 15 miles. I advised them that I was estimating over their station at 1600z. My ADF would still not lock on, and I attributed it to precipitation static.

What I did not know was that just about at the point where I had gone on instruments there had been an almost 160 degree wind shift, with winds of at least 40 knots from 160 to 180 degrees at 12,000ft. This information I got after being rescued from Sonderstrom. This meant that I should have held a minimum drift correction angle of -10, and still holding a +10 meant that I was going off track at about 30 degrees from the desired 232 degree True. Subsequent scaling on a map brought this out almost exactly.

Talked again to Narssarssuaq tower, receiving them very loud. I thought that I must be quite close, as their range had always appeared to be limited. I advised them that I was unable to get a beaming on their homer (NA-359), as there was much precipitation static. They offered to send up a PBY to lead me in, but since I was on solid instruments at 12,000 ft, an interception would have been impractical or even dangerous. Narssarssuaq tower, and the 'NA' beacon started to fade out, and the audio for the Simitug (SI-279) started to get stronger. My ADF started to settle down, and apparently locked on the SI beacon. I got what appeared to be a station passage, and believed it, since my passing or contact with Narssarssuaq, and apparent passing of 'SI' were just about dead on my ETAs. I started a descent about 10 minutes after the apparent station passage, figuring that I was letting down out to sea, and that I would break out at about 5,000 ft since Narssarssuaq had advised me that there was 5000 ft ceiling, and visibility was 15 miles at the coast. I planned to then turn inbound to SI, and fly up the fjord, since I have been there about 10 times and am quite familiar with it.

However, the ADF indication must have been erroneous as, at an indicated altitude of 5,500 ft at 1640z, at position 6142N and 4654W, I felt strong contact with the ice cap, and the airplane came to a sudden stop. The only damage to the airplane was the nose gear bent back badly, under the fuselage, and fuselage distortion on the underside, back to the bulkhead forward of the door frame. There was no other damage to the airplane, the main gear was OK, and the engines were still running. I shut down the engines, got out and inspected for further damage or fuel leaks. There was none, and the props were not touched. The main wheels were buried in the snow to the tops of the tires. Visibility appeared to be about 25 ft, in a complete white-out condition. It was impossible to distinguish where the snow stopped and the horizon and blowing snow started.

After being sure the aircraft was intact, I started one of the engines and made a MAYDAY call on 121.5. I established contact with a PAA Clipper, advised him that I was down on the ice cap, and apparently in no immediate danger, as I had power and heat. Requested that he advise Sondestom, for Air Sea rescue, and gave my estimated position as somewhere West of Narssarssuaq. I advised him that I had a URT/21 emergency beacon, and be sure to tell Sondestrom that, as it would help in locating me. I also asked that he advise Gander, so that they could phone my company and advise them of my problem. After two or three minutes PAA came back, and advised that all this had been done. He was fading out, but I understood him to say that Air Sea Rescue wasn't sure when they would start the search, but that it would probably be at first light. I came back that I would be coming up on 121.5 every hour on the hour, but do not know if he received this message, as I was unable to get an acknowledgement.

Night of Jan 3, 1969

I moved my portable VHF set, so that I would be more comfortable in the cabin, and unknowingly must have loosened one of the antenna connections, as it was not putting out a signal, even though the set was working and giving side tone. Naturally it was not receiving. I kept starting alternate engines, every half hour, and while I was at it, made MAYDAY calls, while I had the electrical power. After about 4 hours, I could not start either engine, as the nacelles were packed solid with blowing snow, and all sources of air were sealed off. I did not activate the URT/21 during the night, and only tried 3 more calls on the VHF as I wanted to conserve the ship's battery. Naturally, those calls were useless, as the antenna connection was still loose.

Day of Jan 4, 1969

81

At first light, I activated the URT/21, but was unable to hold it outside myself, as it was too cold (chill factor about -45F), so I placed it in a snow bank about 20 ft from the airplane. I kept making calls on 121.5 every hour, shutting down after 2 transmissions, and 5 minutes of listening, in order to conserve the battery. After about three hours of daylight, I realised that something was wrong.

I thought that something was wrong with the URT/21 and that the thing to do was check it. Since 243.0 will give a beat on 121.5 I put the URT/21 next to the VHF antenna, and heard nothing. This seemed strange, as new batteries had been installed, and the set checked on Nov 11, 1968. I then placed it right up against the antenna connector on the VHF set, and heard a signal. This made me finally realise that there might be troubles with the antenna connector of the VHF. I checked all the connections and found that the antenna connector at the set was slightly loose. Pushed it in less than ⅛" and tried a transmission.

I immediately worked Rescue 865, loud and clear. He requested that I activate my URT/21, so I stuck it out the window in my hand. He could not receive it. Also, the beat on the VHF was weak. I then reached up through the window, placing the set squarely on top of the fuselage. Rescue 865 then picked it up, and homed in on it. In 5 minutes he was over me and established my position as 6142N, 4654W. He also made some VHF checks with 10 second hold-downs. He then came down to about 100 feet above the terrain, and saw me visually although I could not see him. My ground visibility was zero, as I had no reference points – because of blowing snow, and I could not see too well vertically. I told him that I had to shut down the VHF to conserve batteries, and if he wanted me, to buzz me. After about an hour he came over and advised me that the helicopter (civilian) could not come in after me, as it was not IFR equipped.

They would try to get me out the next day, if the weather improved. He offered to make up a survival pack with rations, sleeping bag, heavy socks and gloves, and more portable radio. I accepted it, as although I was in pretty good shape, I would have liked to have been warmer, especially with the prospect of another 18 hour night coming up. He made a run over me at somewhere about 300 to 500 feet, and dropped the pack with a small parachute. With the 40 knot wind, it drifted several hundred yards away. I started running after it, and it seemed to be fading away as though being dragged by the chute. I went in that general direction for about 150 yards and realised that I was becoming disorientated, as I had no visual reference to go by. I looked back, and the airplane was scarcely visible in the blowing snow. I decided it was prudent to return to the airplane. Going back against the wind was difficult. I arrived at the airplane in bad shape, wet and with about ¼" ice crust on my face. Breathing had been difficult. I called Rescue 865 and advised him that I had not picked up the package. He offered to make up another one and drop it. I said 'N' as I could not think of going outside again in my present condition. Since I had fallen several times in snow drifts that I could not see, and had gotten wet, I became very cold and could not get warm, even though I wrapped myself in the dinghy. It helped some, but I still spent the whole night shivering violently and uncontrollably. I made no attempt to communicate during the night, as the 865 had advised me that there was only slight chance of the helicopter coming out during the night. If they wanted me to come up on the radio, they would buzz me, or drop flares to alert me.

Day of Jan 5, 1969

In the morning the weather was bad, with no surface visibility. At about 1245z I talked with Rescue 184. They advised me that they were trying to lead the helicopter in, but that conditions were bad, and he could not make it. I shut down the VHF and started waiting for conditions to improve. At about 1330z Rescue 865 buzzed me, and I came up on 121.5. He advised me that the weather was better from where he was, and that the helicopter was going to try again. At about 14:15, the helicopter was in the area and 865 vectored him to me. Communications became difficult as the helicopter was on 118.1, and when 865 wanted to talk to me, he had to change frequencies, as he only had one VHF. I resolved this by coming up on 118.1, so we were all working together.

865 got the helicopter about a mile from me, but he had trouble seeing me, so I lit my first orange smoke to help him, and also to give him a good indication of the wind. As he approached, he advised me

that he had no depth perception because of the white-out, and that he could not judge his height above the snow. I took over control, giving him advice about apparent altitude, since I could see the belly of his machine, and knew he must be above me. I then lit my second smoke flare. I also advised him of the snow banks downwind of the airplane, that I had found by falling in them. He could not judge his height within several hundred feet. He finally got down on the snow, very cautiously. The mechanic helped me get my gear aboard the helicopter. During this operation I again stumbled in the snow drifts that had formed around the airplane, fell against it, and bruised my knees. I may sound clumsy, but there is no way you can see the snow banks as everything gets white, and there is no way you can distinguish the contour. The mechanic helped me aboard the helicopter, they took me to Narssarssuaq, where I got something to eat. Rescue 184 then took me to Sondestrom where I had medical attention and a complete physical examination, including X-rays. Everything was good except for the bruised knees and some frost burn on my hands and face."

***

By the middle of February 1970 the fifth Islander had been completed and flown by the Romanians, from kits of parts supplied by BHC at Cowes and they were beginning to fabricate parts themselves. Some assembly jigs had been supplied, overland, along with the early kits, whilst others were being manufactured and set up by the Romanians on site. To establish the separate identity of these aeroplanes, a discrete numbering system was introduced which started at 600. In fact, there was not an Islander with Constructor's No. 600. The kit of sub-assemblies which left BHC in the summer of 1968, as components of Constructor's No. 85, became re-numbered as Constructor's No.601 for its return to the UK as the first completed 'Romanian-build' Islander. This new co-operation began to call for ever more assistance, at technical and business levels, necessitating the initiation of a Commercial Department. There being no reciprocal trade agreements to facilitate the purchase and supply of American-made parts, directly to the plant in Romania, meant that all the business had to be done through UK channels. A young man called Peter Graham was appointed by Desmond Norman, under his 'Sales and Marketing' hat, to look after this most intricate and challenging task.

Initially all the Romanian built Islanders were ferried back to Bembridge, under their own power, in a standardized 'green' condition. This alluded to their newness in a pre-set modification state and the grey-green etch-primer, only, paint protection. Customer specifications and final paint finish were attended to by Bembridge and Marshall's of Cambridge. This latter company had been contracted to complete final painting, and markings, to customer specifications, on account of an oversight when planning the paint shop in the new hangar at Bembridge. A full-width partition had been included, closed off by a double set of folding doors, to form a paint finishing bay, between the production lines and the flight shed facilities. It made a fine paint shop, with full extractor fans and small side bays for detail finishing, but could not be used without precluding movement of aircraft whilst it was in operation. Freedom of movement was paramount in the fever of early production activity and so it made more sense to get the paint jobs done by outside specialists, in the circumstances. By this time Desmond was employing several Sales Demonstration pilots, under his Sales Directorship, and one or other of them would get the jobs of local ferrying, between various establishments such as Marshall's, or another paint finishing facility at Bournemouth (Hurn) and CSE, the engine distributors, at Kidlington near Oxford, for instance.

One of these pilots was Colin Newnes, an ex-Fleet Air Arm officer with an enthusiastic, ebullient approach to things. On one occasion, while John Allan was in office as Chief Designer, Colin returned an Islander to the ground with a somewhat buckled tail fin. It appeared that, in spite of the prohibition of aerobatics – clearly stated in the Flight Manual limitations – he had had some fun in 'rolling' this particular aeroplane which, of course, drew the opprobrium of the Chief Designer. A searching special inspection of the aeroplane had to be done after this escapade, together with repairs to the fin, that did nothing to improve the costs or economies of the day. Colin was a great protagonist of the 'Performance Data Handbook' as an effective sales aid. In no time at all he convinced Desmond, I remember, that the Islander should have one. As interest in the BN-3 Nymph had receded, after the first flush of enthusiasm at Paris, I was quite pleased to be without the task of thinking through the seemingly endless permutations of its graphic build instructions. In the words of the old proverb, however, 'when one door closes another opens' and it was not long before we had the job of devising Performance Data Handbooks for the Islander – not one but two. Since the aircraft with carburetted engines had quite different data from the ones with fuel-injected engines, it was better to separate them to avoid the development of likely complexities.

During April of 1970, I was facing a period of severe handicap by Penny's decision to leave, after her recent marriage. Penny had typed all of the text for the Maintenance Manual, Maintenance Schedule and the many Flight Manuals, for the Islander up to that time. She had done, and was continuing to do, all of this work manually on an IBM 'Executive' typewriter with a 'Bold Face 2' impression. Having accomplished all the teething troubles and knowing all the quick fixes involved, it was going to be difficult to replace her skills on reprographic typing, let alone her invaluable secretarial assistance. Our Illustrated Parts Catalogues were, fortunately, all professionally typeset due to their requirement for distinctively contrasting typefaces and columnar indentation. In the event, fates conspired to introduce a young German lady with a good grasp of English, by the name of Gabrielle. Gabrielle, or 'Gaby', had worked for an automotive distributorship in Dusseldorf and was, therefore, quite used to the industrial scenario. She settled in very quickly and was soon at home, although her incisive German logic was sometimes upset by our occasional English obfuscation. A rash of Service Bulletin work had come upon the scene about that time and it provided a good entree for Gabrielle to cut her teeth on.

Quite a few defects were beginning to appear, so the business of finding answers, deciding repair and/or special inspection schemes, was exercising the ingenuity of the various Technical and Service Department offices. Throughout the flight testing processes, with the Islander, Jim Birnie and Andy Coombe had, on certain occasions, experienced a transient vibration in the elevator control circuit, which Jim would describe only as 'a buzz'. It had proved impossible to replicate this phenomenon for, say, evaluation by the ARB test pilots, or Desmond Norman for that matter. Desmond had taken the controls, after Jim, in some instances, and had been unable (or maybe unwilling) to fault the particular aeroplane. It seemed to be attributable to a singular combination of geometry and adjustment, perhaps, of the elevator and elevator trim tab, in relation to one another, in situ on a particular aeroplane. Jim's big worry was that a more serious condition may be triggered, leading to the deadly 'flutter' that could rapidly disintegrate the strongest components. Although a most conscientious and diligent test pilot, Jim's avowed motto was '… I don't want to be the boldest, only the oldest' and he would always err on the side of caution as a result.

Now, an in-flight incident had occurred on an American registered Islander which had brought the subject back into sharp focus. Somehow or other the elevator trim tab had separated from its attachments and connections, leaving the pilot with diminished control when landing. Immediate inspections and reportage on all Islanders in the field had to be arranged, following which a rectification plan would be developed. This defect was only one of a number as mentioned, but it was the one with the most serious implications which would produce many difficulties for the Company in the not-too-distant future. Nevertheless progress on all other fronts carried on regardless; the aeroplanes in French territories were carrying French language Flight Manuals as a matter of course. After all, what self-respecting Frenchman would put up with an English language manual when a French version was available – even though originally intended only for the 'Private Category' pilot? We had managed to avoid the translation of all of the aeroplane's maintenance literature, by offering to translate, only, the single sheet Progressive Maintenance Check list. This was modelled on an American document, much used by Piper and Cessna, to abbreviate the 50hr, 100 hr, 500hr and 1000 hr checks. It was preferred by many (mainly American) operators for the more frequent checks, over the formal Maintenance Schedule which required a record card system for implementation. Bureau Veritas, in its wisdom, accepted this approach and further helped us by not insisting on the 500hr and 1000hr Checks which they reckoned to be above the scope of the 'Private Operator' in any case.

During the May of 1970, after much thought and enthusiastic

discussion in the ante chambers of the 'Propellor Parliament', plans for the 'Trimotor' finally broke onto the surface. One day John Britten asked me to call on a commercial photographer, in Ryde, to collect a scale model which had been provided for photographing at different angles. Jim Nettleton, the photographer concerned, had done quite a bit of work for the Company and knew what was required. He handed over the model of the 'Trimotor' to me along with the batch of prints ordered and I returned the effects to John, as requested. That was only the start, of course, because before I left him, he thrust several pages of typescript my way saying that Desmond's secretary was producing more and would I get on with producing a brochure for the proposed aeroplane. Another urgent job on the rails, this one, due to the fact that Desmond had arranged to host a Distributor's Conference at the end of the month, when it was intended to formally introduce the Islander's big brother. A few days later, on 26th May in fact, Andy Coombe and I had a quick meeting with John Britten concerning both the Trimotor brochure and the Performance Data Handbook work, after which John referred us directly to Desmond. Apparently he was deeply into a bout of influenza, at home in bed, but would get up to receive us upon prolonged ringing of the door bell, as there was no one else in the house at the time.

A quarter of an hour, or twenty minutes, later we were ushered into the house bearing the Trimotor model and the first draft of the brochure as annotated by John Britten. Andy and Desmond were soon in animated conversation, between sneezes and groans, about the tail fin mainly. Desmond had not wanted the fin to protrude above the upper surface of the tail plane and the model was made accordingly. He felt that the aesthetics would be upset by further vertical extension but Andy argued doggedly for additional fin area. Directional stability would be compromised, said Andy, with the squat fin as it stood. He lost the argument in the first round, the prototype being made as per the model. Desmond was forced to concede, later, that the aeroplane was down on directional stability and would benefit from a vertical extension of the fin, above the tail plane. Listening to all this, I was wondering what ill effects, if any, might upset the draft brochure, already on a tight deadline, if it was to be ready for the weekend; this day was Tuesday. Desmond scanned the text fairly quickly, made one or two minor alterations but, otherwise, expressed his satisfaction, dismissing us as quickly as he could in the circumstances.

I cannot remember, exactly, when the 'Trislander' name was chosen but we referred to it, at that time, as the 'Trimotor'. Its official designation was a 'BN-2A Mark III' and that was the title we used on the brochure. At any rate the brochure was now cleared for production, after I had attended to the necessary changes. Graham Montrose and I had already chosen the paper, bindings and cover boards, which had been cut to size and stood ready for the machining of 500 copies. My diary records that we both worked until 7:30pm on Saturday 30th May 1970, to collate and finish this first batch of Trimotor brochures, on time; we left one copy of the brochure on each of the desks of John Britten, Desmond Norman, and Andy Coombe. On the following Monday afternoon, 1st June, I note that 200 Performance Data Handbooks for the Islander, were delivered to us, by the Isle of Wight County Press who had helped us out in the printing and readying, simultaneously, of these important 'sales aids'. For the time being I was able to return to my temporarily neglected work pattern.

July of 1970 saw the final retirement of my valued illustrator colleague, Eric Jacobs (Jake), upon reaching the age of 65. His dedicated work in producing realistic perspectives, together with accurate graphs and charts, detailing flight manual performance data, would be sorely missed. Feelers were out for personnel of all kinds, just then, so I was only another one looking for the right replacement. Farnborough Air Show was looming again and it was not long before John Britten was asking for another 1000 Trimotor brochures. John was pursuing the line of approach to operators, that the Trimotor was 70 per cent Islander and 30 per cent new aeroplane, In the Drawing Office, Taffy Lloyd was the man charged with bringing the project to fruition in the quickest possible time. It is doubtful whether Taffy would have completely agreed with John's view of the situation, since the wing, although seemingly identical, was a much 'beefed-up' structure, In addition, the fuselage included a 105 in (266.7 cm) stretch which influenced most of the installed system parts. Fortunately Taffy was ably aided by several keen young draughtsmen, chief among whom were M.J. (Mike) Dore and Patrick (Pat) Gallagher. Again the gloves were off and the time ticking away to that magical week in September. They were all working their socks off now, to ensure that the new prototype would receive a showing at Farnborough. A dedicated band of shop floor workers, once again, translating the Drawing Office Instructions (DOI's) into a finished entity; they just made it for the final four days of Farnborough.

This prototype was formed from the additionally stretched fuselage of Constructor's No. 2 (G-ATWU) Islander – which already included a 33 in. (838 mm) insertion from the 'Super Two' project – married to a strengthened new wing. Following that year's show and in the light of the very obvious strength of customer interest, the Company's effort was firmly directed towards, early, full 'Public Transport (Passenger) Category' certification of the new aeroplane. I was instructed by both John Britten and Desmond Norman to give consideration to the subject of providing suitable Air Publications, along with costing and time estimates, for the Trimotor. Therein lay a quirk, however, because, although the new aeroplane would have a new name, technically its Model No. was still a derivative of the Islander's. It all came back to finance, of course, due to the fact that the grants could be obtained to develop existing type numbers, whereas they were not available to finance new ventures. I made my submissions in due course, recommending that we raised a new and completely distinct range of publications for the Trimotor instead of trying to invent supplementary inclusions for the existing Islander volumes. This latter course would have been John Britten's preferred way, I could tell, but I was very pleased to receive Desmond's support for my ideas – which I was sure the ARB would condone – and that swayed John's opinion in the end. By November I was seeking tenders from sub-contractors, towards the urgent implementation of that programme of work, alongside the development of the prototype, into a representative production aeroplane. Constructor's No. 245 was, in fact, the first such production model, bearing the name 'Trislander', although, itself, an Islander conversion which first flew in March 1971; it was, however, classed as the 'pre-production' aeroplane.

7.1 The BN-3 Nymph in flight with Jim Birnie at the controls. The wing-fold joints are visible at the root fairings and each wing bracing strut had knuckle joints, top and bottom, to allow the wings to rest almost flat alongside the fuselage, when folded

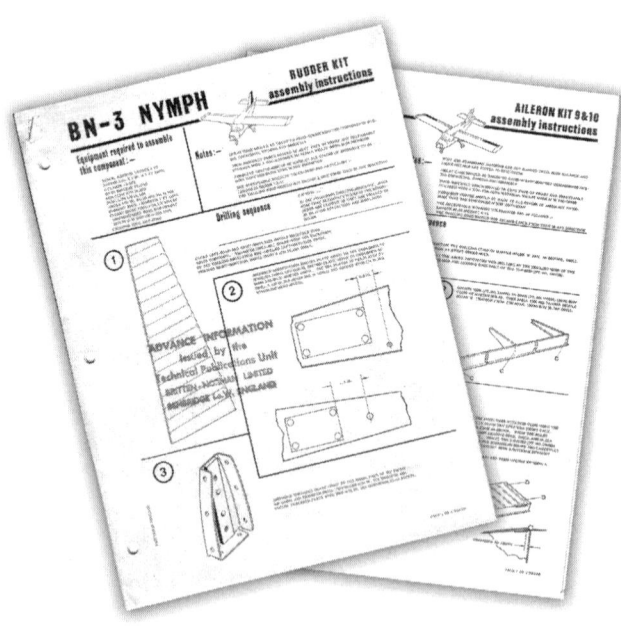

7.2 Specimen component build instructions for the BN-3 Nymph. The aim was to condense the data into no more than five or six pages, with the final one or two carrying the complete list of parts required and space for the authenticated engineer's inspection stamp, certifying component build history

7.3 The BN-3 Nymph taxying towards the original hangar. The tower above the treeline, on the right of the picture, belongs to Bembridge School.

7.4 Scale model of the tri-motor. This was about 1/24th and was used for initial PR purposes

7.5 Constructor's No. 2 Islander 'Whisky Uniform', having evolved into the Trimotor prototype taxying across Bembridge airfield. The new assembly hangar in the background, with finished Islanders awaiting customers

7.6 'Whisky Uniform' flying, after the initial extension to its fin. This was still considered less than aesthetically pleasing and was, later, broadened to full chord-width

Chapter 8

Turbulence

In leaving behind the psychedelic times of the 'Swinging Sixties', with all their optimism and promise, entry into the eighth decade of the twentieth century was altogether more volatile and increasingly uncertain. This was the case for the whole of Great Britain, not least the industrial manufacturers amongst whom our small company was numbered. Harold Wilson's Labour Government was in power, busily changing the national values away from individualism, towards a style of command economy, decimalisation, including closer ties with Europe, together with a gradual running down of the nation's defence capabilities. On the aviation front, once again, just as in the late 1940's when a Socialist Government ruled the country, a bright star was extinguished. This time it happened to the English Electric Company's TSR2, a brilliant supersonic aeroplane with very advanced engines and systems that could have had a great export potential. Other worthy projects to suffer cancellation, although not at such advanced stages of development, were the Armstrong-Whitworth 681 VTOL/STOL heavy transport aircraft and the Hawker P.1154 – a Mach2 version of the Harrier. Coventry based Armstrong-Whitworth did not survive the former cancellation and collapsed shortly afterwards. Much damage was done to the supporting equipment manufacturers as a result of this cancellation. To their advantage, John Britten and Desmond Norman had always recognized the inherent dangers of contracting for the British Government and would have nothing to do with that area of business in normal circumstances. Desmond, however, had been considering a militarized version of the Islander and, as a result, the Technical Offices had put some considerable effort into scheming alterations to the airframe. Hardpoints in the wing undersurfaces, a Weapons Control console, machine gun mountings in the cabin, along with gunsights and other military impedimenta could easily be embodied by simple modifications when necessary. All these modifications were installed and trialled in a specimen aeroplane which had no difficulties in carrying the specified war loads, demonstrating a useful strike power for such a utilitarian weapons platform. My attention to these matters was called for one day when Desmond mentioned that there would be a need for '... Air Publications for the Defender'. This was to be the chosen name for such a version of the Islander if a customer was forthcoming. Upon mentioning this fact to Dickie Bird, relative to authority to proceed and likely additional personnel requirements, I found him less than helpful at that time. Dickie's attitude seemed to be along the lines of '... if that's what he wants then do it for him'. It was not possible to pin Desmond down to definite facts about who the customers might be, or what the definitive Model Numbers of such an Islander might be, only that it was to be dealt with as a priority matter. It was another case of *déjàvu*, when we had all the stops out to produce the new range of Air Publications for the Trislander – now formally named. In November of 1970, from the various contenders for the sub-contract preparation of Trislander publications, I had decided that the parts cataloguing function should stay with Gloster Designs whilst another 'one only' contractor should deal with the Maintenance Manual and Maintenance Schedule. This would avoid three or four other offices, as well as ourselves, trying to co-operate (sometimes ineffectively) as had happened in the early days of the Islander. Now that the Islander's engineering publications had become reasonably settled and had an established pattern – if John Britten's 70 per cent 'existing' + 30 percent 'new' theory held up in practice – it should be a relatively easy, mainly editorial job for one interested party to accomplish. Thus I had concluded that the Production Engineering Research Association (PERA) at Melton Mowbray, Leicestershire, would be the most suitable organization for our purposes. After a hastily-convened meeting with Joe Mark, their Technical Publications Manager, PERA allocated four experienced men to our job at the end of November, following receipt of our purchase orders, and they had started work by visiting Bembridge during the first week of December taking back with them as much information as possible to be going on with.

Taffy Lloyd, in the Drawing Office, together with every available draughtsman, was well into the Islander/Trislander conversion work by now, with a stream of instructions being conveyed to the shop floor workers by sketches, notes and verbal means (but very few, if any, formal design drawings) to speed progress. Constructor's No. 245 Islander was taken out of the production line for the purpose of fuselage extension and strengthening. A new purpose-built wing, which included integral strengthening, was being produced by BHC at Cowes, from earlier and parallel instructions. Effectively, this aeroplane would be a pre-production model. At this particular time about 33 Islanders had been received from the Romanian factory and some were passing down the production line, or had already been delivered, alongside the island-produced ones, accounting for about 280 completed aeroplanes altogether. Some idea of the phenomenal activity can be gained by the note in my diary, of Tuesday 2nd February 1971, relative to Andrew Henry's arrival at Bembridge, that day, to photograph and glean as much information as possible on the Trislander wing. Andrew was PERA's lead illustrator on the job and we had been told that 15th January was the date set for the first flight of the pre-production Trislander, to be registered as G-AYTU. In fact the wing was still in the jig at Cowes and Mr Spall, who was BHC's shop superintendent, agreed that Andrew could go and do what he needed to do '... so long as he didn't get in the way of the production personnel.' Mr Spall indicated that every effort was being made to deliver the completed wing to Bembridge by the following Tuesday, 9th February. Whether it happened just like that, I have no recollection but, further on, my diary clearly records that G-AYTU made its first flight at 11:10am on Saturday 6th March 1971; seven weeks late.

Jim Birnie was the test pilot that day and my notes say that he took off into lowering cloud, disappearing into a sharp snow flurry at an altitude of about 300 feet. The flight lasted approximately 35 minutes and Jim reported numerous troubles on take-off which were obviously exacerbated by a strong crosswind at the time. Nosewheel steering was difficult, with poor direction control, the ailerons and the trimming systems were heavy in operation and he was plagued by an overspeeding propeller on the starboard engine. Although all the engine controls worked well, Jim felt that the tail plane incidence ought to be decreased slightly, because, in his words... "it was trying to fly the aeroplane".

A negative incidence setting of minus one degree from the horizontal was adopted as a result. Constructor's No. 2 (G-ATWU) the prototype Trislander was, by now, laid aside from flying duties and was relegated to a regime of static testing that was to take more and more Stress Office time and effort from Dick Stowe and his colleagues as the programme developed. I found the Trislander project a very odd one really, because although I could not avoid being head over heels in its progress myself, it was quite evident that Dickie Bird had been 'sidelined' in the issue. Whether that was by his own choice, or the choosing of the directors, was impossible to ascertain. At any rate Dickie had no time for the Trislander. When G-ATWU had appeared, as the prototype, at the previous year's Farnborough show, in a bright yellow colour scheme, originally without the upper fin extension, he had rather scathingly referred to it as '... the flying banana'. Similarly, I sensed that I was on my own, as it were, with the Defender project if it ever developed. Desmond was looking towards some early signs of progress from me on this matter, so I had decided to push the boat out quietly, along with the burgeoning Trislander work.

There was a likelihood of the Defender order being placed for about 40 aeroplanes, plus equipment and spares, I gathered. From hints in very brief discussions about his requirements, I also gathered that a potential first customer of Desmond's might be a South American country. Giving him some suggestions about how we might do the job most expediently and how a new range of quasi-military publications might look, in olive green coloured binders, I was almost surprised by his ready agreement to cover the anticipated costs. In an attempt to control these more closely, in a disciplined way, a system of 'Sanctions' had, earlier, been devised. The Chief Accountant, Jim Munn, had a new assistant by the name of Peter Lightfoot, one of whose jobs it was to monitor these Sanction forms, making sure that no work or liabilities were incurred until the necessary authorizations, including those of the directors, had been signed. My Sanction forms for the initial stages of work, for both Trislander and Defender Air Publications, had received clearance on the basis of materials and sub-contract labour expenditure. It was borne in upon me that the Company had no intention to employ further technical staff of its own. Hence, the engagement of PERA and the involvement of its staff members in our work. Their terms of reference were to provide finished illustrations and two copies of finalized draft text; 'camera-ready copy' was not priced in, because of the non-availability of an identical typewriter to our own with a 'Bold Face 2' impression. Something in the nature of a contretemps existed here, because I had to be able to match up with the ultimate production using our own equipment after the dust had settled. To produce the Trislander 'camera-ready copy', I had chosen a young lady from Chandlers Ford, who was operating on a freelance basis and who had a machine identical to our own. The drill set up was for her to receive the finally agreed draft from PERA and type it out onto our page masters incorporating any last minute changes at that time. Carole Line was a most personable and efficient lady whose quality of work perfectly matched her own impeccable turn out. The PERA chaps were charmed to visit her, in transit, with work packages for her attention, or completed ones for our final printing. Meanwhile, Gabrielle, my own typist was wading through the changes necessary to convert an Islander Maintenance Manual and Maintenance Schedule for use on the Defender. Nowadays, such a job would be relatively easy but it was quite a pain to do, manually, at that time, when there was more than enough run-of-the-mill work on hand anyway. She was, of course, following my mark-up of specific and notional changes on Islander handbook pages – 400 or more were concerned – so that we could use them, directly, as 'camera-ready copy'.

Loose-leaf binders, for all this anticipated volume of finished material, were on order; tan coloured for the Trislander (to contrast with the blue of the Islander) and olive green for the Defender – each with stylized silvered title blocking for their respective purposes. Of course, there was a great deal of effort and consternation across all the disciplines in the Company, but my area of responsibility was unique in that one had the satisfaction of handling almost every stage of progress from blank paper to finished and marketable commodity. In the case of the Trislander, this latter stage would all too soon be with us. Yet again I note from the diary that Andy Coombe (now acting instead of Dickie Bird) and myself, with current draft copies of Trislander Maintenance Manual, Schedule, and Flight Manual, were required to visit the ARB, at Brabazon House,

Redhill, preparatory to a final certification date in mid-May. I have a note on the 16th May – which happened to be a Sunday – saying that this is the final day for readying all the necessary Trislander documentation for the Certification Meeting. It seems likely that this meeting happened on Wednesday 19th May 1971, when Andy and myself were flown up to Redhill in the company's Cessna 180. I believe Peter Ward, the Weights Engineer, who also held a pilot's licence, would have taken us. On the previous day, I see that we, ourselves, had issued the first official Trislander Flight Manual for Registration G-AYWI which was the first so-called production Trislander, emanating from the conversion of Islander Constructor's No. 262. The ARB, themselves, had insisted on doing the official Flight Manual for the pre-production aircraft, G-AYTU, first flown by Jim Birnie 6 or 7 weeks earlier, on 6th March; and they were still working on it! That situation does not appear to have compromised the granting of the UK Transport (Passenger) Category of Certification, however, which must have been implicit.

Delays and disruptions of all kinds were affecting us just then, mainly to do with strikes in the postal services, or on the railways. Harold Wilson's government had given way to a Conservative administration, with Edward Heath as Prime Minister, but no apparent improvements ensued. Important consignments were best made, personally, by car or van to or from the Isle of Wight Ferry terminals, with meetings of messengers at one side or the other. Sometimes one of the apprentices, or office juniors, had to be dispatched with an urgent communication or package to an address in London, or elsewhere, to be sure of its safe arrival. I remember, on one occasion at about 6:00pm, receiving a telephone call from Antigua, or somewhere in that region, from a man who would be in London within the following day or two, requesting a particular Islander Flight Manual. He was only passing through London, on his way to some other destination, and would be staying at Claridges Hotel, I think, where he had arranged with a certain doorman to accept the parcel for him. Later, he wrote a very nice letter of appreciation for the Company's co-operation in what had been an important matter for him. I still have his letter amongst my effects. This was a typical incident of the times in which reliable communications could not always be guaranteed.

It was a period when the Company's Cessna 180, which had been rebuilt out of a Brazilian crash landing a few years earlier, came into its own as a general 'hack and runabout'.

That summer of 1971 was proving to be a hot one. The Drawing Office personnel had been moved back to the old hangar premises, already, but we were beginning to be very uncomfortable in the hot roof space of the new hangar as the days wore on. A revised system of working hours was agreed, whereby we would start work at 6:30am and finish at 2:30pm, before the worst of the heat built up. The PERA sub-contract input of Trislander work was coming through nicely and finding its way onto Graham Montrose's print production line in convenient batches, along with our own Defender material. Some of the new binders had arrived, with others to follow on completion, allowing us to collate initial quantities of the new publications. As in the case of the Islander, immediate applications for American FAA Certification of the Trislander were underway, because those regions were the ones seen to have the best promise of future sales. Andy Coombe was, therefore, heavily involved in the compliance procedures (which Dickie Bird had handled, in the Islander's submission of earlier years) necessitating several visits to Brussels, for meetings with the US European Region representatives of the FAA. Andy's flight test engineering duties were progressively taken over by Bob Wilson, his performance engineer colleague, who later assumed full responsibilities for all those areas of activity. From my records it appears that Andy's final meeting with the US officials, of whom a man called Craig Beard was the senior, took place on Tuesday 27th July, whereafter full American Public Transport Category Certification would have been confirmed, subject to the granting of its UK Type Certificate. During this period of time I do remember a group of FAA officials coming over to Bembridge, for a meeting on the subject, and going through our engineering publications, along with the Trislander Type Record (raised by Dick Stowe) and other Master Build documentation (provided by Reg Hobbs, the Chief Inspector). Unfortunately my diary is devoid of all details about this event, so I'm unable to recall whether it was before, or after, Andy's visit to Brussels on 27th July. At any rate the way would shortly be clear for the export of Trislanders to the USA and countries

97

associated with its jurisdiction.

***

While all these events were in train, however, there had been another case of elevator trim tab failure on an Islander, this time in Finland. Again, the spotlight was turned onto the apparently persistent problem. As well as special inspections, revised adjustments had been applied to the trim tabs in earlier actions but attention was now centred on the trim actuating jack and its connecting rod ball-end joints. Dennis Berryman's flight control squad was taxed with finding a solution and it had been decided to introduce an improved trim actuating jack, with a connecting rod having upgraded ball-ends. There was a tremendous amount of pressure created by this defect which the ARB was decidedly sensitive about. Accordingly it became the subject of a Mandatory modification, which was preceded by a 'Campaign Wire' to all known Islander operators. This latter procedure was the usual method adopted when some considerable time was likely in making decisions and obtaining parts. In essence it meant that we had to agree a form of words with the ARB, to cover the initial recommendations, and telex or cable it to all the necessary addresses, including the supervising local Airworthiness Offices.

This action took place and the modification procedure was detailed in mutually agreed form, whilst urgent orders for new parts were put in hand. Peter Mallinson, the Service Department Manager, had the job of urging all the parts and making them up into self-contained kits (which would include our Mandatory 'red-top' instructions when finalized) for addressing and despatch to all parts of the world. Needless to say it was a disruptive and expensive process which was, itself, subject to delays in parts supply and acceptable decision making. Jim Munn and his accounts facilities were close neighbours of ours, in the roof space of the new hangar, and he would sometimes come over and have a few words with me about things, generally. Jim was another ex-colonial service man who had spent a number of years in West Africa but was very close to retirement at that time. It became clear to me that he was perplexed and worried by the trend of events in the Company. Cashflow problems

98

obviously assailed him from all angles but he was too loyal to complain, or to 'let the cat out of the bag'. In retrospect, I now think that Dickie Bird was well aware that the governors were coming off the financial engine, so to speak and had positioned himself on the footplate for a safe evacuation before it left the rails. Dickie had experienced such times before and knew how to take care of himself. In the light of my own experience I, also, had begun to take certain precautions myself.

Out on the Bembridge airfield there were 14 or 15 unsold Islanders during the summer of 1971. Officially they were supposed to be allocated to customers, but the USA had recently imposed a 15 per cent tariff on all aviation imports which dissuaded all but the keenest and most desperate buyers. These were the ones who found it harder and took longer to raise the necessary finance in the first place. By now, Desmond's elder brother Sir Mark Norman, had joined the Company as the Sales Director, but he was not helped by the creeping depression spreading through industry generally and aviation in particular. Sir Mark had been the Company Secretary to the Bristol Aeroplane Company before he came to Bembridge and they, of course, were about to launch the Concorde into service – but with far fewer on their order books than at first expected. Sir Mark was a keen cricketer, wanting to raise a team from the Company to play a few games, during the otherwise favourable conditions of that summer's weather, I remember being invited to play in a match arranged against the BHC team. Derek Osborne, one of our Shop Planning Engineers, Ian Wilson (Bob Wilson's middle brother) who was working on Product Support and others from all areas of the Company, whose names now elude me, made up the required number with Sir Mark as captain. We had an enjoyable game on the BHC sports ground at Cowes, which boasted more mature and congenial facilities than we could offer at Bembridge, but I fear we lost the match.

Warning tremors of the forthcoming troubles had been felt in the spring of 1971 when a notice, citing a number of imminent redundancies, was suddenly displayed on the factory notice boards. Following the re organization in the wake of Jim McMahon's departure, 18 months or so before, the Company had engaged a Personnel Officer, known as Monty Plomer; he was one of the number who left at that time. This was happening simultaneously with the Mandatory modification action to the Islander elevator trim jacks and, as to be expected, had a serious effect on the general morale of the Company's employees. Not long afterwards it became known that Sam Oppenheimer, who was a highly placed director in the Westland Helicopters Co., had initiated moves to recover £600,000 worth of debentures held in Britten-Norman Ltd. which added further depression to the lowered morale of all concerned. Desmond had suddenly gone quiet about the Defender project which seemed to be fading away just when I had 50 copies of each publication coming up to completion, in their new livery. In the circumstances I decided to keep my own council about this matter and only volunteer information or evidence when it was requested by Desmond himself. When that commission was complete I had all the stock parcelled up and innocuously labelled, away from general view. Some time later, several copies of one or other of these handbooks surfaced, upon requests starting with Desmond, but as time went by, the project (and the need for handbooks) failed to materialize. I was eventually to dispose of the printed contents and had the binders re-covered and re-blocked for Islander or Trislander use.

Trislanders now began to appear as the aeroplanes with most promise but our inability to produce them effectively was all too apparent. The conversion process from Islander fuselage to extended Trislander fuselage, incorporated a host of additional contoured doubling plates, of differing gauge thicknesses, built up on top of one another in some cases until the areas around the cabin centre section looked more like an armoured vehicle than an aeroplane. Properly productionized design drawings and manufacturing aids, such as jigs and fixtures for the job, were not available to the shop floor workers who were still reliant upon Taffy Lloyd's fluctuating compendium of instructions (and his memory) to complete the job. Each of these early Trislanders was, therefore, a handbuilt one-off job, so far as the fuselage was concerned. The wing construction was better ordained, under the more disciplined conditions in the up-rated wing jig, in BHC's Cowes Works. Similarly the fin and tail engine nacelle benefited, at least, from elementary jigging. After the conversion of Constructor's No. 262 Islander into Trislander Registration G-AYWI, there were two other conversions completed before October. These were from Constructor's No. 279 Islander into Trislander registration G-AYZR, and Constructor's No. 299 Islander into Trislander Registration G-AZFG. The first so-called production Trislander, G-AYWI, was destined for Aurigny on the Channel Islands routes, whilst the other two were both for export to the USA.

Whereas the Islander's structure had been rated by the ARB as an 'On Condition' airframe, a different rating was to be applied to the Trislander's structure. In the Islander's case that rating meant that it could be operated under any conditions, anywhere in the world, provided the approved maintenance procedures were observed until, and unless, causes for repair became evident. It was decided, by the ARB, that the Trislander airframe must be 'life-limited', according to hours flown and conditions encountered. The approved maintenance procedures had to be observed, of course, but now a more particular regime of monitoring flying hours and route conditions would be necessary. The latter would, perhaps, only be required in parts of the world where severe turbulence may normally be encountered; Tasmania, New Zealand and the Caribbean for example. Then, it might be necessary to record gust forces in those regions. All of these considerations meant a lot more ongoing work for Dick Stowe and his structural engineering colleagues Those relatively simple static tests on the Islander wing which Max Wall had overseen, in the polythene tunnel, years before, had been effected by progressively loading the wing structure with heavy 'shot bags' until it deformed or failed. Now there had to be a continuous full-scale fatigue test programme on a representative Trislander wing, to establish the structural limitations, against the target estimations. Since there were no possibilities of Bembridge having space, or equipment, to perform the required tests, it fell to BHC's facilities to help out, once again. There was no wonder that Jim Munn's financial worries were very real ones. Dick had to get the tests set up and then ensure that they ran continuously and spasmodically, over a period of time, representing about 30,000 flying hours, to include the load variations associated with take-offs and landings. All this was done using an array of pulsing hydraulic jacks and electro-mechanical measuring equipment, whilst constantly being 'eyeballed' by a human operator for any premature failures.

Back in the Islander arena the 'Propellor Parliament' had finally come to realize that, in spite of the recent improvements to elevator trim actuating jacks and connecting rods, the problems had not been resolved. John Allan, along with a number of other people, instinctively disliked this cabal method of working and referred to the gathering as '... a mutual admiration society'. The ARB became ever more insistent that new elevators and trim tabs were the only sure way of conquering the troubles once and for all. The ARB was always uncomfortable with the prospect of FAA domination, in the event of a catastrophe to an American registered aeroplane which may have received its original Type Certificate in Britain. In the situation and realizing the magnitude of the decision, John Britten and Desmond Norman had no alternative but to authorize the design of a new elevator and matched trim tab, embodying revised mass balance criteria. The additional work, together with its conditional testing, was once again sandwiched in with all the other work under the Company's 507th modification. It was only normal practice, of course, but in our straitened circumstances, with so much unfinished work on hand and the daunting aspects of costs and logistics in re-equipping all in-service Islanders, the situation was critical in the extreme. Although I can't be certain, after all this time, it does appear that the design work and its trialling must have been completed by the end of July 1971 because the Bembridge factory closed for one week's annual holiday on 2nd August. From the design instructions, extant, the new elevators and trim tabs were being manufactured under sub-contract, by Aviation Traders Ltd. (a company originally started by Freddie Laker in the days of the Berlin Airlift) whilst I had the duty of raising the mandatory embodiment instructions for agreement by the ARB. Reference to my diary shows that we had achieved this by Wednesday 1st September, when we despatched a bundle of 250 'red-top' leaflets, for inclusion in the modification kits of parts, then being readied by Aviation Traders Ltd. at Southend. These would have to be supplied and shipped to all affected operators, free of charges, under the terms of the Mandatory instructions.

***

102

Before we actually arrived at this date, however, almost the whole of the Drawing Office staff was suddenly made redundant – on 27th August 1971. On that day 17 people received letters of dismissal, by hand, ostensibly citing lack of further project work due to the immediate absence of finance. Though quite shocked, at the time, as was everyone else, it was not entirely out of the blue to myself. About a month before that, I had been told that no further sub-contract work on the Trislander Maintenance Manual and Maintenance Schedule (with PERA) and Illustrated Parts Catalogue (with Gloster Designs) could be authorized. Accordingly, I had forewarned those companies not to exceed the limits of their orders, but to provide me with as many completed batches as possible without running into part-finished work. For the past year, or so, I had also had the benefit of a BHC Technical Writer, Douglas Wyles, working on site in my own office, to expedite changes to the various publications, on a kind of 'firefighting' basis, as they arose. Doug was an ex-BOAC line maintenance engineer who had been employed, by them, on Lockheed Constellations among other types of aircraft. He was a thoroughly useful chap but I was instructed to write to BHC and terminate his contract, with effect from 30th September1971. On the 15th September, Len Townend and Andrew Henry, who were PERA's project leaders on the Trislander commission, arrived at Bembridge to inform about the arrangements for completing their tasks. The financial engine had not yet left the rails but the ride was certainly becoming a 'white-knuckle' one. Friday 8th October saw the retirement of Jim Munn and, though I don't have the exact date, Dickie Bird had already disappeared some months earlier, with the stated intention of looking after family business affairs in Norfolk . He had, in fact, returned to the Miles organization to take up works managership of their Ford (Sussex) factory.

Almost as if foreseen in detail, the forthcoming events had been preceded by a frantic rush to get the pre-production Trislander (G-AYTU) away on tropical trials by Friday 20th August. Its final UK Type Certificate clearance and Certificate of Airworthiness for airline use were, of course, contingent upon the successful completion of these trials. Without the results of 'hot and high' performance scheduling, we could not complete

103

that part of the Trislander Flight Manual, so that it was operating only on a 'Special Category' basis. Until a satisfactory outcome was achieved, no final deliveries to customers could have taken place, even if the Company had been able to produce the aeroplanes more quickly. Geoff Tomms, a shop foreman who was going along to look after the ground engineering duties, borrowed some part-finished engineering manuals, on that Friday afternoon, to help him on the job. Three days later, on Wednesday 25th August, I had to raise another package of part-finished Trislander Air Publications for Andy Coombe to take to the Australian Directorate of Civil Aviation, in Melbourne, on the following Friday. Once again, Andy's limitless energies and enthusiasm were following in the pattern set by Dickie Bird, to achieve Australian certification, which would open Far-Eastern doors to the acceptance of the Trislanders.

In the three weeks, or so since the dismissal of most of the Drawing Office members, plans were made to bring the remaining key people back to the new hangar. It was intended that the old hangar should be cleared and the small band of Works personnel and effects were also relocated to the new hangar during the third week in September. Again this meant a tremendous amount of work and effort for the long-suffering factory maintenance team. Urgent business, connected with an error in the American F.A.A. Approved Islander Flight Manual, caused me to be flown to Redhill, in the Cessna, on Thursday 14th October to agree an immediately authorized change for the subject manuals. Returning, in the dark by Islander, via Goodwood airfield, I remember we had to stooge around a couple of times until a car with powerful headlamps came out to the runway threshold. There were no landing aids, apart from this typically British solution, and so we landed downbeam of the car lights. The Islander had to depart, the same way, for some other destination, according to the young Sales Demonstration pilot, whose name I'm unable to recall; I was left to tie up with two shadowy figures lurking under the wing of an equally shadowy Cessna. These two gentlemen turned out to be John Nielan and Hugh Kendall who were none too pleased to be on the wrong side of the Solent at 7:30pm. Scrambling into the back seat, with Hugh in the right hand one and John as captain, I noticed we were started up and rolling almost before the doors were shut and the belts fastened. Away down the car headlamp beams we went, looking back to see them switched off when we were airborne. Descent down into Bembridge Airport, a little while later, was not even assisted by any lighting, of any sort, on the ground and was not a comfortable experience. John rounded on the Cessna, saying she was a good flyer but a bitch when landing. Exactly four days later, on 18th October, one of the pilots 'pranged' her at Blackbushe aerodrome whilst visiting Fairoaks Aviation Ltd. This was a company run by a flamboyant character named Douglas Arnold, which was acting as a distributor for Britten-Norman Ltd. Severe damage to the propeller and front end would necessitate a rebuild of that area but, fortunately, there were no casualties.

How the costs for this escapade, along with all the other feverish activities, would be settled, was no longer a cause for worry by Jim Munn. A few days later, on 22nd October 1971, the financial engine finally left the rails. About 4:00pm on this day which also happened to be my wedding anniversary, an official notice appeared on the factory notice board downstairs, informing that the financial backers of Britten-Norman Ltd. had called in a Receiver. Not long afterwards TV film crews and reporters, were at Bembridge Airport to gather what they could for the evening's news bulletins. Jim Birnie parted company with the firm, just before this happened I think, because he had suffered for some time with a heart defect which finally put an end to his long and distinguished flying career. Jim and his wife Wendy, bought a large secluded house in Bembridge which they turned into a country house hotel that they called 'The Elms'. Jim's test flying duties were taken over by Hugh Kendall, who must have been on the Company's payroll, because his services were retained by the Receiver. Figuratively speaking, Sir Mark Norman's innings was a short one, however, his wicket being taken about this time by the "change in bowling", no doubt! On Monday 25th October the appointed Receiver moved into Bembridge Airport and began to take stock of things. Price Waterhouse and Partners, as it was then, became the controlling authority with, Mr Maurice (Monty) Eckman of that Company taking over the management of Britten-Norman Ltd. My first contact with Monty Eckman's management team came in a meeting with one of his highly capable lieutenants, called Mark Homan, who told me that all our field service information, from that point on, must bear the printed note: 'A Receiver and Manager has been appointed.' Furthermore, nothing must be posted without first having the Receiver's scrutiny and agreement.

A few days later our Company received a letter from the ARB, to the effect that Britten-Norman's Design Approval was being revoked, until that Authority had made a review of our denuded Technical Staff and the outstanding bills of approximately £6000, owing to the ARB, were paid in full. All these matters were developing to the disadvantage of the delivery schedule of that first so-called production Trislander G-AYWI, for Aurigny Air Services, now with all the airworthiness requirements (apart from its de-icing system) cleared for service. Andy Coombe, accompanied by Mr Macdonald of Price Waterhouse, had to make an urgent visit to the ARB on Friday 29th October, I note, to plead for the re-instatement of the Company's Design Approval and, presumably, pay the Authority's bill, before the aircraft could be formally released. Here was the form of things that would set the pattern as the Receiver's management team gradually penetrated into all of the Company's activities.

Monty Eckman's intention was to sell the Company on, as a viable and worthwhile business, so that the continuing supply of part-finished aeroplanes was of crucial importance. BHC's contracts had been extended two or three times, already, and that company had built and supplied about 305 Islanders, in the form of sub-assemblies, for completion at Bembridge. Its current contract which would take the total up to about 380 units was ratified by the Receiver who decided against any further renewal, relying instead on a supply of Islanders from the Romanian production line, now functioning quite well. Accordingly, the contract with that company (known as IRMA, from the initial capitals of its difficult-to-pronounce full name) was ratified by the Receiver, thus allowing Islander construction and supply to continue from that source. John Britten and Desmond Norman, chastened by these experiences, had been relegated to lower profiles than those to which they had been accustomed, but their presence was not completely banished. Of the remaining key personnel in the Technical Offices, Andy O'Connell and Dennis Berryman were closest to John Britten, perhaps, while Andy

Coombe was maybe nearer to Desmond Norman. The formal Chief Designer was still John Allan but there was no Chief Technical Executive in the absence of Dickie Bird so that I was, myself, officially answerable to the Chief Designer it seemed.

Harry Ellis, at the ARB's Brabazon House Headquarters, was still the Authority's responsible Chief Design Surveyor who was becoming more uneasy about the situation at Bembridge Airport, as indeed were his superiors. Harry well-understood the difficulties presented by the unfolding conditions, and was concemed by the Company's lack of a well experienced engineer at top level. Someone with deep experience of field service conditions, as well as design work, who could handle affairs with a high degree of impartiality to the satisfaction of the Air Registration Board, was seen to be needed. Consequently Miles Aviation and Transport was to help out once again. Ronald Dack, who had been George Miles' Chief Stressman for many years, was persuaded to join Britten-Norman Ltd. as Chief Engineer. Ron was a well qualified and practical aircraft engineer, whose in-depth experience went back to the wartime years, when he had served with the Air Transport Auxiliary (ATA). He was no stranger to Islanders either, becoming involved at the beginning of the Miles consultancy period; Ron had also been involved with quite a few 'Special Purpose Roles' that were introduced along the way. Installations concerning the carriage of Micronair Spraying equipment and Aerial Survey Camera fitments, were among those which Miles had advised upon after the original consultancy assignment had been completed.

One month into the Receivership, on the morning of 22nd November, Monty Eckman informed me that he was going to dismiss three members of my staff, thus leaving only three of us to carry on. During the afternoon, he called a meeting, at around 4:15pm, making a speech about what was going to happen immediately and informing us that a further number of employees would be dismissed; about 39 people in all, including several more from the Drawing Office. He also informed us that the name of the Company would change, the following day, to Britten-Norman (Bembridge) Ltd. When that happened, a High Court Injunction was served, against the Receivership and new Company, by

107

Jim McMahon's Company, Micronair Ltd. to claim recompense from the sales of all new aeroplanes. Wily, as ever, Jim had been watching events develop and was not going to lose out on a 'Royalty'-type of agreement, struck with his former partners, which gave him a share in each new production aeroplane delivered.

Almost in parallel with our own difficulties, industrial tremors were also affecting that great, hitherto unquestionable, cornerstone of British engineering, none other than Rolls Royce Ltd. In its almost ignominious descent into management by a Receiver, it gained the new styling of Rolls-Royce (1971) Ltd. for its Company name. These industrial difficulties were becoming widespread during Edward Heath's government. Vickers Aircraft, at Weybridge, was winding down, after the VC-10 airliner failed to win sufficient operator interest in competition with the Americans and the rising European Airbus Consortium. Only a couple of years or so before, the once-famous name of Handley-Page had disappeared, in similar circumstances, following the introduction of the Jetstream, in its original and unpopular form. As if to mirror these changes, the Society of British Aircraft Constructors subtly renamed itself as the 'Society of British Aerospace Companies Ltd' thinking, perhaps, to reach for the stars in the absence of aerodynes. They were not alone in this form of thinking either, because the ARB, which liked to promote itself as a self-financing organization, was watching its plants of sustenance wither away. In moves toward ensuring its survival, the Authority became wedded to the Civil Service echelons and metamorphosed into the 'Civil Aviation Authority' before the end of 1971.

It was not long before most of the remaining, once independent, aircraft manufacturers were swept into the consortium named British Aerospace. The Vickers factory at Weybridge, home to Barnes Wallace, was sold up for commercial development, most of its airfield now forming a theme park. Likewise the de Havilland factory and its airfield, at Hatfield suffered a similar fate, the site being scheduled for housing when the last of the DH 146 work was transferred to Hawker-Siddeley's former Avro factory at Woodford near Manchester. The long established Hawker factory at Kingston-on-Thames, home to Sidney Camm of Hurricane fame, also became a donor to housing requirements during the decade of the 1970s. I had friends and acquaintances in most of the Companies, among my peers, who were doing similar work, because the SBAC had an organization of committees to cover all of its interests. The Society maintained offices in King Street, St James's, in London, where regular meetings, concerning current developments, took place. An interchange of ideas and discussions helped to keep one in touch with outside affairs, providing a welcome – if very temporary – relief from the humdrum tasks. The manufacturers had representation on these committees, dealing with every aspect of the industry, from engineering design, structural, power plant, electrical and accessories, through to airworthiness and test pilotage. The aspect of Air Publications was dealt with by a sub-committee, devolved from the Airworthiness Committee. At the top of the tree was the 'Boardroom' which boasted a magnificent bow-sided table, around which the principals of the member companies would, on occasion, take their places. Needless to say this room was sacrosanct and only a quick, veiled, glance was permitted to the lesser mortals who foregathered in more Spartan conditions. Our Company's inclusion in such affairs had come in the final stages, if not at the eleventh hour, of the British aircraft industry.

8.1 An Islander embodying military modifications, enabling the attachment of underwing pylons and warloads. (Several were sold as 'Defenders' to minor forces, but all production aeroplanes were required to have civil certificates of airworthiness, as Islanders, before release from the factory)

8.2 The pre-production Trislander. (Constructor's No. 245: BN-2A Mark III). Photograph shows the final shape of the upper fin extension, to full chord width

Chapter 9

Amalgamation and Separation

At the beginning of 1972, under the tight control of the Price Waterhouse Receivership, the Company was beginning to get used to functioning with even fewer staff. Monty Eckman had put out feelers to attract potential buyers, for the going concern of Britten-Norman (Bembridge) Ltd. which soon seemed to produce interest. There was an early rumour, of some strength, that the BHC was set to buy the Company for £4.5 million, but other contenders were in the loop and we never heard any more about that one. A great deal of business interest was building up, in January and February, concerning the possibility of 100 Islanders being supplied to Portugal. The plans, as broached, called for 30 complete aeroplanes to be built for that customer (whoever it was) supported by the further supply of 70 complete kits. John Britten was at the forefront of these matters and insisted upon me providing a fully costed statement for the supply of 100 sets of Islander Air Publications, for inclusion in the Company's overall quotation for the job. Whether or not it was a smokescreen set up by he and Desmond, to inflate the Company's worth, is difficult to know – but nothing materialized in the end, despite intensive work across all the other departments concerned in finalizing the voluminous quotations.

About the same time, we had a visit from the Canadian aircraft manufacturing concern, Canadair; their executives had talks with Price Waterhouse but, again, there was no final outcome. Interestingly, I note, the exchange rate between the US dollar and the pound sterling stood at $2.55 to £1:00 on 14th January 1972. All of our products were priced in dollars at the time and one of the Receivership's inflexible rules, was that nothing must be supplied to any customer, unless full prepayment had been received, and verified, at our bank. Up until the onset of Receivership the Company had always used Lloyd's bank, who were then dropped and superseded by the National Westminster bank. Customers were none too pleased by these arrangements, often being disadvantaged by what they regarded as a slur on their credit-worthiness and by the unwarranted delays.

Delays were unavoidable in the circumstances; from our own, internal, viewpoint they were beginning to be critical, in that purchase orders could no longer be placed for materials or sub-contract services, in a timely manner, to ensure smooth continuity. The Sanction system of cost control was still in existence but each one was now subject to scrutiny and final signature by a member of the Receivership team. Full justification had to be shown for the 'spend' or it would be dismissed out of hand. With the order of priorities which had to be followed, naturally enough, the need for manufacturing items had to be addressed first, even to the threat of compromise upon airworthiness. In the latter case it was often quite difficult to persuade the accountants' mind that, unless certain unpalatable costs were met, a train of even more expensive and/ or dangerous events may follow.

Production of Islanders and Trislanders, side-by-side, was continuing at reduced volume, with each unit being carefully monitored to ensure customer take-up. BHC-built Islanders had momentarily peaked at around Constructor's No 306; this aeroplane had its first flight on 28th March 1972 as a Model BN-2A-8. As such it was delivered to Cavico Aircraft at Fort Lauderdale, in Florida, a couple of months later. At this particular time the Model BN-2A-8 seemed to constitute the prevailing Islander Build Standard. It was tailored to the optimum specification for the American operators, in having the cheaper and lighter, normally-aspirated, Lycoming 260 hp engines, together with the aerodynamic improvements of short sections of drooped leading edges (between the cabin and each engine) and a slightly drooped flap setting. In this form the Islander's maximum take-off weight had grown to 6,200 lb (2812 kg) for operation to FAA Regulations, and by a further 100 lb (45.36 kg) to 6,300 lb (2857 kg) for use under UK BCAR's. With the more powerful, more expensive, and heavier 300 hp fuel-injected Lycoming engines (in place of the 260 hp ones) the FAA maximum take-off weight was also raised to 6,300 lb (2857 kg) for the same airframe standard but the Model No. changed to BN-2A-2 resultantly. There was no additional weight benefit under UK BCAR's for this model, however, its main advantage being conferred by an enhanced performance capability when operated out of high altitude airfields, say above 4000 ft, in the elevated temperatures of the tropics. If the extended wing-tip fuel tanks were fitted, to customers' option, a further Model No. change was applied to each of the above mentioned versions.

Trislanders, however, were a different story. They were still evolving out of the conversion process, presided over the by the effervescent Taffy Lloyd.

The pre-production Trislander – out of Islander Constructor's No. 245 conversion – was still with us at Bembridge but had been sold to Air Gabon. Consequently there was great activity on all fronts to get this aeroplane cleared for delivery. Given that Air Gabon was under French Territorial jurisdiction, I was keeping a low-profile (and my fingers crossed) in case the subject of French language publications was raised. There weren't any for the Trislander just then. In the event everything came together and the faithful old work-horse was delivered to its new owners during the first week in March. From a strictly personal situation, I was becoming worried by the constant drain on my stocks of publications which would soon have to be supplied without binders, unless I could win the Sanction argument with John Britten and the Receivers. Similarly, since the stoppage of sub-contract assistance for Trislander manuals, the previous September, there remained a significant amount of effort to get that range of publications nearer to completion. It took a considerable amount of lobbying and re-submissions, before things were agreed, but on 15th March 1972 my purchase orders were ready for signature by Directors and Receivers. Upon enquiry for John Britten and Ted Tylee (the relevant member of the Receivership team) I was told that they had both departed for Romania – more delay, since the work could not be actioned until they returned and had time to sign the orders.

Following upon the delivery of the third Trislander to Aurigny Air Services, in January, all the stops were out now to get three more consecutive Islanders converted into Trislanders for earliest deliveries. The Receivership was realizing the benefits of the higher value units, but not the vagaries of the associated shop floor 'birth-pangs'. Constructor's

No. 320, 321 and 322 were the Islanders earmarked and they would constitute the 6th, 7th and 8th production Trislanders, when completed. These aeroplanes were destined for operation in three different regions of the world, under the Certification Authorities of the United Kingdom and Australia. Constructor's No. 320 was ordered by a Safari Tours operator in Kenya, under the name of Sunbird - Linblad Tours, who required a special 'non-standard' cabin interior. For this arising the Drawing, Weights and Stress Offices were again engaged in a 'bespoke' job, which then translated into a similar one-off task, on the so-called production line, down on the hangar floor. The other two Trislanders would go to a UK Operator and an Australian one, in New South Wales, respectively; just to further complicate matters, this latter one (No. 8) was being readied for earlier delivery than No. 7. All the while, the Receivership was finding customers for the intervening Islanders – onwards from Constructor's No. 306 – which were steadily being completed and delivered.

During the last week of May, Andy Coombe told me that important decisions about the future of Britten-Norman (Bembridge) Ltd. were likely to be made over the weekend, 27th/28th May. Apparently an Israeli delegation was eyeing the Company over with a view to purchase. Once again, however, it was a 'damp squib' and nothing worthwhile emerged from the negotiations. Rather selfishly, perhaps, I had begun to feel very sanguine about the affairs in general. In the preceding month I had managed to get the Trislander Parts Cataloguing work re-started and was more than fully occupied with that and urgent Flight Manual work including a constant stream of enquiries. That May was one of the worst on record for weather, with heavy rain storms and lashing gales. Having suffered again from rail strikes, postal delays, and other disruptions, during April, one began to feel like a victim of politico/industrial masochism. More and more we were being driven to use people like Securicor and other courier services, to be sure of meeting deadlines and promises to customers. Soldiering on through June and July, with the advent of better weather, and Farnborough once again in prospect, there were problems with failed rudder bar linkages which had to be addressed by the Design Department, myself included, that called for urgent Service Bulletin action. Likewise, further faults suddenly affected the pilots' seat adjuster mechanism – on the seat unit of yet a third Accessory manufacturer's design. A turbocharger installation, of American design and manufacture was successfully embodied in Constructor's No. 307 Islander. This was another attempt towards enhancing the performance of the production standard Islander, with equipment, marketed by the 'Rayjay Corporation,' for application to Lycoming 260hp engines. No fewer than 27 queries and hitches arose, in installation, however, and it did not become a popular option.

Once again the factory closed for the annual holidays during the first two weeks of August. Among many other, mostly mundane, matters, my diary reminds me that I had my first flight in a Trislander on 23rd August. John Nielan was the pilot and Bob Wilson, in the co-pilot's seat, was acting in the capacity of flight test engineer. We took off at 5:15pm and were airborne for about twenty minutes; this was the first flight of a Trislander at the maximum gross weight of 10,000 lb (4,536 kg). Previously the aeroplane had been limited to a maximum gross weight of 9350 lb (4241 kg) and this was to be the next stage in raising its maximum take-off weight. Afterwards, Bob's carefully plotted results of take off and landing distances, times and airspeeds in the climbs and descents, together with the obvious extensions to the aeroplane's centre of gravity limits, would be carefully analysed and set out in an Airworthiness Approval Note (AAN) for submission to the Civil Aviation Authority – CAA as it was now styled. Once agreed and approved the data would be passed to myself for preparation and inclusion in the Trislander Flight Manuals. In this particular case, however, the CAA conservatively rounded down the weight to 9850 lb (4468 kg). Almost exactly one week later, on 31st August 1972, the Price Waterhouse Receivership announced the sale of Britten-Norman (Bembridge) Ltd. to the Fairey Aviation Company. It had been Monty Eckman's avowed intention to keep the Company in business and, so far as was possible, to keep the Island workforce and facilities intact and still British. In spite of the difficulties and risks, he had managed to pull off a skilful business deal which justified the Receivership's faith in the enterprise headed by John Britten and Desmond Norman.

Amalgamation with the Fairey Aviation Company progressed

quite quickly. Despite the fact that Fairey's had long since ceased the manufacture of aircraft in Britain, the company had retained its headquarters and some factory space at Heston, its traditional home in Middlesex. From this base it designed and manufactured filtration equipment for aviation and general purpose use. Furthermore the company still had a good aviation design and manufacturing facility in Belgium, known as Fairey S.A. (Société Anonyme).

This sprang from the mid-1930s contract agreements, between Fairey's and the Belgian Government, for the production of 'Fantomes' and 'Foxes', ordered by the Belgian armed forces. The factory, with adjoining airfield, had been set up at Gosselies, a mining township, adjacent to Charleroi, not far from Mons. Its prime purpose, at this time was to service the needs of NATO requirements, in modification and re-furbishment work. (There was a time, when commandeered by the Germans during the second World War, that these facilities had been used to produce Messerschmitt 109s). A big programme of ongoing work was expected, from the American General Dynamics Corporation, in the design liaison, building and product support, for the F.16 Strike Fighter project. As often the case, however, the F.16 programme had been delayed such that Fairey's workforce in Belgium was in danger of being laid-off. This state of affairs, not to mention redundancies, cost Continental companies dearly, when they occurred, and the Islander/ Trislander acquisition was seen as a valuable 'in-fill' project to tide over the difficulties foreseen. It had, obviously, already been agreed that the first priority was the preparation of fully productionized design drawings and build jigs, for the Trislander. This action would transform the 'make-shift' process of Taffy Lloyd's sketch-book compendium and locked-in mental data into more permanently accessible and conventional manufacturing aids. Not less important, but following on from that, was the need to take over Islander construction work, as it neared the end of the final contract with BHC at Cowes. Arrangements were made, in this context, to transfer the associated build jigs and fixtures to the Gosselies factory where they would be put back into production use again, as they became available. The Romanian production line at Bucharest was now functioning very well and had produced about 80 Islanders at this juncture, so ensuring continuity while the transfer of BHC production to Fairey SA took effect. Indeed, the Romanian production effort was providing about 3 Islanders per month, into Bembridge Airport for finalizing to customer requirements.

Accordingly, on 18th September 1972, the Fairey SA Chéf d'Études (equating to Chief Designer) M. Marcel Leleux, arrived at Bembridge with two of his draughtsmen and one stressman. Marcel returned to Belgium after two days, but his staff members were to stay on for three months, to assimilate as much Trislander knowledge as possible. John Brenchley was still at Bembridge in the following month of October, I notice, because he was deeply involved in the rudder bar defects, mentioned earlier, along with John Allan, Dennis Berryman and Ron Dack. Between them, they had the job of strengthening these units, which were also identical to the ones installed in Trislanders. Eventually, through the Sanction procedures, costs, materials, logistics and Service Bulletin issuance, another problem was laid to rest. It was about at this time that the question of Canadian certification for the Trislander arose. I received a telephone call from Larry Robillard, who was a principal in the Canadian Phaega Corp., asking for the urgent supply of Engineering and Flight Manuals for the Trislander, to further the cause in that direction. It appeared that the Canadian Department of Transport, which was charged with responsibility for Aircraft Certification in Canada, was undecided about whether to accept the American FAA status, or whether to change to the UK BCAR standard instead. To help them in their combined deliberations, Larry wanted copies of both the American and British-style Flight Manuals for the Trislander. The aeroplane concerned, turned out to be No. 3 production Trislander (converted out of Constructor's No. 299 Islander) which had been supplied to Jonas, in New York, with full expectation of American registration.

One of the main issues, perhaps, related to the tail-mounted engine; this was out of sight of the pilot. A major concern was the possible sudden loss of power, from this third engine, during take-off and climb out. For UK Certification purposes, a power failure warning lamp system, in conjunction with an external rear-view mirror, had been adopted and accepted as effective monitoring devices, for just such an emergency. The FAA, however, were unconvinced and had insisted upon the installation of an automatic feathering system for the rear propeller, in the event of power loss. Their case was mainly hinged upon a potential 'panic situation' on the flight deck, caused by a flashing red light in the critical phases of take-off and climb out. These decisions had been taken in spite of the background history of 'autofeather' systems sometimes having malfunctioned and actually contributed to such a power loss. Thus, the Phaega Corporation in Ottawa and the Canadian Department of Transport, were working to resolve the situation for an operator in the Quebec region, by the name of Baie Comeau Air Service, who was anxious to get No. 3 Trislander into service.

**

By November 1972, John and Desmond were once more in their driving seats, to all intents and purposes. This time, though, more in the guise of chauffeurs than principals, perhaps. Indeed, one wag was reputed to have asked Desmond how he liked working for Fairey's; drawing himself up to full height and addressing the enquirer coldly, Desmond informed him that he worked *with* Fairey's and not *for* them. A big chance had presented itself just then for a medium sized freight and troop carrying aircraft in the Lockheed Hercules mould. It was not long before I was drawn into the preparation of an urgent brochure for this project, to be known as the 'Mainlander'. At the root of the project was a surfeit of Rolls-Royce Dart turboprop engines, looking for cheap homes in suitable airframes. Our resultant proposals to the Fairey hierarchy resembled a 100 per cent scaled-up Trislander, powered by three Dart engines.

This project was another of John Britten's inspirations. It was an altogether new aeroplane, despite a passing likeness to the Trislander, with the capacity to carry either 100 troops, or several armoured vehicles. Low to the ground, with 'podded' main undercarriage units and ramp-down rear loading door, the concept had every favourable practical prospect but nothing in the way of financial ones. The mother company, having adopted an expensive orphan, was not in a position to indulge its whims. The task of trying to introduce other interests was an enduring one, however, carrying on well into1973 and involving John and Desmond in much lobbying, lecturing and travelling on its behalf. I remember being involved in costing a notional set of Air Publications for the Mainlander, which came out at about £400,000, in that year's money. It was, I note from diary details 'tentatively agreed with John Britten'. We had to do a series of lecture slide originals, for the anticipated performance data; maximum weight take off and landing distances, climb, cruise and descent graphs and so on. In spite of the enthusiasm and effort expended, however, there were no positive results forthcoming.

Because of the need for regular liaison with the Gosselies facility, as the amalgamation gathered pace, the Company earmarked an Islander as an inter-factory communications aircraft. A pilot by the name of Geoff Boston was engaged to fly the 'Gosselies Shuttle' service as it became known. Geoff was a very capable and trustworthy pilot who set about putting his mark on the operation from the start; every morning at 8:30 am prompt, the little Islander left Bembridge Airport, rain or shine, bound for Gosselies. Urgent parts, design drawings and personnel were transported out, the latter sometimes returning the same day, or staying on if the need arose. The flight usually took about an hour and a half, but a bit longer on the return home, because of the need to clear customs procedures at Manston. There were no facilities for this requirement at Bembridge Airport. A regular quota of Continentally procured liquor and cigarettes accompanied the passengers on their homeward journey. Conveniently placed, just across the main road from the Gosselies factory gates, stood a hyper-market which sold everything from hairpins to motor cars. Taffy Lloyd was, of course, an early patron of the shuttle service, along with other design colleagues and shop planning engineers, one of whom was Ray Jacobs. On one occasion when I made a visit, I remember being in the lunch time company of Ray, and others, when he pulled out a particularly fuzzy-tipped ballpoint pen and proceeded to sketch out some obscure modus operandi on the canteen's crisp white tablecloth. Not having been used to such civilized works canteen facilities, I was mildly shocked by this act of desecration but the others never seemed to turn a hair. No doubt the Gosselies laundry services took it all in their stride.

The gross weight increase to 9850 lb (4468 kg) for the Trislander had received its CAA approval, together with the necessary Flight Manual amendments, by the third week in February 1973 and, as a result the Model No. was changed, from the original designation of BN2A Mark III, to: BN2A Mark III-1. This was the definitive build standard for the early production Trislanders, built at the Gosselies factory; it was not until the introduction of the long-nosed version, with increased baggage capacity, about two years later, that full advantage of the 10,000 lb (4536 kg) gross weight could be claimed and then, only for UK BCAR Certification. In that form the Model No. changed again to: BN2A Mark III - 2. For American Certification, under FAA regulations, the 10,000 lb (4536 kg) gross weight claim had to wait until a full-blown 'Autofeathering' installation for the rear engine's propeller had been FAA approved. When that stage arrived, it marked the end of the production Trislander's development, in the form of the Model BN2A Mark III - 3. By that time the Gosselies factory had cracked Taffy's code, so to speak, and done a thorough job in translating design information into working drawings, supplemented – at last – by workmanlike build jigs and fixtures.

Meanwhile, on Monday 2nd April 1973, Desmond laid on an impromptu Champagne Party at 4:45 pm, in the Bembridge flight sheds for all personnel. This followed the same pattern as several other celebratory ones in the past; this time it was to mark the achievement of 20 aircraft having received their Certificates of Airworthiness, 18 of them having been delivered to customers, in the previous month. It was certainly the best monthly production output up to that time and I don't think it was ever surpassed. In this spirit of revival the year wore on quickly and the atmosphere within the Company began to improve as the association with Fairey Aviation developed. A holding Company had been set up, by Fairey's, under the title of Fairey Britten-Norman Ltd. with its own board of directors that included both John Britten and Desmond Norman. It was the job of this holding to look after the two, still separate and independent, companies of Fairey S.A. and Britten-Norman (Bembridge) Ltd. in their association. It can be seen, therefore, that John and Desmond were still in a strong position, at the top of the tree after all.

Andy Coombe was nominally functioning as Chief Airworthiness

Engineer but was hardly ever available. His Will-o-the-Wisp existence was devoted to almost constant negotiations with Airworthiness Authorities, world-wide. He was, by turns, in Australia, New Zealand, Portugal, USA, Canada or Brazil, perhaps. From any of these locations he might telex us with details of actions necessary, or in the pipeline, to keep the decks clear as it were. His home base responsibilities were largely shouldered by Bob Wilson and Dennis Berryman, who dropped in for a lot of the administrative work in steering the Design Office policies, Sanction procedures and Works liaison duties. Ken Mills, as the Production Director, now became heavily involved in the Gosselies factory activities, having only just recovered – so to speak – from the Romanian experience. His mainstay at Bembridge was the Shops Superintendent of long standing, Len Lathwell. A tall, spare man, of very few words, but with needle-sharp powers of observation, Len had been used to keeping things going on a shoestring, since Jack Sullivan's time. There had been changes in the Buying Office during the Receivership which had resulted in Andy O'Connell taking on the duties of Chief Buyer. That was a succinct move to make the most of Andy's knowledge and experience, for the purchase of accessories and systems components in use, whilst at the same time retaining his name on the CAA Design Approval list; this for the loss of one additional Buying Office job, to satisfy the accountants' dictates. It took some time for him to return to his former position in the Drawing Office as a result.

Through the winter of 1973/74 we continued our publications work in the roofspace of the big hangar. The Accounts Department had moved away and we were more or less alone up there. Bad weather, however, lack of heating and roof leaks combined with threats (and occasions) of electrical power cuts, forced the Company to accept the need to re-house us in order to upgrade the roofspace offices. In the worst of the cold weather we had a phalanx of mobile calor gas heaters brought up to help in raising the temperature. They did so, but only in a very local area. Of course we couldn't do anything about the electric power cuts which were symptomatic of the industrial aggravation then affecting the Heath-led Conservative government. The lack-lustre administration of Edward Heath was soon to give way to another Socialist one which, in due course, demonstrated even greater propensities for industrial unrest and mis-management.

In, and around, the everyday workload and the industrial emergency, we made hasty plans to return to the first floor of the old hangar, once again adjacent to the Drawing and Stress Offices, and our own in-plant printing unit. These arrangements eventually became agreed but, for one reason or another, the move could not be accomplished until the week after Easter bank holiday of 1974. It so happened that the 'Five Nations Grand Slam' rugby international was slated for this weekend in Paris. Ireland were to play against France. Always an ardent rugger fan (especially of Wales) Taffy Lloyd had made sure that a working visit to Gosselies positioned him on the Continent, ready to take the train to Paris for this match. He would return home by scheduled airline service afterwards. So far, so good, but fate had decreed otherwise. The scheduled flight on which Taffy was booked happened to be the ill-starred Douglas DC-10 of Turkish Airlines, on which a partially unlocked baggage loading door separated soon after take-off. The subject door was a large one and the consequent sudden, disastrous cabin pressure loss, caused the aeroplane to crash, uncontrollably, into the Bois de Bolougne with the loss of every soul aboard. It was the first over-land accident to an airliner in the 'jumbo' category; the media coverage showing the starkly horrifying consequences. Taffy's expertise and good humour were taken away from his colleagues and his family alike, at a stroke. It fell to Andy Coombe to deal with affairs, on behalf of Taffy's family and Andy represented the Company at the Memorial Service, in Paris on Thursday 9th May 1974. There was another, more personal one, for Taffy, at Bembridge Parish Church, the following week.

The show went on, of course, the Company being lucky in having M. J. Dore (Mike) who had been a close colleague of Taffy's for several years. Mike was an ex-shipbuilding draughtsman who had been employed by J. Samuel White's Shipyard at Cowes. He was able to take over the duties of liaison with Fairey SA, along with his Bembridge work, continuing where Taffy had been obliged to leave off. Jim Birnie, and his wife Wendy, took Taffy's widow, Eleanor and family under their wing at the Elms, where Eleanor was a valued helper for some years.

This year was proving to be a very unsettling one for me. I was trying to update the different Flight Manuals for the later versions of the Islanders BN-2A, in -20,-21, -26 and -27 forms, in particular. I was also suffering several changes of staff, into the bargain, at the same time. A number of new and revised Service Bulletins were overdue for issue, because of failure to agree their terms, at director level, or inertia there, due to other preoccupations. The situation was causing difficulties with the CAA who were becoming very cross with the firm's sluggish responses. John Britten was greatly involved in a series of lectures on Business Studies and Desmond was requiring a lot of preparatory work for a forthcoming visit to the Philippines. Distractions were manifold.

Through the summer months the Company was working on two specially equipped Trislanders for mineral survey duties. These were production No. 12 and 13. No.12 was earmarked for delivery to a South African Operator, on behalf of a London-based gold mining company. No. 13 had been ordered by a Canadian prospecting company in Ontario, called Questor Surveys. On test flights, above the Isle of Wight, No. 13 was particularly distinctive by its extended nose and tail probes that housed magnetometers. A considerable amount of work and expertise was bound up in these two projects that occupied Ron Dack and Andy O'Connell, along with Andy Coombe, in lengthy negotiations and at least two visits to Canada. Some time later Questor also acquired No.12 which ended up in Canada as well. Pressure again built up towards September and Farnborough week; Desmond was poised to announce a big order from the Philippines after his rounds of negotiations there. Furthermore, the Company could now announce the fact that its production of Islanders and Trislanders had exceeded that of de Havilland's with the DH 104 Dove. This was a major breakthrough because de Havilland's had produced 548 Doves and held the British record for the most multi-engined commercial aeroplanes produced since World War 2. Another champagne party was predicated!

I was, myself, saddened to learn of the death of Percy Braisby. Percy had been poorly for three or four months and passed away on 10th September 1974. He had been a friend and colleague of many years, as well as a valuable business associate in the sub-contracting organization upon which I had relied. His deputy, Julian Partridge, took over his position at Gloster Designs and became my reference point from then on. Julian was an old Gloster Aircraft employee, like Percy, whose experience dated back to the Gladiator biplane era. Their work, in preparation of our Illustrated Parts Catalogues continued, although I had not managed to re-start the Maintenance Manual work with PERA as yet. Towards the end of the year, after a good deal of fraught effort and remote negotiation, Andy Coombe and Ron Dack succeeded in gaining approval for a ski-equipped Islander, to operate in New Zealand, using skis of a proprietary manufacturer's design. The skis were attached with fixed fittings and shock absorbing units, designed at Bembridge. This installation was trialled on a particularly tricky ice field in the French Alps and I remember Andy Coombe excitedly telling me about an adverse incline there, which terminated in a precipice edge and a sheer drop beyond. The operator who had ordered this aeroplane (Constructor's No. 719 Islander) was Mount Cook Airlines, who would be using it in just such similar conditions to transport skiing and mountain rescue parties.

For most of 1974, I had been engaged on and off with all sorts of budgetary exercises at the behest of John Allan, Andy Coombe, Dennis Berryman, or John and Desmond directly. These gambits had considered all manner of permutations to do with the production of Air Publications; staffing requirements, salaries, materials, methods, equipment, sub-contract assessments, annual printing costs arising and so on, for any given circumstance, or combination of such. The deliberations were projected onwards into 1975 and there never seemed to be any satisfactory conclusion forthcoming. Early word-processing capabilities were coming onto the market at the time, but were not sufficiently developed then, to enable one to make a well-informed choice. It was evident that Fairey Aviation Ltd was doing some very deep thinking and some unpleasant sums, across the board. At the end of January 1975, Desmond was hosting a Distributor's Conference, in an expensive London venue, as had become his standard practice in recent years. Following that occasion, my diary records that a top-level Board meeting of the FBN directors took place on Monday 24th March at Heston. Ostensibly this was to have discussed and agreed Company budgets but, a week later, it was made known to us all that no further recruiting or capital expenditure was to take place.

There was another similar meeting, I notice, on Friday 11th April after which I had hoped to know whether I could get the Trislander Engineering Manuals underway again It seems that I was successful, because I had PERA's manager Joe Mark, to see me on 6th May. He took back with him outline details to prepare a quotation for this (now urgent) work. As a result, his leading man Len Townend, who had set up the initial work, came to Bembridge to discuss details on Friday 6th June, along with an illustrator named Wally Wright; tragically, Andrew Henry had been killed in a recent car accident. The Sanction procedure must have ground through, because Len and his colleague appeared at Bembridge on Monday 21st July to 'pick up sticks'. Such was the atmosphere in which we did our business. The Paris Air Show had come and gone, almost without noticing this year, but Desmond now had, in place, a firm commitment to supply at least 20 Islanders to a newly set up organization in the Philippines. This was the Philippines Aerospace Development Corporation, or PADC as we came to know it. On paper, it had every prospect but in practice, as our Service Engineers found out later, there was little to commend the association.

***

To understand what happened next, it is necessary to go back five or six years to a time before the Price Waterhouse Receivership. A young businessman, turned flyer, named Wreford Fisher, had gained the assent of John and Desmond, as well as the owners of Bembridge Airport, and the Local and Aerodrome Licensing Authorities, to set up a flying school- cum-air taxi business at the Airport. Despite the fact that no spare facilities existed, Wreford determined to provide his own. He was the kind of character who liked to do everything himself and was soon engaged in marking out the footings for a new building sited just within the airfield boundary and opposite the forecourt petrol pumps, near the Propellor Inn. A prefabricated building, built around a steel framework, soon appeared on the site and became connected to the services. It was neither a jewel of architecture, artisanship or aesthetism, but it served its purpose in providing several offices and a 'school room' for instructional purposes. Wreford was inordinately proud of it. Soon, a couple of red and white Cessnas appeared – one, a two seater for flying instruction duties and the other a four seater for air taxi work. The Bembridge Aviation Centre, as he called it, was in business. Wreford was a restless chap, however, and soon wanted to move on, leaving the facilities unoccupied for a time.

The Fairey Aviation Company had an active operating arm at Heston besides its filtration interests – going under the name of 'Fairey Aerosurveys Ltd.' This company was engaged in aerial photography in and around the UK. Part of the main plan in Fairey Aviation taking over Britten-Norman (Bembridge) Ltd. had been to re-open their old 'Ringway' plant (now subsumed into Manchester Airport) as a Repair and Overhaul facility. In order to connect the operations, Fairey's had decided to start an air-link between the Isle of Wight and Manchester, calling at Coventry, hoping to build a viable air transport business in the process. Accordingly, it was not long before Wreford Fisher's old premises were being acquired and put into use for these purposes. A new, splendidly liveried blue, white and gold Islander was soon occupying the greensward where Wreford's Cessnas had stood. Engaged to fly the service was a former mercantile marine officer, turned commercial pilot, called Hugh Townsend. The new operating company was named 'Fairey Britten-Norman Airservices Ltd.' and it just happened that Hugh was the son of Fairey's former manager at Ringway in days gone by Bob Townsend, who was now retired on the Isle of Wight. The company's days were short-lived however, because one corollary of those April budgetary and financial meetings, resulted in the winding-up of Fairey Britten-Norman Air Services Ltd. during the middle of August 1975. The Bembridge Aviation Centre would, once more, be vacated.

***

Almost in parallel, and going on from there was the burgeoning requirement upon us to obtain French Certification for the Trislander.

This process began in earnest during October of 1975, on the strength of a sale to a company named SATAIR in French Martinique. The Trislander on order was one of the first long-nosed BN-2AIII-2 models – Constructor's No. 1013 – which provided for extra baggage capacity. It caused a monumental effort to steer this process through the channels of French bureaucracy, in such a short time, because SATAIR had specified delivery before the end of the year. Furthermore, we had not applied for certification, to French Requirements, of the preceding short-nosed Trislander models, BN-2A Mark III and BN-2A Mark III-1, which did nothing to improve the trust of those Authorities in *les Anglais*. All told, the procedure caused a good deal more than the usual intercourse between the DGAC (Dirécteur Genérale d'Aviation Civile) and the CAA (Civil Aviation Authority) to sort out the inherent complications of the situation.

Fortunately I had developed a very useful business connection, through a Southampton-based translation agency, with an associate company of their's in Paris. That company was run by a Franco-American gentleman named Réne Rollande, who was absolutely 'pure gold'. He had on his books a young man called Jean Gauthier, who lived at Rouen, and was, himself, of similar value. Jean had been working for us, on and off, during the various phases of the Islander's French Certification and had acted directly for us with the relevant officials, in some cases of urgency. Besides providing the necessary translating work (all subject to Sanction permission of course) we had begun to use him as our Interpreter/Agent at the inevitable meetings with the French Authorities. The culmination of these frenetic efforts occurred on 5th/6th November 1975 when, together with Andy Coombe and Hugh Kendall as pilot, I was present at the 'Aircraft Appraisal Meeting' in Le Bourget. Jean Gauthier had been notified beforehand and had come out from Rouen to help us through any complicated procedural aspects likely to arise.

While the 'Technical Inspection' of Constructor's No. 1013 took place during the afternoon of the 5th, the real business began on the following day. The responsible French official who had dealt with our Islander French Certification matters, in a similar capacity to our ARB Senior Design Surveyor, was a man by the name of Martiniére. A tall spare man with the visage and attitude of a Foreign Legion colonel, he always conveyed the impression that he was not a man to be trifled with – nor was he! M. Martiniére was our interrogator, here again, along with seven other specialists, who went through all our submitted documentation, whilst the Trislander was test-flown by a pilot and flight test engineer, from the Centré et Vol at Istrés – broadly the equivalent of the Royal Aircraft Establishment (RAE) at Farnborough – who were called in for the occasion. M. Martiniére had, earlier, indicated that he expected to receive the Trislander in a similar set of circumstances to those in which his Authority had accepted the Islander for French Certification. This meant that Andy Coombe, with all his flight testing and airworthiness approval data and myself, with all the aircraft engineering and flight manual publications, went through more or less the same hoops that pertained at the Islander's certification, six years or so before. For myself, I was eternally grateful that I could table a discrete range of Trislander handbooks, at this stage, rather than a compendium of supplemental inclusions to the Islander publications, which would have been John Britten's preferred method. I fear that the results of such a presentation would have had an electrifying effect on the countenance of M. Martiniére.

My diary records that we arrived back at Bembridge at 8:30pm, on 6th November, with a list of high priority adjustments to pursue, before the all-important rubber stamp of the French DGAC could be attained. The next few days were crucial because, besides meetings with our own CAA specialists, Andy Coombe was scheduled to visit Greece, in connection with other business, on Saturday 15th November. One of Andy's performance engineer assistants was dispatched with a hastily marked-up version of the Trislander Flight Manual, by hand, on the train to Redhill, for further CAA consideration, on 12th November – on the promise of a 'letter of approval' by return! The letter duly arrived on 13th November and Bob Wilson, acting for Andy Coombe, had to go to Paris on Friday 14th November for a 2pm meeting with M. Martiniére, and others, at the DGAC headquarters, in the Rue de Louvre. Jean Gauthier had again been appointed to assist Bob in every possible way.

It was still not accomplished, however, and Bob had to put in another appearance at the Rue de Louvre, on 25th November, with Jean Gauthier filling-in and accommodating instantaneous translation corrections as they were brought to light. A number of illustrations, pertaining to performance graphs in the Flight Manual, had to have their captions changed and re-translated so that Jean, who had done the work initially, had to return these to us by telex for re-processing and re-printing, to satisfy the DGAC's requirements. Meanwhile Constructor's No. 1013 was being finalized and kitted-out with its ferry-flight fuel system for delivery. By 18th December everything was more or less ready and, the following day, Jean rang to say that although certain consequential matters were still outstanding, M. Martiniére had informed him that they would not compromise the certification. Accordingly, we received the vitally necessary rubber-stamped title page for the new Flight Manual, together with the DGAC's formal letter of 'Type Approval', just in time for the aeroplane's departure from Bembridge on 23rd December 1975.

Back to work after the Christmas Holiday saw the Company involved with its first true military order. George Paul, one of the senior salesmen – and others in Desmond's departments, had been working hard in the background for some time to secure this valuable business. There had been other para-military Islanders, of one sort or another, supplied to minor forces, but this was to be a significant order for 12 Islanders to the Belgian Army Air Corps. As such the aeroplane would find its way into the front line forces of NATO for the first time. I was asked to go to an early meeting with the Air Corps officials, in company with Andy O'Connell on 19th /20th January, in Cologne. Andy's presence was required to discuss equipment installations, mine because the Air Corps had decided they wanted their own discrete Flight Manual.

Whether it was on principle, or just co-incidence, no-one will ever be able to say, but John Britten and Desmond Norman both resigned from the Company on 1st March 1976. Their separation from the Company which bore their name and their legacy of inspiration and high endeavour, marked the end of an era in British Aviation. Each had decided to pursue his own interests and that fact made the separation all the more complete.

9.1 Islanders and Trislanders under construction in FSA's Gosselies factory – 1977

9.2 Islanders in final assembly at Bembridge – about mid-way down the line, ready for the wing join-up

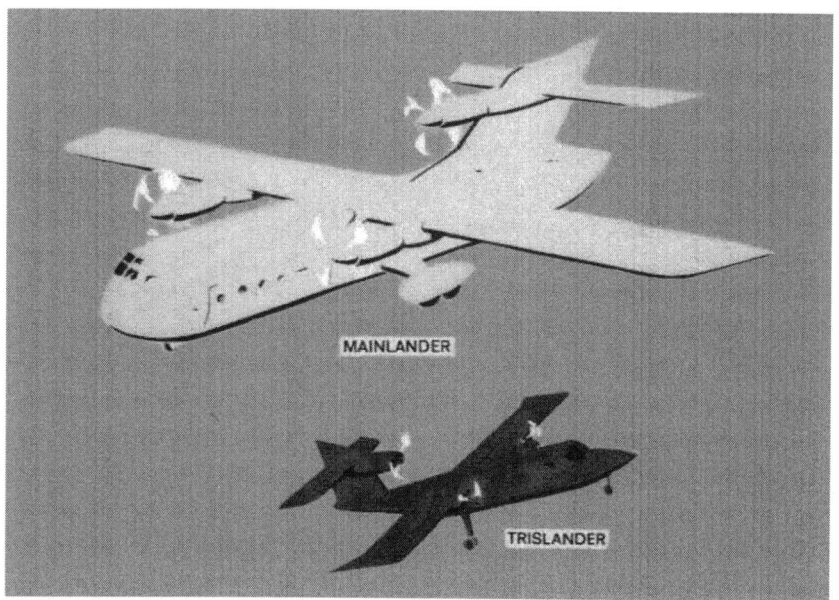

9.3 An artistic impression of the projected Mainlander, in scale comparison with a Trislander silhouette

9.4 One of the early production BN-2A III-2 Trislanders: Const. No. 1010, in service in the Pacific Islands – circa September 1975

9.5 Const. No 1012 Trislander in flight, following final painting in airline livery – circa October 1975

Chapter 10

More Turbulence

Following the departure of the two founding directors, John Britten and Desmond Norman, from the Bembridge Airport scene, there was a curious though not unexpected anti-climax. General industrial conditions, throughout the country, continued to be unfavourable. These were the unsettled times of the Wilson/Callaghan Socialist governments, between 1975 and 1978, when attempts were made to placate union leaders with beer and sandwiches at No. 10 Downing Street. Inflation rates were also running at high levels, showing no signs of coming under control. All told it was a very difficult climate in which to pursue business of any kind, let alone the manufacture and sale of aeroplanes. Desmond's Sales organization had never been a very stable one since its original inception, having run through eight or ten generations of staff, up to that particular time already. Just then, however, the man in charge was an ex-de Havilland Aircraft executive named Pat Hatswell. Pat had managed to build up an experienced team of sales people, among whom was George Paul the man dealing with the Belgian Army in their negotiations for 12 Islanders and support back-up.

Going along, more or less in parallel, was an order for 3 Islanders to serve with the Indian Navy. George Paul again being the responsible salesman for this business. Much importance was attached to this order because, although only three aeroplanes were concerned initially, it was apparent that follow-up orders would materialize if the contracts were properly fulfilled and the aircraft were satisfactory to the naval authorities. Fully productionized, long-nosed Trislanders were coming through to Bembridge by the turn of 1975, when the eighteenth one to be produced by the Gosselies factory arrived on 29th December. To distinguish these aeroplanes from the previous Islander conversions, it had been decided to 'Serial Number' them from 1001, onwards; the one referred to above was Constructor's No.1018 in consequence. Islanders were more quickly assimilated into the Gosselies system, by virtue of their build jigs being complete already and needing, only, transfer from BHC at Cowes to Belgium as BHC's contract terminated. This occurred somewhere about Constructor's No. 370 and no changes to Islander serial numbers were made, except to add the prefix letter G to denote their origin.

Arriving at Bembridge about the same time as Trislander Constructor's No. 1018 was Islander Constructor's No. G480 – ostensibly the 110th out of Gosselies – which was earmarked as the first aeroplane for the Indian Navy. It was Constructor's No. G466, however, that was claiming much attention, as the first Islander of the Belgian Army order. Despite the efficiencies of the production lines, there had been momentary staggers and delays, during the changeover period, not least in the business climate and 'fitting-out bottlenecks', associated with Bembridge. It was quite evident, too, that the latter effects were having a serious influence on the overall situation. The cost controls, via the Sanction form procedure, became more and more obstructive in their implementation, requiring time consuming case formulation and justification before any outside work could be commissioned. This was particularly debilitating to my own area of responsibility since a large proportion of the workload was always dependent upon sub-contract services. Sanctions were pored over at length, by accounts management and by directors, both locally and at the Heston headquarters of the Fairey Britten-Norman Company. Frequently they were delayed, either in transit or prolonged consideration (which sometimes resulted in requests for re-submission in, perhaps, more palatable portions) or simply shelved until the appropriate official was available. It was no way to expedite the timely delivery of aeroplanes, as forthcoming experience was to prove.

Just a few months before, in the summer of 1975, the Technical Offices at Bembridge – and what facilities the hard-pressed Works teams could provide – had been turned on their heads to produce a prototype turbine engined Islander. This happened partly because of increasing pressure from Operators, felt as feedback to the Sales Department, during those Distributor Conferences and, generally, in their approaches to the field. As well as the desire for better performance, there was a sound reason for turbine powered aircraft in many areas of the world, on account of the various effects of fuel crises. Avgas (aviation petrol) was becoming increasingly difficult to obtain while Avtur (aviation kerosene) was more readily available, as the staple diet of turbine engines internationally. Such influences made themselves apparent when Sales Department personnel were, perhaps, trying to persuade a potential buyer who may already be operating turbine engined helicopters, for instance. A 'mixed-fleet' operation would not be attractive in such cases.

At any rate, in true Britten-Norman fashion, the end was intended to justify the means and work had gone ahead on the design drawings and conversion of Islander Constructor's No. G 504 as the host aeroplane. A long nose, similar to the Trislander's with provision for an extra baggage bay, would be incorporated at the same time. There was no great range of choice in the smaller turbine engines of the day and the one selected for the Islander was a 600 hp unit of Avco Lycoming design and manufacture. It did not prove to be a suitable engine because of installation difficulties with the airframe and a little known service history, on the one hand, together with an overly powerful and extravagant performance, on the other. In these respects the initial attempt at introducing a turbine engined Islander would not prove to be a successful one and would, in fact, defeat the aeroplane's *raison d'être* in the first place. Occurring when it did, it meant another upset in manpower, materials and timetables, just when those effects could well have been done without. Along with numerous other matters, including unfinished follow-up business concerned with the recently negotiated French Certification of Trislanders, the workload kept the Technical Offices on their toes well into 1976. It formed the background of activity, against which the visit of Andy O'Connell and myself to the Belgian Army base, near Cologne, took place in the middle of January 1976.

George Paul, from the Bembridge Sales Department was already at the base when we arrived and effected the necessary introductions whilst outlining the Contract obligations. The Belgians, as part of the NATO front line forces, had chosen Islanders to replace their ageing battlefield support aircraft which were of German origin. Whereas those aircraft could only carry one stretcher case apiece, each Islander could accommodate three, as well as two medical attendants. A keen Project

131

Team had been set up by the Army to ensure that their needs were met in full, by any replacement aircraft. We found the four officers concerned with our particular inputs to be Commandants (equivalent rankings to British Army Majors) Albert Dooms and Flourent Behitz, along with their colleague Lieutenant Vandormael, who doubled as their unit's Engineer Officer. Their Commanding Officer was Colonel Doumodin. The Army was, naturally, very anxious to get its new equipment into service at the earliest possible time and a high degree of priority centred on Islander Constructor's No. G 466 as a result. Accordingly, the Contract specified penalties in the advent of late deliveries, which was never good news to an aviation salesman.

There was no doubt, however, that this Contract represented the best multiple order for the Company, to date, because a further value of approaching 40 per cent was involved in the supply of spares and training support programmes, on the back of the 12 Islanders ordered. Although the advent of this order, and the emerging one for the Indian Navy, were obviously anathema for John Britten and Desmond Norman, they were viewed differently by the seniors of the main Fairey directorship. The romantics among whom – if there were any, after the unpleasant revelations of the previous year's accounting results – may have been lulled into reminiscences of old synergies at work between Fairey's and the Belgian Armed Forces of the 1930s. At any rate, a lot of importance was attached to these contracts, so that they would not easily be interrupted for another quick prototype, or interesting special-purpose aeroplane, to lure a mercurially elusive buyer.

The Fairey board of directors had allowed John and Desmond a lot of control in the affairs, since the buyout from Price Waterhouse, rather than their just being constrained to the roles of 'Consultant Advisers to the Company,' as had been indicated at the time. In fact John and Desmond had been, more or less, still in control and when they were in control, they were virtually uncontrollable! New directors were appointed to Britten-Norman (Bembridge) Ltd, after the departure of the two founding partners, when Dr Gordon Watson became the Managing Director at Bembridge. A man by the name of Derek Thurgood was installed as the Managing Director of the Fairey Britten-Norman combination and the Sales and

Commercial Departments were moved out of Bembridge to the parent Company's headquarters at Heston. Some part of the Sales Department had been housed in Wreford Fisher's old Aviation Centre Building (after the demise of Fairey Britten-Norman Air Services Ltd.) and, as soon as those premises were vacant again, my own facilities were moved into two of the empty offices and an adjacent Portakabin. The latter was used to house our collating/stockroom and mailing service impedimenta. At the same time Ron Dack and some Stress Office colleagues were moved into the remaining two or three Aviation Centre offices, to vacate the first floor of the old hangar. Our canteen provisions had taken a long time to establish, in the rooms next to the Propellor bar, but were now suddenly closed, leaving everyone to cater for themselves again.

The two Belgian Army pilots, leading the acceptance programme for Constructor's No. G466 Islander, were in regular visitation and correspondence with us. They were Commandants Flourent Behitz and Albert Dooms. It was Albert Dooms who seemed to have been given particular responsibility for procuring an acceptable flight manual for their Islanders, as distinct from the civilian version. Over several months I was required to work in close conjunction with Albert to ensure that their aims were met. He and Flourent often had massive arguments about the way forward, constant changes being necessary so that, along with other delays in the equipment selection and trialling, George Paul got very nervous about impending late delivery penalties. Bob Wilson became deeply involved in re-scheduling their specific performance data requirements and had to pay numerous visits to meet the project team in Brussels, before agreement was reached. Finally, I was able to complete the Belgian Army Flight Manual, sandwiched in between my other work, and produce the 30, or so, copies which they had ordered. By the middle of March, things were almost finalized and Commandants Behitz and Dooms arrived at Bembridge, for their official Islander conversion courses, on 22nd March 1976. Acceptance formally agreed, delivery of the first Islander to operate under the auspices of NATO did not, however, take place until 21st May 1976 and then it was G468, instead of G466 (which was delayed by equipment defects). The requirements of the Indian Navy were making themselves felt by now, George Paul again being the responsible sales executive. A similar performance ensued which kept us all extremely busy for the rest of the year which, I note, was a 'Farnborough' one. Gosselies was supplying kits of semi-completed Islander components, wings, fuselages, empennages, and associated equipment to the Philippines Aerospace Development Corporation (PADC) at that particular time and someone suddenly woke up to the fact that Air Publications were also needed. Those particular aeroplanes would not, of course, come back to Bembridge for finalization and so, their allocations had to be forwarded. The job of acquiring the publications from Bembridge, for onward shipment to Manilla, was delegated to the Gosselies Technical Librarian, an expatriate Irishman named Paddy Macdonald. That cheerful worthy arrived on the Gosselies shuttle flight of 9th September, just in time to visit the Farnborough event, before making his return with a quantity of publications which reduced my stocks considerably. They were even further reduced, later, when a typhoon and tidal waves struck the Philippines, damaging or washing away stocks of materials and equipment, to the ultimate disadvantage of the whole project.

***

Despite the reservations about interruptions to the Bembridge finalization of production aeroplanes, two more special purpose variants had been sanctioned. Dennis Berryman, carrying John Britten's torch, had embarked upon an agricultural version of the Islander – with two huge external spray tank pods outboard of the engines – and a 'water bomber' version with cabin-mounted internal tank, for forest fire-fighting. In the case of the former, there were doubts over the 'engine-out capability', at take-off, with both tanks fully loaded, which went unresolved in the course of events, due to lack of interest. There had been a lot of pressure to get these aeroplanes into operational states, in time for Farnborough, with a view to helping in the sales drive but, regrettably, with no discernible benefit. An unfortunate train of defects also began to interpose in the already stretched resources – propeller blade failures, faults in the propeller governors, corrosion appearing in aileron mass balance weight arms and corrosion, also, in Trislander main undercarriage legs. All these defects caused consternation at the highest levels in the CAA and brought on a rash of activity in the Service Bulletin preparation and negotiation procedures. Harry Ellis had retired from the Authority and his place had been taken by one of his former colleagues named E. Y. (Eddie) Bramble. Eddie was a rather fussy little man who was determined to hold our noses to the grindstone until every finite detail had received check and double check. Although no different in those respects, to previous practice, everything now seemed somehow more tedious and exhausting than before.

Interspersed between the Islanders delivered to the Belgian Army and the Indian Navy, throughout the year, were numerous civilian and quasi-military aeroplanes, but it was evident that sales were not keeping pace with production. There were increasing re-allocations, as initial deals fell through, causing Sales and Commercial Department personnel to be under constant pressures as a result. Towards the year end of 1976, still without American certification for the BN-2AIII -3 Trislander, an all-out effort was made to attain that goal, so that no impediment should affect the sales effort to move such aeroplanes. This, the ultimate model development of the Trislander, already had its UK Type certification at the gross weight of 10,000 lb. (4536 kg) in BN-2AMarkIII-2 form, but – as will be remembered from earlier details – was not acceptable to the FAA, without the provision of autofeathering for the rear engine propeller, at that weight, for operations in the USA. December 17th, a Friday, was seen as the clinching date for submission, to the FAA, of the Trislander autofeathering installation. Due to the fact that the FAA's European Regional Office in Brussels, closed down on that date to allow its American staff members to return home for Christmas leave, there was no time to be lost. Furthermore, most of them would be absent for the following 6 weeks after that date.

Accordingly, there was a hectic couple of weeks or so, for the Technical Offices to get everything ready for FAA scrutiny. The autofeathering equipment, itself, had been installed and trialled on Constructor's No 1029 Trislander. Approaches between the Company, with CAA backing, and the FAA's Brussels office had been continuing, tenuously, since late

135

July in fact, but still without a successful conclusion. The crux of the matter lay in the fact that the FAA was relying on the UK certification of the BN-2AIII-3 to take effect beforehand so that they, then, would 'ratify' it in their usual manner. That there was no necessity, in UK terms, for the rear propeller autofeathering system, was neither here nor there in the FAA's cogniscence. Therefore, a series of meetings between ourselves and Eddie Bramble, together with a retinue of other CAA specialists, went on more or less continuously, until Friday 3rd December, when the CAA declared its acceptance of the autofeathering installation modifications. The resultant flight manual changes which I had to make, equally urgently, took several days longer before they were approved. I note that they were consigned with a courier (someone from the Product Support Department) on board the Gosselies Shuttle flight of Wednesday 15th December; the courier, no doubt, had instructions not to return if he failed to find the FAA's address in Brussels!

Two more links in the original chain of the Company's Design Approved personnel were broken in that final month of 1976 when John Brenchley resigned, to work in the USA, and Andy Coombe handed in his notice on Monday 20th December. Andy had been poached by Desmond Norman to join him in his new ventures. Bob Wilson now had another step up the promotional ladder, to be fully responsible for the airworthiness and certification procedures in Andy's stead. As soon as the new year of 1977 rolled in, the CAA now alarmed by what they saw as the Company's diminishing technical capabilities, began to exert even more pressure. John Allan, functioning in a more or less administrative role, was called upon to prepare a 'Design Manual' and to overhaul the Company's Exposition – part of an aircraft manufacturer's responsibilities under the British Civil Airworthiness Requirements. There had been no satisfactory outcome, as yet, to the propeller blade failures. Hartzell, the American manufacturer of the propellers used on Islanders and Trislanders, had thousands of similar propellers in service around the world and was not anxious to begin remedial procedures without extensive background research. No troublesome history of such defects existed and they were thought, at first, to be peculiar to the Britten-Norman installations; particularly on account of the co-incidental problems affecting some of the Woodward propeller governors. These were the product of another American company, also with thousands of such units in operation.

Nevertheless both Hartzell and Woodward took the matters very seriously, Hartzell having earlier despatched one of its senior engineers (Gill Howe) together with advanced straingauging equipment, to monitor a special flight test programme. Matters were steadily progressing, without any definite leads, when on 11th February an accident occurred in the Virgin Isles. A fully loaded Islander, in the process of take-off, suffered the loss of a propeller blade on the starboard engine whilst passing through about 70 feet of altitude. Resultant out-of-balance forces caused the starboard engine to separate from its mountings and come adrift from the aeroplane. That incident, of course, galvanized the Airworthiness Authorities and everyone else alike. A CAA delegation arrived at Bembridge the next day, deploring the fact that the situation had remained unresolved for four months, and insisting that Service Bulletin action must be taken within the next seven days. This was accomplished, as promised, but was only the start of what proved to be a much more complicated and expensive set of circumstances, as time went by.

All these matters, along with the development of others – a resurgence of uncleared problems associated with the French Certification of the Trislander, together with the FAA's now detailed concentration on the autofeathering modifications, coupled with impending completion of the prototype turbine Islander – swept us along on a wave of activity until Easter. A few days before which, on 6th April 1977, at 7:30pm, the original turbine-powered Islander first flew, in the hands of John Nielan with Bob Wilson as flight test engineer. This work had taken about eighteen months, so far, but had very little to commend it to potential operators. The Avco Lycoming LTP 101 engine was not in service in any numbers and there were question marks against the engine's reliability, besides its unsuitability for installation in Islanders. About this time Ken Mills, who had led the production activities in one way or another, since Jack Sullivan's day, decided to leave the Company and join up with John Britten in his new venture. Ken's push and 'know-how' would be badly missed. Since production matters were rather less important than clinching aircraft sales, just then, the position of Production Manager/

Director was to remain vacant in the prevailing circumstances.

Another change also occurred, around that time, when Reg Hobbs the Chief Inspector for so many years, succumbed to a heart attack, leaving his deputy, David Bishop, to carry on in his place. Looking back, over my records, I notice that the factory Production Meeting Minutes, as at the 18th April 1977 which was the week after Easter, showed 49 unallocated aeroplanes. There were 41 new Islanders and 8 new Trislanders awaiting customers. Most of the aeroplanes were still at Gosselies, in fact, because Britten Norman (Bembridge) Ltd. only took delivery of, and paid for, those aeroplanes for which it had hard and fast orders, secured by deposits. These arrangements meant that FSA at Gosselies suffered a huge and increasing cashflow problem, directly related to its own production efforts. It became obvious that the Fairey group of companies was facing grave and worsening difficulties. Gosselies could not easily be 'switched off' since the prime intention had been to keep its workforce engaged, pending receipt of the long delayed F16 contract – still in abeyance – and Bembridge could not move aeroplanes out unless it could sell them. The flywheel of production impetus was, once again straining at the tightening outlets of the sales initiatives. It appeared to be a near repeat of the 1971 situation and so it proved, when word spread on Tuesday 30th August 1977 that Fairey's had sold out to Short Bros. & Harland of Belfast. Little over a month before, a shadow had been cast over the Bembridge scene, by the premature death, at 49, of John Britten.

***

Amidst rumour and counter rumour, our work went on, my always tenuous sub-contract work again under threat of stoppage at any time. Eventually, it became apparent that Short's interest was falling through and, on 11th October 1977, at 4:30pm, we were told that the Fairey Group of Companies had gone into liquidation.

The appointed Receiver, this time, was Sir Charles Hardie of Dixon, Wilson & Co. and his manager at Bembridge was a Mr John Godfrey. On Friday 21st October the Receiver addressed the Works Council, at Bembridge, telling them that there was sufficient work and orders, on hand, to carry through into the New Year. Further, the Receivers indicated that three companies had exhibited interest in buying Britten-Norman (Bembridge) Ltd. which would be kept in business as long as it was possible. Meanwhile Bob Wilson seemed to be regularly 'emplaned' for Brussels, Paris or elsewhere, chasing up the loose ends of French, American, or other certification matters. Ron Dack, John Allan, Andy O'Connell, Dennis Berryman and others were completely immersed in the propeller, propeller governor and corrosion defects business. (The Hartzell Propeller Corporation eventually 'grasped the nettle', revising some of its propeller blade manufacturing and overhaul procedures accordingly). Dancing attendance over the whole scenario, and exhorting everyone concerned to ever greater effort was Eddie Bramble and his colleagues at the CAA's Brabazon House headquarters. On Tuesday 8th November 1977 Dr Gordon Watson was relieved of his duties, as the Managing Director of Britten-Norman (Bembridge) Ltd. and departed forthwith.

The Receivership operated by Sir Charles Hardie, over Britten Norman (Bembridge) Ltd, was complicated by the fact that a Continental Receivership was also necessary to administer the affairs of Fairey SA in Gosselies. Things were not quite as straightforward now as they had been in 1971. There was also the question of the continuance, or otherwise, of the production contract with IRMA in Romania. Three-way communications and negotiation, in what was no longer a wholly British debacle, were being required. About 260 aeroplanes had been produced by the Romanian facilities at that time and it proved easier to 'throttle back' IRMA's effort, on account of the fact that they had other irons in the fire just then; the contract being kept alive, however. A different situation affected the Gosselies plant which, by then, still had a stockpile of 40 or more Islanders and over 20 Trislanders waiting for transit to Bembridge and consequent payment. The Receivers had no alternative but to cease the work there and concentrate on a deal with the Belgian Government, which eventually resulted in a takeover of the Fairey SA factory, in their own national interests. Subsequent revelations indicated a financial 'black hole' approaching £28,000,000 in 1977, as compared to the 1971 total of around £4,500,000.

Our day-to-day routine carried on much the same, however, and I was still in regular contact with the Belgian Army personnel, who began to run a fortnightly shuttle service of their own, to collect spares, equipment, and up-dated publications material, as developments dictated. Lieutenant Eddie Vandormael and, perhaps, an NCO would normally fly in for these purposes. Sometimes Albert Dooms would come with him, or in his stead, and they always had interminable questions when they arrived. It was, for me, a decided advantage that the Indian Navy Headquarters, at Cochin, was further away, because they also had interminable questions. We received regular eight to ten page letters from Cochin, or sometimes from Delhi, with closely spaced questions and/or assertions which needed time-consuming attention, if the enquirers were to be fully satisfied. All told, there was a great need for assistance at Cochin and John Oversby, from our Bembridge Service Department, was a regular visitor there (together with his colleague Ken Dye, I seem to remember) while the liaison was in its infancy.

On Monday, 16th January 1978, the Receivership at Bembridge had a decisive meeting in the afternoon which resulted in notification of imminent redundancies. The old spectre was stalking us again. A list of people affected was posted, Max Wall, the ex Miles/Beagle structural engineer, who had overseen the original Islander wing testing programme, being one of those named. Max had been with the Company for 13 years and he left it on Friday 3rd February, along with approximately 40 other people, of varying lengths of service and departmental occupations. For several years I had had a young man working as an Improver Technical Illustrator, who was also used to pulling his weight in any related capacity where needed. James Morton had started in my department soon after the 'Mainlander' feasibility study, because his uncle thought that the experience would be good for him; his uncle happened to be John Britten and James had turned out to be a very useful member of my small team. Now, in the wake of John Britten's death and the likelihood of James having a vested interest in his business affairs, it seemed probable that I should soon lose his services.

Recalling the antipathy of John Britten and Desmond Norman, for the Swiss aircraft manufacturer, Pilatus, it was ironic, in the extreme, to discover that one of the leading contenders to purchase Britten-Norman (Bembridge) Ltd. was none other than Pilatus.

Despite a brief renewed interest, by Short Bros., who sent an evaluation team to Bembridge, Pilatus was eventually successful in its bid to Sir Charles Hardie of the Dixon Wilson Receivership. Things did not happen quickly, however, because it was not until Wednesday 12th April 1978 that we had a small and quick advance delegation from the Pilatus company, at Stans. There were only two or three people, who had an early morning meeting with John Godfrey before giving an address to the Technical Offices' personnel at 1:30pm. On the way to that meeting, John Godfrey brought two of them into my office and introduced them; one was the Financial Director, a man by the name of Oscar Brundtler, and the Technical Director, Dietrich Klöeckner. They were with me for 10 minutes, between 12:30 and 12:40pm! Then, for me, it was back into the vagaries of our complicated procedures, associated with the completion and circulation of updated field service information and chivvying of sub-contractors, whilst being harassed myself. In May I received James's notice, reducing my complement of staff to a typist and a lady tracer, who was employed on the preparation and amendment of wiring diagrams.

Top level meetings went on, at regular intervals it seemed, with Pilatus, sometimes with our Design Office members, Ron Dack, Andy O'Connell, or Bob Wilson, going to Stans. Dennis Berryman was always a reluctant traveller because he did not like flying; he had a Company car and would use that if he had to make a continental visit. In August, Dennis Berryman's leading electrical design draughtsman, Brian Groves, left the Company to join Desmond Norman and, in November, Peter Mallinson left his job as manager of the Britten-Norman Service Department. On Wednesday 29th November, a team from Pilatus visited Bembridge and expressed their intentions of taking control of the Company from 1st January 1979. Their intentions did not work out quite so quickly, due to the complexities of the situation, though Dietrich Klöeckner was installed as the Chief Executive on Wednesday 7th February 1979. He gave an address at 2:00pm, I notice, probably to the Technical Offices' personnel in that early instance. There was much to do in all areas of the Company because, besides our technical business, it was a fact that Pilatus was

141

reviewing the roles and necessities (or otherwise) of all personnel, prior to its full takeover. Arriving at Bembridge about the same time as Dietrich Klöeckner, was one of Pilatus's Production Engineer executives named Joe Keller who took direct charge of factory affairs. Caught in the middle of the muddle, as it were, was an already late, facelifted model range of the Islander which included many much-needed improvements, highlighted by operational experience. Among these was the introduction of full airline-standard cockpit instrumentation and lighting which had moved on considerably since the 1965 original design layout. This improved version was designated as the '1978 Model BN-2B Islander' and its UK Certification date had been set for Friday 16th March 1979. A lot of work had been put into the project and the CAA had been kept in the picture all along, so that it was mainly a matter of formality, but the necessary certification was not completed until Thursday 12th April 1979.

It seems that the combing through of personnel requirements was completed by the third week in July, because another announcement of redundancies was made on Wednesday 25th, when I note that my diary states that Company morale was at an 'all time low'. John Allan became very ill with heart trouble about this time and had to give up his position as Chief Designer. Dennis Berryman had been shadowing the post for some time and he was the one to whom the continuing responsibilities fell. Plans were being made to bring the Sales and Commercial Departments back from Heston and to make Bembridge an homogeneous unit once again. Lateness in time of the BN-2B model range and the production standard Trislander, would do little for the Sales potential and the Commercial Department would be further saddled with difficulties, by being left with only the remote Romanian production facility for future arisings. Such was the scene, as it developed around my own small, but always volatile, area of activity; constant urgent updatings of all the Air Publications – now to incorporate the 1978 Model BN-2B facelifted versions. Sanctions, meetings with sub-contractors, CAA and other agencies, where and when required. The weeks went by extremely quickly until 21st September 1979, when on that day, the Receivership of Dixon Wilson, under Sir Charles Hardie, finally came to an end.

Britten-Norman (Bembridge) Ltd passed into the control of Pilatus Aircraft of Stans, Switzerland, and was officially no longer a British company. Not that these matters had much effect on day to day working, however, which continued in much the same way as before. There were a number of high level meetings with the CAA, concerned with the renewed Approvals and the legalities of Romanian built Islanders, that may be certificated, in future, to FAA Requirements. It had always been possible, up to that time, to keep the eastern European built aeroplanes out of the USA market, where they were not acceptable because of a lack of reciprocal trade agreements. These influences would matter less, as the time went by, because of changing marketing conditions and fashions in the USA, where Islanders came to be viewed as an obsolescent species, with no evident successors in the offing. As the new masters of Britten-Norman (Bembridge) Ltd, Pilatus would soon be called upon to address this latter situation, if there were to be any long term future ahead. Pilatus had already decided not to continue building Trislanders, but was acquiring all the jigs and tools for them, at Gosselies, pending decisions for disposal. Although it was a highly economic, utilitarian workhorse for many areas of operation, there was no doubt that the Trislander lacked passenger appeal. Its long narrow cabin, housing pilot and 17 passengers, in nine twin-seat rows, without aisle or cabin attendant facilities, precluded operations on all but the shortest of routes.

Such, then, was the state of things towards the end of 1979, in the middle of another big shake out at Bembridge when, on 5th November at 5:00pm the unthinkable happened; the Propellor Inn was suddenly closed! Since the departure of John and Desmond from the company, the 'Propellor Parliament's' influence had been on the wane, but it was still regularly used and would be missed by those customers who were faithful to it. In truth, the closure turned out to be of a temporary nature and probably had more to do with a change in licensing and managerial arrangements than anything else. Even so, with Christmas approaching and the need to boost morale, rather than shatter it altogether, this was hardly a welcome development to see out the eventful year of 1979 and the turbulent decade of the Seventies.

10.1 One of the Belgian Army Islanders. These aeroplanes were well equipped with state-of-the-art avionics and fully detachable ambulance interiors

10.2 An Indian Navy Islander, photographed outside the Bembridge flight sheds. These aeroplanes were equipped for maritime surveillance duties and carried search radar; the scanner was attached to the front bulkhead, forward of the nosewheel mountings, inside a GRP radome which replaced the standard nosecone

10.3 The first turbine Islander project. Constr. No. G504 modified to accommodate Avco Lycoming LTP101 engines and a lengthened nose, which incorporated an extra baggage bay

10.4 A view of the upgraded BN-2B series cockpit facilities. The 'Jim Birnie type' control handwheels were fitted, as standard, by this time and the instrument panel background was changed from black to grey

Chapter 11

Reprieve

It might be said that here was an end to the 'Grand Adventure' as it had developed and run out of its "Britishness", so to speak. With its principal motivators gone and all that they held dear, in the way of historical foundations and potential for progression into a Company of unassailable strength, all the indications certainly pointed that way. So long as the aspirations and efforts remained on British soil, however, there would still be an essentially British connection which would take years to weaken. Pilatus Aircraft of Stans, in Switzerland, took its name from the 'green mountain' under which the local community stood, 10km or so, up from Lake Lucerne. Although an independent company, it was one of almost 80 others, owned by the immensely powerful and private Oérlikon-Burhle group which had subsidiaries in the USA, as well as other countries; there was one at Grantham in Lincolnshire, devoted to ordnance. There was a desire, by this group, to strengthen its aviation activities, through association with other similar organizations, which had led to the acquisition of Britten-Norman (Bembridge) Ltd. One of the first things to happen was a change of our Company's name to: Pilatus Britten-Norman Ltd.

If John Britten and Desmond Norman had dreams, Dietrich Klöeckner the new man in charge could be said to harbour a vision. He had spent some years in the USA, in the General Aviation design and operation spheres, and had his own strong ideas about what should happen at Bembridge. Dietrich was tasked, first of all, to make a success of the association between the two companies with paramount priority on the success of Bembridge. The taskmaster was Dr Burhle himself, since the whole group undertaking was of a private venture nature. In true Teutonic fashion there were moves to educate the Bembridge workforce in management courses, inter-personal skills, measuring, analysing and grading the results, as they went along. Failure to succeed, said Dietrich, could not be countenanced but if such a situation appeared to be at all likely, then Oérlikon Burhle would turn the whole enterprise into a huge chicken farm!

In order to get to know the people in the Technical Offices better, and on a more personal level, he started his own 'pub group' by inviting some of us to meet him – not at the Propellor Inn – but at The Anglers Inn, a couple of miles up the road at Brading, after work. Since this was the opposite direction to the way home for many folk, it seems doubtful whether he achieved the truly representative sample of opinion which he sought.

Dietrich Klöeckner's big ambition was to design and build a high altitude, economical turboprop powered aeroplane, in the 6 to 12 seat executive jet class, popularized just then by the Learjet and Cessna Citation. He was very anxious to compete head-on with the Americans, with what he saw as a viable alternative to their expensive twin, pure jet, engine formats. His solution was to use a single propeller turbine engined machine, flying higher and further than the normal prop-jet – a 'Trans-Am' range was predicated – for lower power plant and fuel costs, with easier and cheaper maintenance routines. Such an aeroplane was not a natural successor to the Britten Norman products and it was pointedly made clear to him that the chances of Public Transport Certification, for operation over water, with only one engine, were practically nil. These were aspects easily overlooked by people who populated the large land masses of the world and had no need to overfly any large expanses of water throughout their working lives. Dietrich Klöeckner was not convinced but the well-reasoned opposition which he encountered made the initiation of such a project untenable at Bembridge.

All was not lost, however, because there was still the worthwhile venture of a practicable turbine engined Islander to pursue. Accordingly, thoughts and efforts turned towards developing work along those lines. During 1980 the design work on a successor to the prototype turbine Islander of preceding years, began with a new enthusiasm. A breath of fresh air seemed to be present in the political landscape, also, with the advent of a Conservative government under Britain's first woman Prime Minister, Margaret Thatcher. As if to underscore a resurgence of business emphasis and entrepreneurial spirit, 'Thatcherism' had arrived. My own situation began to improve and I was able to get some long-neglected areas of work underway again. There had been changes in the accounts department leadership along the way, with Brian Whitehead following Jim Munn for a while and, latterly, a man by the name of Arthur Woodthorpe. George Paul had departed from the Sales Office and a new man called Trevor Ward had picked up his ongoing duties concerning liaison with the Indian Navy, for example. A marketing director was appointed, once the Sales Department had completed its relocation, along with the Commercial Department, back at Bembridge.

The design studies concerning the second attempt at re-engining the Islander with turboprop power plants, had been more thoroughly effected than the first one. This time a more suitable engine, in terms of size, weight and adaptability, had been chosen. Like most of the engines in this range of small turbines, it was primarily designed for use in helicopters and, again, there was no meaningful service history in fixed wing use to rely on. The engine specified was designed and built, by Allison's, as the Type 250 B17c rated at 420 shaft horsepower, but down-rated to 360 shaft horsepower for the Islander's installation. All in all it was a very neat little power unit that would permit 3-bladed propellers to be used for the first time, without the fairly drastic changes to engine cowlings that would have been necessary for the piston-engined installations. At the heart of the installation was a relatively high tech, high grade steel mounting cage, featuring an inverted U-shaped frame at the front, to accept the main engine mounting points. The design work entailed, with the manufacture and testing of the new parts and systems interconnections was quite extensive, taking seven or eight months to complete. A Gosselies-built Islander, Constructor's No. G419, which had been used as a demonstrator aircraft, since its arrival in 1974, was modified into a prototype for the Allison Turboprop engine installations and given the Type No. BN-2T

Whilst all the initial work was going on, I was having a very busy time in the wake of the French certifications which had given us a continual harassment, in one form or another, for many months. Our work had been so widespread, over all of the Islander and Trislander Engineering and Flight Manuals, that considerable costs and complexities had built up. Jean Gauthier, who had performed such yeoman service for us, kept ringing up to enquire about payments that were overdue. His patron, Réne Rollande, also, had to put his shoulder to the wheel, across many weeks, to find out why his remunerations had not connected with his variously nominated, and situated, bank accounts. A lot of exhaustive cross-checking was required to trace the positive or negative action, relative to the tasks and dates in question. There had been an increasing emphasis, over two or three years past, on noise abatement requirements, particularly on 'climb out' which had taken up a lot of Bob Wilson's time and ingenuity, on the flight testing and negotiation of acceptable mitigation procedures. Of course, all of the results had to be transcribed into the aircraft Flight Manuals; quite involved in the case of English language publications, but even more so in the French ones. Hence, we had come to some quite sticky business with our translating services. These were unwelcome effects and it took a lot of undercover work to maintain the enténte cordiale so that goodwill continued to be exercised, even in the face of sustained gimlet-eyed accountancy.

Pilatus had, nevertheless, carried on its intended investment programme in the company's facilities at Bembridge. A major disadvantage of the grass airfield was inadequate drainage from the centre, where there was a shallow depression. War-time exigencies had decreed that the aerodrome should be ploughed-up, to deny the enemy a landing ground and the after effects of that action did nothing to help matters. On some occasions, in extremely wet weather, it was impossible for anything other than a lightly loaded small aeroplane to get airborne. I remember once, in retrospect, when Desmond and John were to attend an important financial meeting (just prior to the first receivership) the Islander they were using became bogged down halfway through its take off run. The airport fire engine and its crew had to turn out and drag or push the aeroplane clear, for Desmond to make another attempt. By that time he and John, both contributing to the 'heave-ho', had gone over the shoe tops in mud and their suits, as well as the sides of the aeroplane, were also unsuitably decorated with the stuff. A paved runway was the answer, of course, and work was commissioned on that project, along with a small control tower and reception-centre building, just off the new hangar approach road. Energetic efforts were being made by Island business interests and Local Authorities, about then, to start an Air-Link between the Isle of Wight/Southampton/Gatwick and there were high hopes of using Bembridge as the Island Airport. Stores facilities had been a problem for some time too, with the expressed intention of improving Product Support services, more space and better handling had to be provided. Another new hangar building was erected, alongside the big one. Though not quite as large, it was able to accommodate all the foreseeable parts and spares inventories, leaving a useful workshop area, at the northern end, sufficient to house 2 or 3 Islanders.

Our quarters, in Wreford Fisher's old Aviation Centre building had become very uncomfortable due to leakages and draughts from ill-fitting windows, doors, and general neglect over the years. The building was in a very sorry state, in fact, looking extremely dowdy, both inside and out. Several attempts at weatherproofing the flat roof were made by the gallant Works Maintenance Team, who had lately applied a latex rubber overseal compound, but the rain still managed to percolate here and there. I can't imagine what the first reactions of Dietrich Klöeckner and his financial practitioner colleague were, when they had first passed over my office threshold, with John Godfrey, nearly two years before, but now we were set to move once more. Back to the top floor of the new hangar again – another job for Jan Maley's long-suffering maintenance men who, by now, did not much look forward to moving the Technical Publications Department with all its stockholding impedimenta. The transition was made over the last weekend in March 1980, when Ron Dack's (and his colleagues') offices were also moved across to the same location. The Technical Offices were once again together, instead of being spread between different buildings, because the Drawing Office and Weights Control, with some Stress Office people, were already installed in the upgraded roofspace accommodation of the new hangar.

***

For several years there had been serious attempts to capitalize on the use of computer systems, for the benefit of design and manufacturing facilities, as yet without any positive decisions or commitments. A couple of years, or so, before the Fairey era, a young chap by the name of Paul Wells was engaged to make pilot studies of what was likely to most suit the Company's needs. It was following the time of the Nymph and it's 'Parts Classification' scheme, when those ideas were still prominent, that Paul began his work. His outlook was much shaped, perhaps, by those influences, particularly as he had a background of local authority/accounting experiences. All that was about to be elbowed out, however, by Pilatus's decision to bring in one of their own computer specialists who had been working at their Grantham factory. He was Hans Heurlimann, a large, bearded, Swiss who was just as remote from aircraft design and manufacture, but wedded to the philosophy of 'central computer control' across all disciplines of activity. Of course, the very idea of any so-called central management (with overtones of corporate surveillance) did not find favour with the freeborn spirits of Bembridge Airport, who were a decade ahead in their perception of laptop PCs, which had yet to emerge.

Such matters, so important and yet seen to be only at the fringe of our everyday affairs, went unresolved and became 'political footballs' for too long. My own area of work was crying out for word-processing capabilities, which would have needed investment and dedicated staffing that I could not hope to justify in the circumstances.

By 9th July 1980 the BN-2T's starboard engine subframe and firewall installation was in position and almost ready for Trial Installation (TI) of an engine. My programme start date for the engineering manuals was 1st August 1980 and I was forewarning Len Townend at PERA and sending them copies of 10 photographs of the subject areas, to help them in the initiation of illustrations. At the same time I had been given the job of a 'Task Definition' to review all of the Air Publications activities taking place in Bembridge and Stans. About the middle of August, Dennis Berryman mentioned that I was expected to go to Stans, imminently, to discuss matters of mutual interest, with my opposite numbers there, in the furtherance of this project. Several telephone calls and telexes later, indicated that the first available opportunity would be 16th – 19th September. My visit to Stans followed in the footsteps, so to say, of Ron Dack, Andy O'Connell and Mike Dore who, no doubt, had similar assignments to myself, and my 'Task Definition' was duly completed. Whether it was ever used, or debated in other circles, I shall never know because I never heard of it again, except in passing references.

At last a new Production Manager had been engaged to replace Ken Mills. A highly qualified and competent production engineer, called David Fear, made his appearance at Bembridge early in October, taking over the reins from Joe Keller who, I note from my diary, left the Company after 20 months service at Bembridge, on 10th October 1980. David had previously worked for the Napier engine company and had dropped in for the completion of the prototype BN-2T; the engine installation of which was probably right up his street. Speaking to him the previous day (9th October), I noticed that there were significant changes going on with the starboard side engine oil system, when I visited to check on progress. A further two weeks would be necessary, he thought, to complete the changes then underway. Besides his vested interest in the BN-2T engine mounting frames, Dick Stowe was engulfed in corrosion protection, and some fatigue failures to do with the Islander elevator trim tabs again, making necessary the issuance of X-ray photographs in Service Bulletins to aid field inspections. These instructions and procedures took up a great deal of time and effort to conclude, at one time the CAA threatening to ground all the subject aeroplanes, unless effective measures could be agreed and promulgated quickly. Dick was also suffering severe nervous strain from years of such arisings without adequate help to rely upon.

About this time I was, at first, rather put out by the receipt of a letter from the secretary of our SBAC Technical Publications Committee. In polite terms I was informed that my continued presence on the committee was no longer admissible because my employer was a foreign company. The damning effects of non-British patronage struck a deep personal chord, but I was somewhat cheered by a later paragraph in the letter which said that my colleagues, on that body, had no objections to my appearance there '… as an observer'. Presumably the same effects were felt by other Technical Office members, of different committees who made representation there. On 12th November 1980 Dr Burhle, himself, paid a visit to Bembridge to inspect the newly upgraded airfield and factory facilities. Looking back, now, I think it was an early sign that

150

things were not working out as well as expected. There were numerous 'big meetings', I note, before and after the master's visit, mainly including the presence of accountants.

Completion of the BN-2T project seemed to be delayed by one thing after another. There now appeared to be difficulties with the Allison engines' propeller installations, relative to the reduction gearboxes and engine mountings. Troubles had apparently manifested themselves during initial flight trials of the BN-2T whilst at RAE Bedford in the third week of November. As a result, it had been necessary to call in Allison's technical representatives, who visited Bembridge on 1st December. Now, my notes remind me, that Dennis Berryman, Ron Dack, Andy O'Connell and Bob Wilson were incommunicado for three whole days to thrash out a solution to the problems; no doubt it was Dietrich Klöeckner who was driving affairs at that important meeting though I cannot be sure after all this time. My own limited horizons were momentarily clouded when Jean Gauthier telephoned, on 16th December, to say that the redoubtable Mon Martiniére, of the French DGAC, was dead. Our 'Grand Inquisitor' had passed away on 22nd November it seemed and it marked the end of a thirteen year liaison which was generally fruitful, in spite of the ups and downs. We should certainly find out who his successor was when the BN-2T was submitted for French Certification.

Sure enough, as soon as the new year of 1981 rolled in, news broke of a ten per cent redundancy overall. In spite of Pilatus's avowed intentions to strengthen Britten Norman by meaningful investment, it looked quite a different picture from our viewpoint. Work had to go on, however, the usual pre-occupation with annual budgets began again, along with all sorts of requirements for estimates of one kind or another. Meanwhile a solution to the BN-2T propeller troubles seemed to have been found. It must have been an expensive one for the Allison Engine Company because it entailed the provision and fitment of new propeller reduction gearboxes to all Type 250 B17c engines in the field. One of the management courses, favoured by Pilatus, took place on 3rd and 4th February, guided as usual by their Herr (or was it Mr?) Wagner, flown over from Zurich for the purpose. In the discussion, afterwards, he was so perturbed by our criticism of their management information and deterioration of 'company government', that he offered to bring in Dietrich Klöeckner to hear our views. That he did and Dietrich Klöeckner sat up and took notice, promising improvements as a result. There was another untoward death about then; that of A.J. (Andy) Coombe at the age of 47. Andy had been poorly for some time, on and off, and I remember visiting him in hospital once, during the previous year I think, when he was propped up in bed, still working on aerodynamic problems associated with Desmond's latest project, even while indisposed. His memorial service was held at Bembridge Parish Church on Friday 6th February and, although not still working for the old Company, to those of us who knew him well it seemed as though we had lost another current colleague. So the year went on with its usual panics and flaps; for me it was regular business with Bob Wilson and the BN-2T Flight Manual programme, amongst all the other duties.

It seems that the prototype BN-2T was finally certificated, after completion of 'rolling through standing water' trials, on 19th May 1981; my Flight Manual work having received internal agreement and waiting, only, for the CAA's approval. Coming up fast behind the prototype was the first production Model BN-2T, converted from Islander Constructor's No. 2030 that was built up from a Gosselies manufactured kit of sub-assemblies. This aeroplane had its first flight on 13th May and was to be used for Tropical Trials, scheduled to start on Friday 14th August. It would be delivered, afterwards, to GKN Mining Enterprises, at Kinshasa, in Zaire. Finally the Turbine Islander was up and running but its Engineering publications were some way behind their subject, I regret to say. The PERA team was working hard to catch up and were now also dealing with a discrete Illustrated Parts Catalogue for the aircraft, which would have all the early non-relevant Islander modifications 'edited out'. Gloster Designs was still concerned with Islander and Trislander Spares compilation, however, and although not at full pitch, a steady programme of modifications continued to be embodied. The liaison with this work caused me to visit the Hucclecote office at regular intervals, as well as their satellite office at Coventry sometimes. This latter location, at Baginton, had historic connections as the one-time headquarters of the Armstrong-Whitworth Aircraft Co. Indeed, the dozen or so personnel working there, formed the last remaining enclave of that Company, having been taken over by Percy Braisby at the end of the A W Argossy programme, some years before.

Clearly the sums at home were not producing the desired results because, once again, a high powered Accounts Meeting took place during the first week in September. This event brought in a party from Switzerland which had the job of considering the old chestnut of inadequate cashflow. The Islander's ageing image in the aviation scene, not helped by the obvious lack of a credible successor, was of major concern now. It really began to look as though the vital opportunities to create such an aeroplane had been lost, for ever, in the unforeseen turmoil of earlier years. Several very possible design studies had been made, so it was not for the want of engineering design initiatives; in every case undercapitalization and over-stretched resources at the time, could be seen to be the causes of the present dilemma. One of the design studies, I remember, resulted in the building of a full scale fuselage cabin mock-up, in plywood, of a rather nice looking 12-seater.

Ron Dack, who had a predilection for radial engines, was behind that one. There were 5 rows of the current twin-passenger seats, on a slightly raised platform floor at the left side of the fuselage, with a narrow foot well at a lower level along the right hand side of the cabin. The passenger access door was on that right-hand side, while a large freight loading door was at the left rear end of the cabin. Of course, two small radial engines were the prime choice and a retractable undercarriage was specified, in which the main gear would have been housed in sponsons, at the lower extremities of the fuselage. Because no suitable radials were available the engines chosen were improved versions of the Lycoming O-540's, so successful in Islanders, or, again, Allison B17c units. For a modest increase in fuselage width and height, of the order of 12in. (305mm) each way, the questions of passenger mobility and possible cabin attendant/toilet inclusion had been addressed. Furthermore, without seats installed, the available cabin volume for freight carriage was approximately doubled. In spite of the promising prospects, it was not possible to proceed any further at the time and another collection of good ideas fell by the wayside. It was now that the price would have to be paid for such failures, together with the insufferably difficult situation of being left with only one, remote, manufacturing facility – and that, behind the iron curtain.

Following upon the financial meetings and the general volatility of affairs, Dennis Berryman, who was functioning as Technical Director, appeared to have been singled out as the sacrificial lamb. On 1st October 1981, his long-time confidant, Andy O'Connell, announced that Dennis was '… no longer with the Company' and that was that, apart from an official notice posted later on the notice boards. Dennis had been a 'workaholic' driver of plans and policies, since his early days at Bembridge, under John Britten's wing. Selected to take Dennis's place in the same role, was Bob Wilson who stepped up from Chief Airworthiness Engineer, after an invitation from Dietrich Klöeckner. Less than a couple of years later, Dennis was dead at the age of 53, another casualty of overwork and heavy drinking.

**

At the end of October a new high level executive appeared at Bembridge, in the person of Dr Egon Haefliger, who was reputed to be very close to Dr Burhle himself. Egon Haefliger was not of an engineering discipline, but more financially orientated it seemed; there was a short overlap of Chief Executive Officers, for a month or two, before Dietrich Klöeckner bowed out of the Bembridge scene and left the helm to his successor. At the beginning of December there was sudden excitement in Sales Department circles, by the prospects from an enquiry by the American Federal Express Company, for tenders for a small feeder liner aircraft to service its outer operating 'hubs'. Federal Express was an influential air cargo company and their requirement for 30-plus aircraft presented a very attractive piece of business. On Friday 4th December, Dietrich Klöeckner ordered that every other activity in the Technical, Sales and Administrative departments must stop, in order to get the basic facts together for a top-level Sales Delegation, which included Bob Wilson, departing on Monday 7th, for Federal Express headquarters in Memphis, Tenn. USA. As usual, in these cases, no immediate decisions were made and 1981 gave way to 1982 without any definite news of a deal.

The early weeks of 1982 were taken up by much 'to-ing and fro-ing' of Bembridge executives to Stans, while there was another redundancy of 26 Bembridge people, receiving their severances, at the same time. Bob Wilson had called the 'Technical Offices' people together in mid-January, telling us that the Company had lost £5 million the previous year and that things hung in the balance, due to only 14 firm orders in hand. On Friday 19th February Bob was off again to Memphis, along with others, to give a crucial presentation to Federal Express. About this time we had a visit by a colourful American aviator character named Ron Hauck and his Chief Engineer. They were much interested by the Trislander, it appeared, although in what particular way was not clear. Ron and his colleague, whose name was Ray Kitchener, spent a good deal of time looking through Trislander Engineering and Flight Manuals, from my stockholdings, accumulating a pile in the process. After a couple of days or so, they indicated that they were ready to go and would like to 'take the pile' with them. On being asked what arrangements they had made for payment, both looked somewhat stunned and gave the impression that they were doing me a favour by taking the publications away. At the current listed prices, $200 or $300 worth of literature was involved and so we presented them with an extra piece of paper to take away with them, in the form of an invoice to the amount in question.

It is co-incidental, and significant, that I received news from the Gloster Designs office on 7th April that the Trislander Illustrated Parts Catalogue would be completed by the Revision (No. 10) then almost finished. When it had been received, from them, for printing and distribution by us, all the relevant design changes for the Trislander would be listed, finally, in the catalogue. In the same message, however, I was informed that 45 design modifications were still outstanding for inclusion in the Islander Illustrated Parts Catalogue. A Romanian built Islander stole the limelight for a while in becoming the 1,000th aeroplane to be delivered, early in May 1982. This was Constructor's No. 2106 which was destined for Cyprus, to be used by the Ministry of the Interior in that country. There were local celebrations and 'Press Releases' to commemorate the event, at which Reg Caudle, the Marketing Director, formally handed over the aeroplane's Flight Manual and keys to Mr Constantinides the Cypriot Government's Agent. John Britten, sadly, had not lived to witness the event which had taken substantially longer to materialize, than either he or Desmond had expected – 5 years longer in fact. That such a benchmark had been established at all, by the small company, in the prevailing circumstances, was remarkable in the extreme.

Despite the shaky state of the aircraft market, in general, the Company continued to find outlets, maybe the Falklands war had something to do with affairs. We had fairly recently supplied at least one Islander to the Falkland Islands Government Air Service (FIGAS). The fourth production Model BN-2T, Constructor's No. 2115 was delivered to the British Rhine Army Parachute Association in June and, about the middle of July, Bob Wilson informed me that FAA Certification of the aeroplane had been achieved. This was on the strength of the efforts by the Technical Offices as a whole, to widen the availability of the aeroplane to Sales initiatives. There had proved to be no future in the Federal Express tenders, however, in spite of all the strenuous efforts to secure the order. American business interests had always been difficult to counter and the original specifications had probably mutated into something quite different, in the end. About the middle of August we had another visit from Ron Hauck, the American with a penchant for wearing red suits and cowboy boots. It turned out that he was making approaches to buy out the remaining Trislanders, still holed up in Gosselies, and wanted to negotiate a license-build operation which would, also, include purchase of the jigs and tools. Dr Haefliger was very hopeful of a lucrative deal at this stage and did all he could to cultivate the association.

There was another Distributor's Conference just prior to the Farnborough Show in September 1982, and I think it would have been there, that the idea of using microfiche for our Air Technical Publications was broached, at my request. For some time we had been evaluating possible improvements, including the word processing capabilities, and the one possibility of microfiche had seemed to offer greatest economy and usefulness for the least outlay. The Service Engineers, particularly, needed a better reference base than the dog-eared manuals they had to carry about with them. Many years before, I had repelled an approach from a freelance American practitioner, who wrote to the Company asking for a set of publications to convert to microfiche, without so much as '… a by your leave.' Finding out some background about them, I discovered that my opposite number in the American Beech Aircraft Corporation, had suffered some embarrassment on their account and he advised me to steer clear of any association. That incident had led to my immediate action in securing copyright on all of our existing, and future, publications. A precaution that I don't think, from later discussions with my own British colleagues, was ever taken by the mainstream aircraft manufacturers of the day. When we replied to that overture, I was able to say that we had our own plans for the work referred to and we would take legal action against anyone compromising the situation. Those plans, a long way over the horizon at that time, now looked as though they were achievable.

Early in 1983 I was approached by a company in the Coventry area, who were actively engaged in the filming and supply of microfiche, specifically for airline use. A meeting was arranged at Bembridge and their managing director came, with his leading man John Wilder who had previously been a line maintenance engineer with British Midland Airways. They knew just what was required and had the equipment and the expertise to provide it, on a low-cost, sub-contract basis. They took specimen pages away with them and, in due course, returned sample fiche with a loaned viewer for our appraisal. John Oversby and his Service Department colleagues were very enthusiastic about the prospect, especially when they were assured that 'briefcase-size viewers' were available for mobile use. It took several more months to obtain internal agreement, including Dr Haefliger's, before we could begin a service but by the end of 1983 we were in a position to proceed. Soon afterwards it became possible to offer all our Engineering Publications, except certain special purpose 'check lists', on microfiche, with consequently much reduced shipping and postal costs, together with benefits to operators in the field.

An extremely tight financial situation prevailed, however, and a new Accounts Department head, named Alan Larwood, was in charge of those affairs. The factory had been reduced to 3-day working weeks, across the winter months of the past 2 years, but receipt of a follow-on contract from the Indian Navy, for 8 more Islanders had helped to keep things going. Pilatus was appearing less and less interested in the civilian aircraft market, turning more towards the para-military authorities in its quest for customers. The Indian Navy aeroplanes were all quite extensively specified for maritime reconnaissance roles and these were the markets that Pilatus appeared to be more comfortable in. A number of BN-2T's soon began to go towards such customers. Some years before, a large nose-mounted radar scanner with a 360-degree viewfinder had been planned and the externally modified nose shape, with internal ballast, had been thoroughly flight-tested. Associations with several airborne radar manufacturers began, including the American Westinghouse Corporation. During 1984 equipment was selected and an operational aeroplane was sold to the Ministry of Defence on the basis of a requirement for a battlefield surveillance aircraft. A somewhat ungainly and sinister-looking Islander, which went under the codename CASTOR, it was unmistakable in the air by virtue of its large bulbous nose that had to accommodate a 42 inch (106.7cm) wide rotating scanner beam. The CASTOR Islander was, in fact, a conversion into a Model BN-2T, from a Romanian built kit of sub-assemblies supplied to Bembridge as a Model BN-2B-26. Romanian built machines were no longer flown over to the UK, but were transported to Bembridge, as semi-complete fuselages, wings, and empennages, by road. The long distance hauliers would return to Romania loaded with "Charitable" supplies and whatever merchandise could be traded. Pilatus had made numerous studies of extending the Bembridge factory facilities and fixtures, for a resumption of work back at home, but nothing was ever finalized. Geoff Tomms, who by now was the Works Superintendent, under David Fear, had made exhaustive ground plans, in all kinds of permutations, with attendant costings, which must have convinced the hierarchy in Zurich that there was no long-term future in the business as it stood.

Unless there was evidence of an upturn in aircraft sales, in the very near future, the prospects began to look grim. 1985 was a Paris Salon year and a note in my diary says that we only had a firm order for 1 new aeroplane, on 3rd June (just before the start of the Salon). At the end of the year, I am reminded by a note on 23rd December, that we would be starting the New Year of 1986 with a firm order for only 1 new aeroplane – could it have been the same one I wonder? In the same space, however, I had pencilled in the better news of three hot prospects for contract signature in the first weeks of January 1986; two of them were BN2T's for the Malawi Police Force. It seemed there was a continuing future for the Bembridge conversion squads for a little while longer at least!

11.1 Second hangar, on left of BN new assembly hangar, with airport terminal building in front. These additions were made at the time of runway construction and general airport improvements; photographed c2003

11.2 The Allison-engined BN-2T turbine Islander, used as a company demonstrator aeroplane. It was an early production machine, appropriately registered G-DEMO

11.3 Two British military turbine Islanders, flying together. A standard army air corps BN-2T, alongside the battlefield surveillance version: the AEW version had almost identical profiles to the latter

Chapter 12

Running Down

One of the first aeroplanes to be readied for delivery in 1986 was Constructor's No. 2146, a Model BN-2T, that received its Certificate of Airworthiness about 10th February. This aeroplane had some last minute changes to cockpit instrumentation which we had not been able, at the time, to include in its Flight Manual. A new Chief Test Pilot called John Ayers was then working at Bembridge – John Nielan was, by that time, retired and Hugh Kendall had not much longer to go – who strongly felt that a 'Temporary inclusion' should be made to cover the changes. This was upheld by the CAA and I had another urgent bit of work to do before the final certification could be cleared. In the Flight Sheds' office of the Chief Inspector, David Bishop's chair had been taken by Jack Griffin who had been the Deputy Chief Inspector. David had become very oppressed by what he perceived as unwelcome protocol and returned to 'fieldside' engineering duties with either Jersey Airways or Aurigny. For a short time, during the changeover, however, it was nice to see the person of Denzil Humphrey helping out once again, although he was not in good health.

Oerlikon Burhle Holdings (OBH) had steadily been improving the works facilities, in spite of the difficult business climate, and had invested in some quite advanced, numerically controlled machinery which helped local manufacturing processes. Hans Heurlimann's computer control influences, though repelled by the Technical Offices, had been put to good use for the Spares and Parts inventories, which had suffered badly from a lack of knowledgeable control during the early welter of modifications. Trying to unscramble the resultant holdings, some of which should have been scrapped years ago, was a dour Swiss gentleman named Gary Rindlisbacher. Hans's evolved solution was to use the bar coding discipline to identify Parts and Spares, irrespective of their original engineering identities but it was more than likely that many unwanted items 'hit the bin', after having been through the bar coding process anyway. Once again there had been short time working, across the previous winter months, for the factory personnel, but my own affairs were falling behind such that I had to solicit help in the making up of complete sets of new publications. Consequently the Senior Foreman, Clive Dove, offered me the temporary services of two of his electricians, who seemed to quite enjoy a diversion from their normal duties.

About the middle of March, undercarriage troubles afflicted both Islanders and Trislanders, in the form of cracked torque links on the Fairey designed and manufactured units. Additionally, on Trislanders, was a further corrosion related defect on the main undercarriage support tubes. Another round of Campaign Wires and Service Bulletin action ensued. During April the BN-2T operated by the British Rhine Army parachute team suffered a complete turbine disintegration on one engine which called for high level action on the part of the Allison Engine Corporation, together with resultant airframe repairs at Bembridge. There were some trials, up in Scotland, of an Islander equipped to carry a guided torpedo, of Marconi design, and then it was Farnborough again. At the end of September, Dick Stowe who had struggled manfully to keep the Stress Office's workload afloat for many years, had to take early retirement, on medical advice, departing from Bembridge on 10th October 1986. A young man called Peter Chivers, who had been working with Dick in the Stress Office, took over his duties under Ron Dack's overall control. Bob Wilson, at the same time, was seconded to a 'Military Sales Department' role for a while, without relinquishing his responsibilities as Technical Director.

There must have been changes in the CAA, too, because I notice that Jim Tucker's name occurs, in the place of E. Y. Bramble who must, himself, have retired about then. For many years I had been fortunate to deal with the same man, at Brabazon House, in the pursuance of Flight Manual work; John Turner was one of the rare veteran Bristol Blenheim pilots of early World War II times, his input always being concise, freely, politely and thoughtfully conveyed. Latterly, I was dealing with another individual named Percy Howlett who assumed John's duties after his retirement. Percy had been an ex-Vickers test pilot and was, himself, approaching retirement. It was as if, metaphorically speaking, the seam across the industry was nearly "mined out".

Almost contrarily, there was a reawakening of national security, and heightened governmental awareness of defence issues, taking place after the Falklands and first Gulf Wars. In June 1987, there was a General Election in Britain, which returned the Conservative administration of Margaret Thatcher to power. Going along with the CASTOR project, mentioned earlier, was an Airborne Early Warning (AEW) version of the Islander, for which a suitable radar installation had finally been chosen. The official 'roll-out' of the so-styled BN-2T AEW Defender, had occurred on Friday 6th March 1987, in front of Lord Trefgarne and 65 other dignitaries, from all over the world. Additionally there were 65 press and media representatives present at Bembridge that day, at which a free buffet lunch for all employees also took place. Pilatus entertained high hopes of meaningful sales of these low cost, efficient, military variants but, despite the best efforts of Bob Wilson and a newly-appointed Military Sales Director, in the person of Anthony Stansfield, nothing much crystallized. Nevertheless a lot of background work went on between the Company and the Ministry of Defence (MoD) with a view towards quantifying Islander applications. Stansfield was, himself, an ex-Army Air Corps Major and carried certain influences, beyond the range of an ordinary civilian, in such approaches.

Towards the end of 1987 a breakthrough occurred when the MoD decided that it could use a surveillance version of the Islander for certain duties. Although the order would not be a large one, there was no telling what it might lead to in the future. Once again an air of urgency and enthusiasm returned to the scene at Bembridge, as the Technical Offices got to grips with the Ministry's specifications. Bob Wilson asked me, on 3rd November, if I would undertake the work of producing a 'Compliance Check List' for the project, putting aside my normal duties for the rest of the month, perhaps, until it was completed. The chosen aeroplanes were Model BN-2T's which were to be operated by the British Army Air Corps, much to the chagrin of the Royal Air Force, in combination with their helicopters. Interservice rivalries had more or less established that the Army could use helicopters, but were not welcome to use fixed wing aircraft of a multi-engined nature. In this instance the Army had been successful in fighting its corner and the RAF interests had no alternative than to go 'grumbling away.'

About 36 pages of 'Compliance Checks' duly emerged, from a study of the military requirements, vis-à-vis the existing civilian-certificated BN-2T, showing where design action would be needed and where a state of equivalence existed, such that no action (or only very minor) would be necessary. It was not long before we were deeply involved in meetings and associations with the MoD, the initial order eventually crystallizing into 5 aeroplanes, plus spares and backup services on a proportional basis. A useful order for the Company, but nothing like the expectations which were entertained. Pilatus was, no doubt, disappointed by the general situation because it had been working hard to promote its latest 'homegrown' Swiss product into MoD circles as well but, regrettably, without success. Possibilities had arisen in connection with the RAF's need to replace its ageing Jet Provost two-seat advanced training aircraft. Pilatus had had great success with a family of very competent two-seat trainers starting with their PC-3 model, which was piston-engined, running though to the latest PC-9 which was a turbo-prop model. A substantial number of various trainers had been sold, world-wide, and the latter aeroplane was highly regarded by the pilots who had flown it, including those of the RAF.

Once again, however, the dead hand of politics had intervened to ensure that work would be directed to the Northern Ireland factory of Short Bros & Harland in Belfast. It was in the form of a package deal between the Brazilian Embraer Aircraft Company and the British Government, whereby the similar 'Tucano' trainers would be built, supplied and supported by Short Bros., thus maintaining the fragile backing of that region's voters for as long as possible in the difficult times prevailing. It was, perhaps, significant that the Army's new BN-2T Islanders were to be used, largely, in Northern Ireland as a less vulnerable alternative to their helicopters during the "troubles". Overall, Pilatus Britten-Norman had allowed its civilian sales initiatives to fall away and was at this time mainly reliant on sales to military and para-military operators. There began to be interest from UK and other Police Forces, for surveillance duties, and some very esoteric equipment, including thermal imaging systems, came to be specified as a result. Although such business was keeping the Company going, in a small way, every order was hard won, with little prospect of more than one or two units at the most.

The Trislander situation was still not resolved either, despite the high hopes of three or four years ago, when Ron Hauck – the colourful American character – had purported to buy out the rights to the project. A deal had been struck with Egon Haefliger (and, by extension, the Oerlikon-Burhle Holdings in Switzerland) to take over the remaining ex-Gosselies manufactured Trislanders, amounting to about twenty in all, along with all the jigs and tools and relevant design drawings. A substantial amount of material had already been shipped to Miami where Hauck had a base not far away, in Homestead, Florida, when the man himself was killed in a flying accident. Since it appeared to be a fledgling enterprise of a 'one-man-band' nature, the whole outcome was mired in immense legal and financial difficulties that were not conducive to the early settlement, so badly needed by the OBH. It was understood that a consignment of material, including build jigs, was still on the Miami dockside where it had been unloaded. Naturally enough Dr Haefliger took this situation very badly, because it was one of those that refused to go away.

As 1988 came in and the Technical Offices became involved in the design changes for the Army, I was faced with a requirement for specialized Air Publications for the contract. At first, the indications were that the MoD would take the normal civilian publications that went with the Model BN-2T Islander. The Army, however, raised enough pressure to insist upon having servicing and spares literature in the form to which they were accustomed. New costings and negotiations, leading to contract amendments, therefore became necessary which ultimately delayed the job, because the MoD wanted to seek a cheaper route to the Army's goal. Fortunately my own production capabilities had been upgraded by the installation of early DTP equipment but I should, again, be reliant upon sub-contract assistance, to provide the required volume of work on time. Pilatus was keen on personnel development, through all levels, and Dr Haefliger used to regularly take some of us, from the Technical Offices, on afternoon 'brainstorming sessions', with the intention of widening the field of ideas and expertise within the Company. If not held in the big hangar meeting room – or the new terminal building – we would sometimes convene in the Seaview Hotel, in the little town of Seaview, after a working lunch there. Whether these meetings served their purpose or not, is difficult to judge but there was one last attempt to improve the Islander's appeal, and utility, in a bid to gain increased sales.

These improvements were to be made, based on the Model BN-2T, by re-introducing the 33in (838mm) fuselage stretch – ahead of the wing leading edge – and incorporating a new design of longer nose, having a different profile from the earlier long-nosed aircraft. Intended for para-military usage, there was no need to meet the cabin evacuation requirements, for passenger carriage, due to specialized 'working-crew' cabin layouts. The new nose, although not as long as the previous designs, was made more capacious for electronic equipment installation, by carrying the fuselage chine width two or three feet further forward, in parallel, before tapering to meet a new and enlarged nose cone. Together with overall systems upgrades, uprated undercarriage and an increased gross weight the 'new aeroplane' was designated as the 'Defender 4000'. The '4000' alluded to the increased gross weight of the aircraft at 4000kg, but the Defender part of the designation was certainly unrecognisable from the exercise I had performed, at Desmond Norman's behest, seventeen years before. This was to be the last version of the Islander family to be schemed and built at Bembridge Airport. No decisions had been taken to construct the new buildings necessary if production were to resume in the UK and the only supply of new aircraft sub-assemblies, from Romania, was beginning to cause apprehension on several counts.

***

According to my diary details the first Army BN-2T (Constructor's No. 2184) departed just after Christmas 1988, for trials at the Aircraft and Armament Experimental Establishment (A&AEE) at Boscombe Down in Wiltshire. The other four (Constructor's No. 2194, 2195, 2196 and 2199) were delivered between then and the following April. Amusingly,

I note in passing, Dr Haefliger called into my office on Friday 13th January 1989, to have a word with me about the subject of my potential replacement. This matter was also bound up with my need to replace my current typist/secretary and yet another impending office move. For some time, however, there had been an awareness that my own position was not covered by a deputy and that early action should be taken to rectify that situation. My current typist/secretary had been invited to work with Bob Wilson, the Technical Director, and she would gain a promotion if she made that move. Of course I had to agree to that and, so, the process of indoctrinating yet another person would begin all over again. The next one would be the ninth one since Penny's time with me had expired! Dr Haefliger had, some time ago, appointed a Personnel Manageress who was now deep in a Company-wide Job Evaluation and Classification Scheme, emanating from all the Personnel Development Plans and Courses, which had been implemented. Nothing could happen quickly, in the circumstances, and it was towards the end of 1989 before my Sanction permission to recruit a 'deputy' was agreed and cleared for action. My requirement for a replacement typist/secretary was easier and was filled by a young lady whose great ambition was to become an air hostess; after eighteen months she succeeded and the seat was empty again.

Throughout this particular time the staple duties of support work and updating of our civilian Air Publications went on, alongside the new creations for the Army, with undiminished vigour. A good deal of time was spent, between the Stress Office, Ron Dack and the CAA, on the subject of corrosion control. This was becoming relevant to so many of the earlier Islanders – and Trislanders too, because we still held the Design Authority for those aeroplanes – which began to exhibit deterioration in some areas of their structure. The CAA's preferred method was for manufacturers to publish a 'Corrosion Control Manual' but, for what I like to think were good reasons, we demurred. Instead, it was agreed that we would deal with the subject by Service Bulletin action. On account of this decision the Company's 190th Service Bulletin was the instrument by which about sixteen pages of text and illustrations were released, into the field, to permit approved inspection and remedial procedures.

All of the Service Bulletin material was on microfiche, by now, and it was a relatively easy job to deal with the circulation because we had left 'hard copy' behind for most of our publications output at this stage. It was a good job that we had, because Service Bulletin No. 190 became a regular missive for amendment and addition over the following years. A quick and reliable service, from my Coventry-based contractor's was a valuable attribute in satisfying CAA requirements and reducing postal costs. The Army, however, would be one of those customers who continued to require 'hard copy'.

Eventually the recruitment for my 'deputy' went ahead and, from the applicants, a young chap named Ian Proudfoot was selected. Ian had been working for Richard Noble (the then World Landspeed Record Holder) on a small two-seater aeroplane, with an 'all-new' three-cylinder engine, which Noble had wanted to build and sell from a base at Sandown, on the Island. Unfortunately the then undeveloped engine gave trouble which led to an early demise of the project. Ian made a start with us, at Bembridge, on 9th April 1990 and soon began to contribute to the proceedings. He was computer-literate, to a degree that I was not, and was able to start building a case for suitable advanced equipment. In spite of the difficult business climate, I had been able to convince Dr Haefliger that more of the Company's publications 'know-how', should be held inside the firm, rather than in the hands of sub-contractors. As a result of that, I had gained permission to recruit three more members of staff and a modest amount of improved DTP equipment, all of which happened during 1990/1991. I should have realized, however, that (as before) most rises were succeeded by falls.

About the middle of June 1990, after an acrimonious disagreement with Dr Haefliger, David Fear, the Works Director, quit the Company in an instantaneous resignation issue. There were signs of trouble ahead. Two months later, our Technical Publications Department moved into newly refurbished office space, back on the first floor of the old hangar. Farnborough came and went again and, in November, a delegation of engineers from the Westinghouse Electric Corporation arrived at Bembridge, to discuss mutual interests in a BN-2T AEW project. (It would not be until the following November that a celebratory buffet, recognizing receipt of an order, could be arranged, however). In the meantime, Dr Haefliger's lady personnel manageress had departed for other avenues of employment, while Alan Larwood – the Financial Director – also left the Company suddenly in October of 1991. A few months before, Peter Chivers had also moved on. Peter was an ambitious young man who saw that his future as Chief Structures Engineer was threatened by the general run-down. Before leaving, to join the Airbus Consortium, he had co-operated with Ron Dack in recruiting a replacement engineer in the person of Alistair McCartney, who took up his duties in mid 1991. Although not realizing it, at the time, my own service with the Company was nearing an end too. The BN-2T AEW aeroplane (Constructor's No. 2115) for the Westinghouse Electric Corporation, would be the last one to which I made an input. Immediately after Christmas of 1991, and the return to business got under way, Bob Wilson spoke to me about a specialist Maintenance Schedule which we had drafted for the subject aeroplane. This was to be checked out by Ron Dack and John Oversby (of the Service Department) before finalization. Bob and the fairly newly installed Aerodynamicist/Airworthiness Engineer, Nigel Davis, were scheduled to visit the Brussels Office of the FAA, on Wednesday 15th January 1992, in connection with American certification of No. 2115. Evidence of the aeroplane's Maintenance Schedule, or its near-availability, would be required before certification could be granted; they would take with them a photocopy of the draft, to that all-important meeting.

On Friday 10th January, at the regular Design Office meeting, Bob Wilson advised us all to be 'on hand' for the next Tuesday (14th January) when a Pilatus and McKinsey delegation was expected, to discuss a re-organization plan! The delegation arrived on Monday, in fact, spending two days at Bembridge, and indicated that they would be making a return visit in 7 to 10 days. Now we knew that something unpleasant was about to happen again. The delegation returned on Monday 20th January, to put a re- organization into action, and two days later a notice was issued to the effect that Dr Egon Haefliger was 'stepping down'. His duties were to be assumed by Anthony Stansfield, who became Managing Director. Two weeks later, on Monday 3rd February, the new Managing Director held a Management Briefing at 1:00pm. We were informed that 57 job losses would occur and that the Company's establishment would be reduced to 197 employees. No further sub-contract orders were to be placed after that date. More information, on terms of severance, would be given in a few days, Anthony said, but it was likely that a generous settlement would be made for anyone volunteering to go.

It so happened that I was booked to go into hospital, on 13th February for an operation and I thought this may be a suitable time to finish with the working world, to retire in peace, albeit 15 months short of the official date. The more I thought about it, the more I liked the idea and I also hoped that my leaving might help to preserve the jobs of those people we had recently attracted. My mind was made up and I put my name forward accordingly. The arrangements were made and I went off to hospital in a settled frame of mind, to make a token return for a few days in March at the end of my convalescence. When I bade my friends and colleagues goodbye at Bembridge, I had been with the Company for 26 years and almost 3 months. It did not upset me to leave Bembridge Airport, there had been many good times in the past, but there had also been black days and frustrations. Overall, I had enjoyed my association with the aeroplanes, the authorities and the customers, together with a huge amount of job satisfaction. Looking across the wider spectrum of the British aviation industry, as a whole, it was clearly evident that the running down process had been a general one which had almost disabled it altogether. A company like Britten-Norman was unlikely ever to be replicated, as an all-round Operating, Design Approved, Construction, Sales, Marketing and Repair organization, indigenously raised on British soil again – the Grand Adventure was nearly over. In this vein, my narrative of personal involvement is ended; the rest of the story, like the beginning, becomes an outsider's account of things once again.

12.1 The final production BN-2T version, designated the 'Defender 4000' and intended for maritime reconnaissance/paramilitary operations, at almost twice the weight of the original 1965 BN-2

Chapter 13

Endgame

By the Spring of 1992 it must have become obvious to Pilatus, and the Oerlikon Burhle Holding group, that there was no future for the Bembridge company in their own development projections. There were changes taking place at the highest levels in the Swiss organizations, following the recent death of Dr Burhle which, no doubt, helped to concentrate minds. Margaret Thatcher's dynamics in the Westminster scenario had been replaced by the altogether more mundane premiership of John Major, which augured little in the way of improvements for business sentiment. Industrial activities, particularly in the aviation sector, continued towards steady decline in Britain. Nevertheless, facing even these circumstances and the much reduced capabilities, following their recent re-structuring, the Swiss management must also have harboured hopes for some improvements ahead. From that point, onwards, a renewed attempt was made to carry on the Britten-Norman business in the face of mounting difficulties.

Work went on, in a low-key vein, to keep faith with the airworthiness responsibilities and the requirements of Operators world wide. Bob Wilson remained in his position as Technical Director for some time to come and Anthony Stansfield continued as Managing Director for a little while. Anthony lived on the mainland and used to commute to Bembridge in his 'motorglider'; he was a regular sight in the island skyscape on his journeys to and from work. Andy O'Connell, who was named as 'Project Manager' for the MoD/British Army contract, took charge of the Drawing Office and Mike Dore functioned as Chief Draughtsman ably assisted by Steve Stapleton. They still had a considerable amount of work on hand, most of the time, because about 1300 aeroplanes had been produced, the majority of which were still in service. Once again, however, there was some concern about the overseeing of Stress Office functions due to Ron Dack's impending retirement in July of 1992.

Alistair McCartney had had a lot to catch up with in a very short time and he was not altogether comfortable with 'in-field' repair work, with its insurance and litigation connotations. Consequently the CAA continued to request Ron Dack's services, on an 'as-and-when' basis, even after his official retirement. These conditions applied for a further seven or eight years, until the time of the Bembridge company's sale by Pilatus in 2000, by which time Alistair had suffered a seriously debilitating illness that led to the engagement of yet another Chief Structures Engineer.

The Technical Publications chair was not occupied long by Ian Proudfoot, who appeared to have more of an interest in Information Technology, in general rather than aviation applications in particular. Another person was appointed, within two or three years, who came down from a post with Scottish Aviation, at Prestwick. A Defender 4000 prototype duly emerged and became the subject of a keen marketing drive. It was a very handsome looking aeroplane which represented a worthy ultimate development of the Islander. Being much more expensive, however, it seemed that the less capacious – and less comfortable – adaptations of piston-engined Islanders would continue to interest budget conscious operators in most cases. There was an awkward situation to contend with, now, in that the shop floor work force was depleted to twenty, or fewer, people to make things happen.

In the years that followed, there was one, other notable occasion, on similar lines to previous celebratory ones, at Bembridge Airport. This was the 30th Anniversary of the Islander which occurred in 1995. There was an invited gathering of Operators and Distributors, together with past and present employees. Many of those present flew into Bembridge in a wide variety of aircraft types, causing almost as much interest as a full scale airshow. An air display did take place, in fact, the culmination of which was a fly-past by three Islanders in vic formation. A standard Islander led the formation with the Defender 4000 on the port side and an AEW version on the starboard side, thus making what turned out to be a splendid curtain call appearance over an appreciative small crowd. Such displays had been a feature of British aircraft manufacturing resources, almost since the end of the first World War but were, by this time, almost extinct. With the possible exception of some small and localized

171

gatherings, the 'Great British Public' appeared to be mostly inured to the appeal of flight, for flight's sake, and its history of high adventure. The most pressing need for aeroplanes now seen as mass transit media to escape the British climate for anticipated luxury in the sunshine.

Worthy of note, however, in connection with the above event – although not an intrinsic part of this story – was the appearance of two Pilatus aeroplanes. One was a visiting PC7 two-seat trainer, which gave an impeccable aerobatic display and the other was a PC 12, which had conveyed some Pilatus and Oerlikon-Burhle people over for the occasion. This latter machine was the material embodiment of Dietrich Klöeckner's vision; a single engined turbo-prop executive transport with a distinctive high-mounted tailplane and upswept wing tips in the 'dyna-soar' fashion. A beautifully finished aeroplane, both inside and out, it stood quietly some way away from the rest, vigilantly guarded by its pilot. It was a pressurized six to twelve seater, of the design espoused by Dietrich, 14 or more years before. Apparently PC12's were then in production, in one of the OBH's American facilities where the FAA certification would have been gained on the more favourable grounds of an indigenous product.

Almost co-inciding with these events, was the fall from grace of the Conservative government under John Major's premiership. Yet another catalogue of scandal and ineptness caused the 'Great British Public' to choose, again, the socialist way ahead. Not under the militant Red Flag this time, but altogether more subtly contrived, with the Red Rose as a symbol, came forward the party of *nouveau travail*. There was now little, if any, chance of a meaningful revival of aviation interests in the United Kingdom, despite the shift from any previously applied agenda. Such a situation must have been patently obvious to the powers within OBH and Pilatus, where the original optimism and business opportunism leading to their association with Britten-Norman had now run its course. Accordingly, the Bembridge company was put up for sale, as a going concern, by its Swiss owners in 1997/8. Although its prospects were diminished, there was no suggestion of insolvency and much effort was put into finding a suitable buyer.

There were no ready takers, from what little remained of the British aviation industry, and the process dragged on until the year 2000 before a buyer emerged from the shadows. Eventually a company with the unlikely title of 'Biopharms Ltd' purchased Pilatus Britten-Norman Ltd and began its own searching review of the acquisition. The new owners had no intentions to develop anything this time, except an asset stripping exercise, to raise as much money as possible in the shortest timescale. Accordingly, everything of potential value was identified and sold off to the highest bidders. The Southend-on-Sea firm of Aviation Traders Ltd, had metamorphosed into 'Flightspares Ltd' over the years, but still dealt with the spares and product support work, on behalf of Pilatus Britten-Norman Ltd. That association was cancelled out when the relevant business functions were sold off to R. F. Saywell Ltd, a similar spares and accessories vendor.

Very quickly the essential underpinnings of the Company were dismantled, in this way until Biopharms Ltd placed the unfortunate victim in the hands of a liquidator – the third receivership to handle it! Those employees who remained with the Company, and those who looked forward to receiving a pension when they had to leave their employment, were doubly hit because they found out that their pension fund had disappeared. The pension fund – which had been started in 1972 by Fairey Aviation Ltd – was quite a good one for the times and was reliably run by well-intentioned employers. Its substance, however, was one of the attractive assets that baited the particular buyer.

A state of near collapse was reached at that stage but, just when it seemed that the Britten-Norman enterprise would disappear, altogether, from the aviation scene, another foreign buyer came forward. From further afield this time, but with bona fide aviation credentials, an Omani family syndicate, headed by a Mr Alawi Zawarwi, bought the impoverished company from the liquidator in the year 2000. An aviator, himself, Zawarwi is also an enthusiast who is – at the time of writing – still trying to rebuild a viable organization from the ruins of the Bembridge company. He calls it by the name of the B N Group (BNG) and has gathered some of the original workers back into the fold, along with the few who were retained. It is heartening to see that the cherished, trademarked, logo of B-N is still relevant and has not disappeared forever into the fiery furnace of debt and destruction.

Without the jigs and tools and wherewithal to produce new aeroplanes of the Islander family, however, the situation is a difficult one. Romanian production of the necessary sub-assemblies has dried up, in the absence of viable contracts. Knowing that the Bembridge facility was wholly reliant upon their efforts, enabled the Romanians to dictate terms, in the latter stages of production, so that the association became completely uneconomical. So far as the Islander work is concerned, there is still some turnover in repairs, overhaul and modifications, together with the supply of spares and other product support services. Additional work has been introduced into Bembridge Airport, by assembling kit-built small single engined cabin monoplanes, by which it is hoped to augment the factory's capability. These are American designed and built aeroplanes, a product of the Cirrus Airplane Corp, which are finished and flown in the USA where they receive their FAA Airworthiness certification, before being dismantled and shipped to Europe for re-assembly and sale. In the continued absence of manufacturing jigs and tools, as well as the cessation of supplies of part-finished Islander sub-assemblies from Romania, there is little doubt that the Britten Norman Islander story is over.

Now too long in the tooth for any further worthwhile development, the design has become completely outdated. With its inspirational progenitors gone from the scene, including the 'helping hands' of Miles Aviation, the Islander's home facilities at Bembridge Airport will soldier on for as long as foreign finance will support it. And so it is with the remainder of the British aviation industry, now in consortia with Italy and France for helicopters, Germany *et al* for strike aircraft, and Germany, France and Spain for civilian transport, with connections – of course – to the USA. The confident, competent, design and experimental teams which gave Britain a front ranking in aeronautical competition at all levels, have long been disbanded and scattered to the four winds.

The British Hovercraft Corporation, always linked to Westland's at Yeovil, still carries on in business with hovercraft work but mainly derives its benefit from lucrative sub-contract production work for American aircraft manufacturers. In an ideal situation to help out with helicopter work, should the need arise, the Cowes facility has developed many additional contacts, and skills, since the days when Eric Gilberthorpe first co-operated with John Britten and Desmond Norman to produce the Islander. Those times were still full of promise for the future, even though the superlative Cowes designed and built Saunders-Roe Princess flying boat was never put into production. No one who witnessed the Princess's flypasts, above the Farnborough crowds could have failed to be impressed by that gentle giant; along with the Bristol Brabazon, one of the largest aeroplanes conceived, built and flown in Britain. Thus, in keeping with the times, the Cowes facility has gone from major to minor, in the sense of aircraft design and production work, whilst still managing to keep its factory going somehow.

Elsewhere across the industry it is, sadly, not the case as we have seen all too plainly. At this time of writing, with the first decade of the twenty-first century almost over, there are no new indications of aeronautical inventiveness or would-be business backers, on the British horizon. It is regrettable that aviation in these islands seems only able to thrive in the exigencies of war and threats of war, even though the possession of such advancing technical and productive capabilities is necessary for our industrial survival and international trading welfare. The unique existence of the Britten-Norman enterprize, at Bembridge Airport, on the Isle of Wight, demonstrates that the stimulus of war is not always necessary to succeed, but that the employment of practical, knowledgeable, and consistent management controls, along with careful attention to the build-up and utilization of capital, certainly are. Cavalier attitudes can be fun, and very necessary in some instances, but they cannot be sustained for long without serious damage.

Almost as if by constructive negligence, it seems, our once great national institutions and centres of aeroplane design and manufacture have been allowed to decline to the point of international insignificance. In hindsight, therefore, the innovative engineering and production accomplishments, emanating from Bembridge, can be viewed as a starburst of extraordinary creativity at the tail end of our British aircraft design and manufacturing industry. As the twenty-first century continues on its way, examples of our past heritage – like specimens in an ornithological collection, most inert but some still active – are cared for by curators now, their originators themselves having passed into history.

In this overall process, the experiences of the little Britten-Norman company, during its life and times as an indigenous organization, can surely be described as '… The Last Grand Adventure in British Aviation,' can they not?

13.1 A Pilatus PC-7, two seat advanced flying trainer, which gave the aerobatic display at Bembridge in 1995

13.2 Dietrich Klöeckner's 'Dream Machine'. An early example of the propjet Pilatus PC-12, executive transport, photographed at Bembridge:1995

13.3 A birthday flypast: photographed by the author at the Islander's 30th birthday event in 1995. A standard Islander leads the formation, with an AEW version on its starboard side and a Defender 4000 on its port side

Chapter 14

Retrospective

Bembridge Airport remains much as it ever was, a privately owned airfield and 1920's flying club-type hangar, with appended pub and outbuildings, on the roadside between Brading and Bembridge village. Supplemented, of course, by the later additions of the runway, Airport Terminal Building and the adjacent pair of larger hangars. The wooden hutments on the petrol station forecourt, along with the commercial petrol pumps, were progressively dismantled in the late 1970s. Wreford Fisher's prized Aviation Centre building, being thoroughly decayed and neglected, went the same way a few years later ; to the greater good of the local environment it must be said. In summer the airfield grass is still cut, made into hay, and transported away in bales for animal feedstuff during the harsher months of the year. The 'Propellor Parliament', was dissolved in the spring of 1976, when its founder members left to pursue their own individual futures. Five or six years earlier both partners had been honoured, by the Queen, in receiving CBEs for their services to aviation. In 1974 the Trislander was the recipient of a Queen's Award to industry, for 'innovative design'. For some years, John Britten had been trying to further his own ideas, in the design and manufacture of a light, twin engined, two seat side-by-side, training aeroplane. True to style, he would not be dissuaded from continuing this project, for which there seemed little evidence of backing capital, except his own personal means.

Shortly before this time, F.R.J. Britten had been elected to the ancient office of 'Sheriff of the Isle of Wight', a role which he was justly proud – if a little hesitant – to fulfil. Although a purely honorary one, and lasting only for one year, the duties had interrupted his working life to some extent. With the help of relatives and friends, John took over some available hangar space at the neighbouring airport of Sandown and was soon re-engaged in the work that he loved. His ultimate product would, he

177

foresaw, be mostly in competition with American aeroplanes, of similar types, many of which were named after North American tribes such as : 'Cherokees', 'Navajoes', 'Pawnees' and so on. He joked that it was time, perhaps, to '... put a Sheriff among them' and that may also have had allusions to his recent office as well. In the event, that was his chosen name for his new aeroplane – the 'Sheriff'. Unfortunately, because of his untimely death in 1977, at the age of 49, the project was an unfinished one, in the sense that no marketable machine emerged. Things were left in the hands of his nephew (James Morton) and Ken Mills – who not long before had joined him at Sandown – to wind up affairs. The conclusion was further dogged when Ken Mills, himself, suffered a similar sudden death soon afterwards. James, who had always been fascinated by racing cars and the aura of motor racing circuits, as well as their media, went on to join one of the teams, in some capacity or other.

Desmond Norman's individual move first took him to Cardiff, in South Wales, where he began work on his own two-seat training aeroplane, as well as a big single-seat crop sprayer with a turbo-prop engine. Desmond, in true entrepreneurial fashion, had been able to take advantage of some favourable grants, aimed at introducing new business potential into the region. His trainer was in no sense a competitor to John Britten's, being quite fighter-like in its tandem seating layout and prominent tear-drop cockpit canopy design. No doubt this appearance and the associated aerodynamics, owed a lot to Andy Coombe's influence. This aeroplane was called the 'Firecracker' and, at first, it was fitted with a piston engine. Desmond made an early visit to Bembridge, with Andy Coombe in the rear seat, to show people what they had been up to – afterwards making a 'beat-up' before departing for home. Later on, the Firecracker design was further developed and had a Pratt & Whitney PT-7 turbo-prop engine installed. It seemed unable, however, to better what competition there was in that class, at the time, and nothing much was seen or heard of it again, after Andy's early death in 1981. He was 47 years old.

The crop spraying aeroplane was quite another thing altogether. Desmond had never lost his interest in, and feel for, the 'agricultural' aeroplanes and had decided to concentrate on a machine with a large-capacity chemical tank. Consequently, a somewhat ungainly looking aeroplane, with a high-mounted cockpit, resembling an aerial dromedary, emerged. Christened the 'Fieldmaster', this aeroplane had a 750 Imp. Gal (3409 l) spray tank which Desmond was proud of. He liked to refer to it as '... the biggest tank in the West.' The Fieldmaster, although a simple aeroplane at first sight, had quite a complex electrical system – for the design of which he poached Brian Groves from the Bembridge design team. Plans were made to put the Fieldmaster into production and, indeed, several were built before things went wrong in the administration somewhere, causing a withdrawal from the Cardiff region.

At the outset of his individual venture Desmond had created a new company, under the title of NDN Aircraft Ltd, and it was not long before that company transferred its base and operations back to the Isle of Wight; at Sandown Airport this time. One example of the Firecracker was retained, and one or two Fieldmasters, but there were insufficient financial resources to proceed in any meaningful way, the projects not being developed to full potential. About this time NDN Aircraft Ltd secured a deal with a Turkish company, to take over the production and marketing of the Fieldmaster – which thus transferred the 'biggest tank in the West' to the Near East ! It was hoped to use the aeroplane in a forest firefighting role, whereby the full contents of the tank could be emptied by the use of a 'dump-valve' when required. There does not seem to be any evidence of the aeroplane's widespread existence, however, and one must presume that unfavourable conditions have been responsible.

One example of the earlier Nymph had survived and had found its way, by various means, back into Desmond's possession. An attempt was made to regenerate that project, in a slightly different form, under the name of 'Freelance', without any commercial success. In a 'spin-off' from the 'Freelance', another similar small sporting aeroplane, by the name of 'Weekender', was spawned – but again without success – before the full scale operations of NDN Aircraft Ltd. had to come to a halt. By virtue of his continuous links with the crop spraying industry, not least with Micronair Ltd, Desmond had been able to build up a consultancy function, which included the Coventry-based firm of Air Atlantique Ltd. That company was engaged, among other operations, in the aerial control of oceanic pollution, by spraying oil spills, and such-like potential disasters, with detergent solutions. For this purpose, elderly Douglas DC-3's were used, when fitted out with tanks and delivery systems, utilizing Micronair equipment. It was in this kind of work that Desmond's final few years were spent and it was, indeed, during a train journey to Coventry, for consultation with Air Atlantique, that he died in 2002, aged 73 and still on the job !

Miles Aviation and Transport Ltd, those other consultant helpers of previous years, progressively went out of business during the 1970s era. Failure of the Beagle Aircraft conglomerate, was followed by a sell-out of the Miles Electronics division, at Shoreham, to the Hunting Group. Shortly afterwards the Miles Plastics division, which had dealt with the film-making business, was also sold. G.H. (George) Miles, who had been extremely busy – along with his colleagues – in the aviation consultancy and sub-contract business, at Ford, E. Sussex, was anxious to retire and decided to sell the undertaking to a German company in 1971. Thus it was that the illustrious name of Miles finally disappeared when Dufon – the German buyer whose name was suffixed – ceased trading in 1977/8. F. G. (Freddie) Miles who, together with his wife Blossom, had been founding partners of the 1920s company – originally in association with Phillips & Powis, at Woodley, near Reading – died in 1975. There were no family successors to carry on the Miles tradition but George, the youngest of the three brothers, lived on until the age of 85, after his late retirement from the Company which bore their name.

Bob Iba the veteran ferry pilot and survivor of the American Pacific war theatre, was killed when the aeroplane he was flying was shot down by Central American bandits. Word had it that he had refused to carry the contraband they demanded, thus attracting a terrible retribution.

What of the others, named and un-named members and contemporaries of the times ? Much as one would like to remember, in detail, it is not possible to do so effectively. Jack Sullivan, however, started up a successful market gardening business,with his wife, in Bembridge which prospered, following Jack's severance from the Airport. Jim Birnie and his wife, Wendy, ran 'The Elms' contentedly for some years, from where Jim continued his diligent support of the RNLI. Later on he renewed his aviation interests by assisting his elder son – also named James – with a pleasure flying operation, out of Sandown aerodrome. They acquired a four seat Cessna for this work and Jim's duties consisted of running the booking kiosk, along with other essential ground-borne tasks, until his death in 1998 at the age of 78. Dickie Bird remained as Works Manager of Miles Aviation and Transport Ltd. at Ford, until 1975/6, when he went to Canada to join the Canadian Department of Transport, concerned with aircraft certification matters. He appeared, briefly, at Bembridge once more, at the Islander's 30th Birthday celebrations in 1995. At the same gathering was John Brenchley, resplendently attired in a yellow suit, whilst on a home visit from his American sphere of employment.

Andy O'Connell and Ron Dack continued in service at Bembridge until their normal retirement times; fortunately before the sale of Pilatus Britten-Norman Ltd to the Biopharms organization. Not so for Bob Wilson, however, who was caught in the financial vacuum but retained in a consultancy capacity by the current Omani owners of the BNG. The Drawing Office was moved over to Southampton where it is now headed by Steve Stapleton, one of Mike Dore's colleagues, and a few stalwarts, such as Service Engineer Tim Barton, formerly one of the Flight Sheds' staff, and ex-Shops Planner Bruce Jacobs, now Airport Manager, continue in the time-honoured fashion. (Bruce was no relation to Ray, mentioned earlier, who had taken over a 'Spar' shop across in the West Wight, many years before). The CAA no longer occupies Brabazon House, its shrunken facilities having been transferred to Gatwick Airport. Similarly, the SBAC – if it still exists – has disappeared from its King Street, St.James's, headquarters which are now given over to other uses. Peter Graham, who was Desmond's Commercial Manager, formed his own business and remains active in the aviation scene by cooperating with the 'BN Historians'. This is an independent body devoted to a comprehensive record keeping operation of all the production aeroplanes, by serial number, type, date first-flown, and ultimate customer name and location in the world. At the time of writing, Peter is engaged in a project to restore Islander Constructor's No. 3, Registration G-AVCN (Charlie November), to an airworthy condition once more. This was the first production aeroplane to be completed, over 40 years ago, for delivery to Aurigny Air Services in August 1967 and was lately rescued from dereliction, in Puerto Rico.

David Williams, one of the very earliest of John's and Desmond's employees, lives now in quiet retirement, but remembers well the frenetic activities of those formative years. Years when such pressure of work caused many men to be almost strangers in their own homes and other instances – as in the case of Arthur Rayner, a foreman at the time, who was found wandering on Bembridge Down, a day or so after having gone missing from his duties, not knowing where he was. Such experiences were not uncommon across the industry, generally, when the construction of prototypes was concerned and so, it could be said, that the Britten-Norman episode ran true to form. Peter Gatrell, too, has lived through the iconic times to enjoy his retirement years, after his services to Britten-Norman and Micronair Ltd. came to an end.

The Micronair aerial spraying techniques with their specialized equipment and systems could rightly be considered the foundation stone of the Britten-Norman enterprise and, thus, an intrinsic feature of the 'Last Grand Adventure'. Following Jim McMahon's takeover, and establishment of Micronair, as an independent company at the Bembridge Down headquarters, international business links were maintained and strengthened. This state of affairs continued steadily and diligently under Jim's dedicated stewardship, until the time of his retirement, when the business was sold out to a man named Ted Tylee, and some associates. Tylee was of South African origin, being an accountant by profession and one of the original team of Price Waterhouse's receivership at Bembridge Airport, under Maurice Eckman. He was, therefore, not a stranger to Bembridge affairs and obviously found the local amenities attractive enough to buy a house at Bembridge, taking up residence there. Unfortunately the Company went into decline, following the absence of J.M. McMahon's influence and became another casualty of business failure in that form.

Jim McMahon, the last of the original executive directors of Britten-Norman Ltd, passed away in February 2006 ; he was 83 years old. Always modest and approachable, Jim was nevertheless a competent and determined business man whose clear blue eyes were never clouded by success. He never courted publicity, was never honoured by the establishment and never became the recipient of civic accolades, but was a staunch supporter, in life and in death, of the Great Ormond Street Hospital for Sick Children, in London.

The years go by, the tumult and the shouting dies, people's faces and memories of their triumphs and disasters gradually fade away from the scenes of engagement. The sights and sounds and indefinable, exciting, smells of aeroplane design, manufacture and operation are increasingly distanced from personal experiences, as a new age rolls on and British involvement recedes into the past.